CANADA'S CHINESE GENE

A Sense of Belonging, Ownership and Contribution

By

GUO DING & KENNY ZHANG

Onebook Press

Title   CANADA'S CHINESE GENE

Author   GUO DING & KENNY ZHANG

ISBN   978-1-7775297-0-3

Published by

Onebook Press

(BC, Canada)

https://www.onebookpress.com

Cover and interior design by

YI LIU

CONTENTS

Acknowledgements

This book is an English translation of *Canada's Chinese Gene—A Sense of Belonging, Ownership and Contribution*, which was originally written in Chinese language and dedicatedly published in May 2017 to celebrate the 150th anniversary of Canada. During the re-production, some of the chapters were also updated with the latest Canadian census data which began to be publicly available then.

Nevertheless, this effort is not just a translation, but an extension of ongoing discussion about statuses and roles of Canadians of Chinese heritage in this great country. When the Chinese version was publicly launched on June 17, 2017 at the Poly Culture Arts Center Vancouver, dozens of people lined up for authors' autograph and a total of 400 prepared copies were sold out on site in just a half hour. The feedback from the publication of the Chinese version has been intense and totally beyond authors expectation. Various fellow overseas Chinese and writers from not only Canada but also the United States, Southeast Asia and other regions have asked the authors whether this same argument could be applicable to their respective regions. Rather to give a simple yes or no answer to the question, we would like to invite more readers to join the conversation by making the book available in English.

The publication of this English version of *Canada's Chinese Gene* is the result of the collaborative efforts and supports across the community in Vancouver, the most Asian city outside of Asia. We are grateful to Sophia Zhang who provided a great deal of assistance in completion of both Chinese and English versions of the book. Princemountain Transnational Services

Inc. provided a timely and professional translation that allows the process of getting it ready for English publication to begin. Our special thanks go to Yvonne and Jan Walls, a highly respectable intellectual couple in Vancouver specialized in cross-cultural exchanges, who provided English copy-edits and the second readings after all manuscript was translated. However, any remaining errors if any are authors' responsibility.

In additional to scholarly and technical contributions, the book also benefits financial supports from many individual readers and community organizations, without which it would not be possible to make this book published by now. Special thanks are due to Mr. Bai Jiping, Mr. Kong Qingcun, and the Canada Committee 100 Society (CCS100).

Foreword

Canada's 150th anniversary is being celebrated this year in ways and forms that are as diverse as the country itself—from documentaries to concerts, parades to parks, and much more. Many of these activities are about remembering our history; others are focused on celebrating the present. The most enduring commemorations are those which help us re-think the Canadian story and re-imagining our collective future. Which is why I am so pleased to write a foreword to this volume by my friends Kenny Zhang and Guo Ding, who have assembled a collection of essays that tells the story of the Chinese in Canada from are freshing new perspective.

Perhaps the most important point of this book is the centrality of the Chinese presence in Canada from its very formation in 1867. It isn't simply that Chinese workers built the most difficult stretch of the Canadian Pacific railway—a project which brought the West into confederation and made Canada possible—but also that the very goal of the railway was "to have an ocean connection to Japan and China", as CP Rail President George Stephen wrote in a letter to Prime Minister John A. MacDonald.

This idea is captured in the intriguing title of the book, which can be translated as Canada Chinese Gene. It implies that Canada owes its current (and future) complexion in part to a "genetic" contribution by Chinese people that is as old as the country itself. For many people, this is an unfamiliar way of looking at the Chinese presence in Canada. A more common approach is to frame it as a latter-day phenomenon, a product of enlightened immigration policy starting in the 70s—as "newcomers" welcomed to a multicultural society. The "newcomers" label, however, comes with various kinds of social baggage—from pressures to integrate into "mainstream society" (is integration a one-way street?) to resentment over the impact of their arrival on real estate prices, school class sizes, and social services.

Zhang and Ding employ a similarly intriguing sub-title for their book, using the Chinese term for "nation building" as part of the storyline of "Canada's China Gene". This is borne out in many of the essays which describe the unique nation building efforts of Chinese Canadians, individually and collectively. what comes across powerfully is the wide range of social, cultural, and business activities that Chinese Canadians have been involved in and how they contribute to the Canadian fabric. In a year that also marks the 100th anniversary of the Battles of Vimy Ridge, Passchendaele, and Hill 70, the contributions of the 700 or so Chinese Canadian soldiers who fought in World Wars I and II bear special importance for the role they played in bringing to an end the Chinese Exclusion Act in 1947, making it possible for Chinese Canadians to become citizens of their adopted country.

The longevity of the Chinese Canadian presence in Canada, especially in British Columbia, and the growing density of this presence, have created a new set of Chinese-influenced innovations, tastes, and practices that originate in places like Vancouver and Toronto, but which have since spread to Chinese communities around the world. From gastronomy to media to architecture to contemporary art, the "Chinese gene" in Canada has resulted in offspring far beyond our borders. In this sense, Canada has become not just a home for migrants from the Sinosphere, but also a platform for these globally-connected Chinese Canadians to shape the very places where they came from.

Not all, however, view the modern reality of the Chinese presence in

Canada as a positive one. It is not uncommon these days to hear cries of "too much" Chinese (or Asian) presence in Vancouver or Toronto—with sky-high real estate prices usually cited as a socially-acceptable reason for voicing such an opinion. There are other, less frequently-articulated fears, including community alienation, fear of infiltration by the People's Republic of China, and various form of "culture wars" (most notably over language), especially in areas where there is a large concentration of ethnic Chinese residents. Most of these concerns are vastly overblown and are a result of rapid change in major metropolitan areas rather than issues that are specific to ethnicity or country of origin. All the same, they will have to be navigated by Canadians of Chinese and non-Chinese descent with sensitivity, mutual respect, and above all patience. But there can be no denying the impact of the Chinese "gene" on the first 150 years of nation-building in Canada. This book helps us envision a future where the Chinese presence in Canada is even more closely interwoven with the national fabric and welcomed as such.

The Honourable Yuen Pau Woo
Independent Senator | British Columbia Senate of Canada

Preface

What exactly is meant by the "Chinese Gene"?

The feedback from the publication of the Chinese version of *Canada's Chinese Gene* has been intense and totally beyond expectation. Various fellow overseas Chinese and writers from not only our Canada but also the United States, Southeast Asia and other regions have asked me whether this same theory and concept could be applicable to their respective regions? Some friends have also asked me whether Western researchers and the general public can accept this standpoint and this view? Obviously, this is a topic worthy of continued discussion.

The term, "Canada's Chinese Gene", is not a fabricated idea coined out of impulse; nor is it a new idea created without historical grounding, all for the purpose of forcefully improving the social standing of Chinese Canadians. There are three vital factors which became the foundation for this proposition.

First, the founding of Canada as a nation was based on the gene of multiculturalism, and not one simple "Anglo-French" bicultural gene. Despite the fact that the final negotiation and agreement between the English and French descendants were key in laying down the mechanism of a nation, the country was composed of a multitude of cultures. The Aboriginals (the First Nations) are not only the earliest inhabitants of this land, they were also participants in the war against Americans (1812−1815), during which they fought alongside the British and the French troops and helped deter the American annexation of Canada, thereby making confederation possible. The contributions made by Canadian First Nations received little recognition from mainstream historians, but it is undeniable that Canada has the "Aboriginal gene" at its foundation. The same can be said for the "Chinese gene". This is not a false claim but a restatement and truthful depiction of historical fact.

Secondly, as we have recounted in our book, Canada's "Chinese gene" is substantiated with historical evidence. Based on historical pathways of Chinese people entering Canada, Chinese migrant workers entered Canada's West as early as the late 18th century, followed by more Chinese workers who flooded in during the Gold Rush. All these took place before confederation. Western Canada joined in 1871 after confederation in 1867, but only under certain conditions. One of these conditions was that the confederation must build a railway to connect Canada from coast to coast within ten years. Some people claim that Western Canada could not secede from confederation even without the Canadian Pacific Railway (CPR). However, such a claim is farfetched. Canada's second Prime Minister Alexander Mackenzie (the First Liberal Prime Minister) was tardy in the construction of the railroad. This became the reason for the return of John A. Macdonald, the first Prime Minister of Canada (of the Liberal-Conservative Party), who defeated him. During Macdonald's term, the CPR was completed, and the confederation was stabilized. The entire Canadian society agrees that the Chinese workers were pivotal in completing the CPR, to the point that Macdonald publicly announced that the CPR could not have been built without Chinese labour. Similarly, without the CPR, we would not have the Canada of today because Western Canada would eventually have acted on their threat to withdraw from confederation. Therefore, the "Chinese gene" simply cannot be denied when we look at the historical development and birth of Canada.

Thirdly, in terms of the genetics of the early settlers, such as: the First Nations, the English, the French and the Chinese, the Chinese are closely related to the earliest settlers, the First Nations, to the point that these two groups might even be of the same genetic heritage, both being of Mongolian stock. Furthermore, as mentioned in the *Foreword* to the Chinese edition of our book, written by Jiayan Yan, a tenured professor at

Peking University, there are official historical records in the Liang Dynasty History (*Liang Shu*) about Chinese monks having visited North America on a mission to spread Buddhism about 1000 years before Columbus, and there were even "reliable records of local customs and practices". Based on such evidence, professor Yan strongly affirms that the idea of the Chinese gene is not a figment of imagination.

This book, *Canada's Chinese Gene*, serves to establish a fundamental status for the history of Chinese Canadians, settle pointless debates that have gone on for over a hundred years, and work towards building a new vision of Canada with no ill feelings. Most members of Chinese society have expressed agreement or even excitement over this goal, because for the first time ever we've made such a clear definition of our position in Canada. There does remain one problem: do non-Chinese Canadians identify with this definition and conclusion?

On this matter, I feel confident. As I have had conversations with other Canadians (including various people in media, politicians, scholars and ordinary citizens), I have found that they think the theory is unique and reasonable. This reorganization and repositioning of history can both allow the truth in history to re-emerge by breaking the version of history that is solely Anglo-French focused, as well as embracing the modern Canadian values of acceptance and inclusivity. Much of the prejudice against Chinese people did not simply take root in racism but was caused by ignorance and deviation in historical narratives, and we feel a responsibility to change this situation.

The year of 2017 is the 150th anniversary of Canadian confederation, a great chance for us to rethink the position of this country, the Canadian of our Chinese communities, and ourselves as individuals. 150 years of history is short for a country. Even though still young, is Canada today the same as it was 150 years ago? In the eyes of those in power, the rights and wrongs of today and of history are becoming a mere tale and a decoration, as well as a new form of "political correctness".

Looking vertically through the 150 years of Chinese people in Canada, their position has shown earth-shaking changes, to the point that the desperate dream of reaching "Gold Mountain" is within reach for the Chinese people today. Yet under the banner of "progress", history is becoming weathered, and it is now becoming a "tool" for politicians to grab votes.

As far as I am concerned, however, history is both a record of events that have happened, and a "warning" for the future, because it is not an uncommon occurrence for history to repeat itself in human civilizations.

Thus, true historical records and correct teaching of history are indispensable in preventing the reoccurrence of history's injustices and tragedies, especially for Chinese in Canada. At the same time, there is also a pressing need to summarize the last 150 years of history concerning Chinese people in Canada for their descendants, or for those who are concerned with them today and tomorrow, and for Chinese immigrants who have already settled or are soon to be settled in Canada.

It is an admirable Chinese virtue to remember those who have helped us, and this is also a basis for Chinese people to continue exploring in this new age. It is not easy to depict the Chinese elements over the 150 years of Canadian history in the shortest possible length of a book, but it has to be done, because it is vital to rethink how we position ourselves in Canada. Luckily for me, my life as an immigrant has been in beautiful British Columbia. This place holds more than 150 years of memory for the Chinese people, since even before confederation.

B.C. is the origin of Chinese communities in Canada. The word "origin" has four meanings.

First is that Chinese came among the earliest settlers. As early as the '50s of the 19th century, Chinese people already stepped on this land along with the European explorers. Then from the '60s to the '80s of the same century, tens of thousands of Chinese flooded into the land of "Gold Mountain" during the Gold Rush and the construction of the CPR. At one point, almost half of the population in some Gold Rush town of B.C. was Chinese. Entering Canada through B.C. has become a tradition for Chinese people even to this day, and this has turned B.C. into Canada's Asia-Pacific gateway geographically, economically, and in the increase of immigrants.

Second is the great contributions made by Chinese in Canada. As previously stated, the Gold Rush and railroad construction established the foundation for economic and population growth of this region. The construction of the CPR stands out in particular, as it was a vital factor in Western Canada joining and remaining in confederation and creating the landmass that is Canada today. This must be stressed over and over while we celebrate the 150th anniversary of Canada. I have always emphasized: Chinese people are not outsiders but must be seen as one of the founding peoples of Canada. Outstanding contribution towards Canada's economic development has become one of the most important features of Chinese communities.

Third is the profound victimization suffered by Chinese. White politicians and communities in B.C. have mounted anti-Chinese campaigns historically, from the head-tax to the *Chinese Exclusion Act*, from the stripping of citizenship to the burning of Chinatown, all have brought Chinese families dispersion and loss of homestead. Chinese have suffered all the hardships faced by immigrants, have worked to create the perseverance and dauntless spirit of Chinese communities, and have served to train Chinese communities to work hard to consistently create better lives. In other words, tragedies made the Chinese people recognize that being forced to live as outsiders and being manipulated are not predestined for the Chinese people.

Fourth is the quick awakening. Ever since the *Chinese Exclusion Act*, Chinese communities have awakened and begun to resist. During the Second

World War, many second and third generation Chinese of B.C. abided by the beautiful Chinese cultural tradition to "fight hatred with virtue" and entered the war against fascism as non-citizens. They were not mercenaries like those who are fighting now in the Middle East or in Africa, but they fought with a clear "national identity" and "anti-fascism belief". During the war, they asked Canada to fix its historical mistake of excluding the Chinese by restoring citizenship and voting rights of the Chinese people.

The bloodbaths weathered by the 700 Chinese soldiers have functioned to change the status of Chinese people in Canadian history and forced the government to abolish the *Chinese Exclusion Act* in 1947, which won back the due rights of Chinese people as Canadian citizens. Not only that, Douglas Jung, a veteran and lawyer from Vancouver, became a Conservative member of Parliament in the 1950s. He became the first Canadian MP of Chinese and Asian descent in the Canadian House of Commons and marked the beginning of Chinese Canadians taking part in politics.

The pursuit of freedom and dreams is part of human nature, but it requires great perseverance, hard work, or even payment in blood and lives to have them realized. Today, the dreams of the Chinese Canadians have gone far beyond the "gold mountain" dreams of the Chinese workers 150 years ago. This requires us to take on a more global vision, a heart of compassion and a spirit of giving back, acting with all of our might to achieve a win-win future for Chinese communities, for Canada, and for the world.

Guo Ding

Introduction

*This book is about nothing but Canada. In particular, it is
dedicated to celebrating the 150th anniversary of Canada's birthday.*

In 2015, the year in which I had lived in Canada for exactly 15 years, I
was reminded that Canada's 150th anniversary was just around the corner.
By sheer coincidence, I had an opportunity to discuss with a friend who had
been in the publishing business for many years, about his action plan for a
publication. One of the ideas was to publish a book to celebrate the 150th
anniversary of Canada before Canada day in 2017; this idea resonated with
me immediately. The final decision to publish this book as part of a series was
confirmed after some careful thought and preparation, and I was especially
reassured after my friend, Mr. Guo Ding agreed to join in the effort and
provide support for this book.

This is a book on the 150 years of Canada from the perspectives of
Chinese Canadians and Chinese communities in Canada.

As a book on Chinese Canadians and Chinese communities, the book
inevitably touches upon Chinese phenomena and elements such as: the
Chinese language, Chinese New Year, Chinatown, old and new generations
of Chinese immigrants, etc. However, these Chinese phenomena and
elements that refer to China today cannot be equated at all to the "China"
of 150 years ago. During this period, many historical milestones occurred,
including the fall of the Qing Dynasty (1644–1911), the victory of the 1911
Revolution, the birth of the People's Republic of China in 1949, and most
importantly, the rise of China on the world stage over the last 30 years. Also,
the term "Chinese" here is not specific to any nation or region, but rather to
the internationalized Chinese communities. Therefore, over the 150 years,

Chinese phenomena and elements have also evolved, with new chapters added as time progresses.

The purpose of this book is not only to describe Chinese phenomena and elements in Canada, but also to discuss and reflect with our readers what these phenomena and elements have meant to Canada as a country.

Few would disagree when someone claims that Canada is a multicultural country with many national origins. The multitude of peoples and cultures undoubtedly include Chinese people and cultures. They have been in North America since long before the official establishment of Canada as a country in 1867. However, it would seem strange, confusing, or even questionable to many, if someone were to connect Chinese people and cultures to being characteristic of Canada as a nation and the Canadian people.

This co-author first came to Canada in 1999, the last year of the 20th century, as a visiting scholar to Simon Fraser University, and decided to immigrate and settle in Vancouver a year later with my family. It took a whole 15 years of residing on this land before I started working on this book, which just happened to be one tenth of the 150 years of Canadian history since its founding. During this period, I have encountered a variety of people and events that many other old and new immigrants may have encountered as well. Having come through both blessed and painful times, for better or for worse, I attempt to describe some of the meaningful events in the following two stories.

The first story is about the new policy announced in August of 2016 in B.C., wherein the province would begin to charge an additional 15 percent property transfer tax for foreign buyers who purchase properties in the Vancouver region. This new policy should seem as normal as winter rain in Vancouver. However, the problem is that the factors which determine whether someone is a "foreign buyer" is based on whether the person has a "foreign surname". Typically, Canadian authorities do not check the nationality of property buyers. Yet to prove that it was "foreign" buyers who created the real estate bubble in B.C., causing dismay among local residents who could no longer afford a property, the opposition party and some media collected and published information on buyers with Chinese surnames in order to pressure the party in power to establish new taxes to suppress "foreigners" who try to make money from investing in real estate. It is absolutely wrong to pick out Chinese surnames as "foreign names". Based on statistics from phone directories in Canada, the fact is that among the top 20 surnames, four of them are of Chinese origin, with "Li" ranking number 1, a number far exceeding "Smith" which is in the 2nd place. This does not even include the other spelling of Li, i.e., "Lee", which ranks in 8th place. Moreover, the Chinese surname "Lam" is in 3rd place, and "Chan" in 19th place. By this formula, if we were to count Philip S. Lee, David See-Chai Lam or Raymond Chan and their families as "foreign buyers" if they were to buy any Vancouver property after August of 2016, would that not make this tax reform a laughingstock?

The second story has to do with Chinese signatures on IDs and documents. The PR Card, SIN Card, Health Card, debit cards, credit cards, driver's licenses, passports and others, all these documents and files would require a personal signature to be processed when a Chinese person arrives in Canada. When accompanying newly arrived friends to process these IDs, I was frequently asked by these friends whether they should sign in Chinese or in English. The fact is, the signature only serves to prove a person's identity, that is, that the signer is indeed the person with the signature, which must be kept unique and uniform; whether it's in English or in Chinese is not really a concern. I have kept my Chinese signature as a habit, which was to be in-line with the signature on the only official ID I had when I left China— my Chinese passport. It never occurred to me that this habit would end up causing a senseless fuss at one point. I sometimes represent our company when sending invitation letters to senior executives of Chinese companies to visit Canada as a part of my work duties. My signature on the letter naturally remains as the Chinese one. One time however, after receiving my invitation letter with a signature in Chinese, the Chinese company kindly, implicitly, yet firmly asked me to re-send the invitation letter with a signature in English, because the company's international affairs office suspected the Canadian invitation letter was forged, since the signature of the inviter was in Chinese. I sent the letter again with an English signature to assist their work, and the invited parties successfully passed the authorization from the company's international affairs office and received their visas. This experience still weighs heavily in my heart, and it feels important for me to give vent to it, even though it happened quite some time ago.

Therefore, this book is for Canadians, as well as for Chinese friends who care about Canada.

The first chapter of the book directly delves into the subject of Chinese people being a part of Canada's "founding genes", and that the Chinese "DNA" both exists and extends in the "bloodstream" of Canada's history by revisiting the establishment of Canada as a nation. The second chapter describes how Chinese Canadian soldiers countered hate with kindness and sacrificed their lives to save Canadian troops and fight for Canada during the First World War. Their actions defended the spirit of the Canadian constitution and Canadian values. The third chapter describes the large increases, widespread origins, and complex structures of Chinese immigrants, as well as their contributions to the communities in various fields and professions as their skills diversified. The fourth chapter showcases how Chinese Canadian economic activity is moving out of Chinatowns, out of traditional industries, and into the field of investments—the new field where Chinese people and Chinese companies are making contributions to Canada. The fifth chapter reflects on the difficulties and achievements Chinese people have faced and created in Canadian politics, as well as being awed by the sight of the light at the end of this tunnel full of twists and turns. The sixth chapter highlights the many faces of Chinese communities with examples from Chinatowns, traditional social groups, and online virtual communities. The seventh chapter discusses how Chinese language media have changed, as well as their important roles in the 150 years of documenting the history of Chinese people's struggles in Canada. The eighth chapter concludes short essays on new challenges and opportunities facing to the Chinese community amid the unprecedent COVID-19 pandemic.

At this moment, it feels like we can hear the heartfelt words from every Canadian in our national anthem, "Oh Canada! Our home and native land! Oh Canada! We stand on guard for thee."

Kenny Zhang

Chapter 1

Chinese Pioneers as Founders of Canada

Canada is a geographical giant of the north, and at the same time a small North American country in terms of population. To the west, it is connected to Asia, and has especially strong connections with China across the Pacific; To the east, it is connected to Europe via the Atlantic Ocean, and its relations with countries such as England and France go far back in history. It is a big country in that its landmass is the second largest in the world, exceeding even China's 9.6 million square kilometers. However, with a population of only 37.8 million[1], it is just 1/37 of China's 1.4 billion population. The earliest residents of the country are those who are called "First Nations", the aboriginals.

No one would cast doubt on Canada's claim to be one of the most peaceful nations on earth. Bordering the United States, it has not had a war

---

1 *Statistic Canada*. Table 17-10-009-01 population estimates, quartely. (2019)

in over a hundred years since its establishment. Compared with the history of other nations, Canada's founding did not involve much bloodshed and violence. Therefore, some historians of Canada share the view that Canadians can look back at their nation's development with pride as it was full of peace and clemency in general, which makes it a well-established exemplar for the development of other nations and races.

However, many English-speaking historians only narrate the pre-Confederation history of Canada in terms of the struggles between the colonies of the United Kingdom, France and America, and the effects of America's War of Independence; they ignore, whether intentionally or not, the bloodshed and misery of the First Nations people during this "peaceful" progress of history. Similarly, mainstream historical narratives have given little justified and objective accounts of the Chinese people's contributions towards western Canada joining or staying in the Confederation, nor the hardships they went through. It is interesting to note that many Francophones in Quebec, a major player in the Confederation of Canada, also have retained feelings of bitterness towards the Anglophone majority even to this day. Looking back in history, September 1864, while English and French armies were fighting a bloody battle in Port La Joye, right across the port in Charlottetown a meeting was being held between the delegates of the British colonies in North America. This was the first meeting that drafted the Confederation of Canada. On October 10th of the same year, the various colonies held a conference called "the Quebec Conference" in Quebec—the second meeting on Canadian Confederation. Brought about by the stimulation and pressure of the America's independence, Canada's Confederation happened very quickly. New immigrants to Canada from the American War of Independence also hoped to establish a new nation.

In December 1866, the British Empire footed the bill and delegates from all involved colonies went to London and modified the "Quebec Resolution" to become the final statement for the British Parliament to approve. In 1867, the British North America Act of 1867 came into effect, and a new North American nation was born.

One cannot claim that Canada in its confederation went through a totally peaceful journey with no acts of violence at all. For example, after Confederation, Canada purchased from their Hudson's Bay Company the control of the Northwest Territories in 1869. Fearing destruction of the traditional hunter-fisher lifestyle, the Métis staged two uprisings (rebellions, as they were once called). Peace was reached after negotiations were held in Ottawa, and Manitoba joined the Confederation as a province. However, the leader Louis Riel was hanged for treason.

Chinese people have played key roles in the confederation and development of Canada, but they have also suffered the pain of racism within their "peaceful" surroundings.

Long before Canada's Confederation, Chinese people had already set foot on the lands of Western Canada along with European explorers. Two waves of Chinese immigration happened in the 19th century: first in the 1850s and 1860s during the Gold Rush, and second in the 1870s and 1880s for building the Canadian Pacific Railway. At that time, the Chinese came to Canada not as honoured immigrants, but as hired labourers who came here in pursuit of their dreams.

Chinese people played crucial roles in the history of Canada's establishment as a nation. For one, the First Nations, aboriginal people of Canada had close ties with Chinese people historically, but even without mentioning this, the roles and positions of the Chinese people were irreplaceable in the early days of Canada as a nation. We could even say that Chinese "genes" have existed since the very beginning in the "bloodline" of Canadian history. Unfortunately, the Chinese "founding genes" in Canada were ignored, or even rejected by "mainstream" historians over the last one hundred and some years, whether on purpose or not. The mainstream historical narrative of Canada is being flipped upside down along with the multicultural development, especially since June 22, 2006, the day on which Prime Minister Harper apologized formally in the House of Commons regarding the "Head Tax" and for the history of Chinese exclusion. Along with other acts of apology in different parts of Canada, and the retelling of the more truthful history of the aboriginal peoples and Chinese Canadians, historical wrongs have been righted, people have started to wake up from the ruins of memory, and a truer historical representation of the Chinese people has been established.

Historically, Chinese people entered Canada from the west, along the Pacific coastal region. During the era of exploration in the 18th century, Chinese sailors came with European explorers into the mountains and rivers of British Columbia. They left unforgettable imprints of themselves on this land now known as the "best place to live". Between the years 1788 and 1789, 120 Chinese contract workers, including blacksmiths and carpenters, arrived on Vancouver Island, having come all the way from Macau. They helped to build the first 40-ton sloop of Canada's West Coast, the "North West America". The ship became a trusted vessel of Captain John Meares in his exploration of the North American Coast. Captain Meares had close relationships with the Chinese in his fur trade, because the Qing Dynasty royal families had a high demand of fur products at the time. Meares registered the ship as a Portuguese vessel in Macau which was a Portuguese colony in China because British ships required a permit from the British East India Company to explore the West Coast of North America, while non-British ships were exempt.

That being said, the first mass Chinese immigration into western Canada was prompted by the Gold Rush and the building of the railway; both of these events were critical in the development of western Canada and the growth of confederation. It could even be said that without the Chinese people participating during the Gold Rush, we would not have had the original accumulation of wealth for the economic development of Canada's west. Without the Chinese workers, the CPR would not have met British Columbia's established deadline for completion of a trans-Canada railway, and Canada's Confederation would look nothing like the nation it has become today. Therefore, it is right and proper to define Chinese as one of the founding peoples of Canada.

The Chinese and the Gold Rush

The first surge of immigration of Chinese people into Canada happened in 1858. Between the years 1855 and 1857, Californian prospectors found gold in a valley downstream of the Fraser River in British Columbia, which triggered the well-known Fraser Valley Gold Rush in the area. As adventurers gathered from many places, Chinese merchants in San Francisco, California started hiring workers from China to mine gold. Victoria Harbour was filled with Chinese gold miners from San Francisco during the summer and fall of 1858. Boat after boat, group after group, the miners most likely totaled over a thousand. Due to the low population of Chinese miners coming either from San Francisco, or via San Francisco, there was a shortage of workers; so Chinese miners started flooding into the Fraser Valley region from Guangdong's Pearl River Delta and Macao to join the work force from the end of 1859 to 1860. These gold miners mostly went to Hope and Yale where the gold deposits were discovered, to participate in the hard labour of gold mining. Others stayed in Victoria to set up shops that provided the necessities for the miners, and this became the beginning of Canada's first Chinatown.

Many people believed that the Chinese gold miners went to the "gold mountains" to gain great wealth but forgot the excruciating pain and risks they had to take. On the journey to Canada, these people went through life-and-death challenges in the Pacific Ocean; countless died from hunger and illness. Those who made it to the mines had to work in an environment of racial discrimination, low wages and intensive labour. It was not a cakewalk. The Chinese miners usually had one of two types of migration status. One was for contracted workers who signed a contract with merchants in San Francisco or Guangdong; the other was free labourer. Regardless of their status, the Chinese miners were discriminated against by white people; they were solicited for protection money, bullied, and beaten up. Many of these people were robbed or even murdered.

Apart from the gold miners, Chinese people were also hired to construct roads that led to the newly discovered gold mines. Many Chinese people died from epidemics, freezing temperatures, and falling off of cliffs during this process.

Even today we can find the remains of abandoned gold mines along the Fraser River into the mainland; the most famous of these is the "Chinese Wall", as named by the locals. Gold mining of those days required workers to dig out sand that might contain gold and bring it to the riverbanks, then remove the large pieces of rock. The workers laid a wall of these rocks piece by piece, forming a "little great wall", which served to both shield them from the wind and avoid making trips to dispose of the rocks.

It is fair to say that the Gold Rush brought to western Canada not only economic activity, but also the population and incentives required for future development. Chinese miners made incredible efforts in developing the gold mines and gave much in the way of contributions towards the development of western Canada and its diverse communities.

What also needs to be mentioned is that these workers mostly came from the tri-city (Nanhai, Panyu, Shunde), quad-city (Taishan, Xinhuì, Kaiping, Enping), and Heshan county areas. These people later became the foundation for Canada's Chinatowns and Chinese communities, with their influence still lingering today. We can also say that the early communal development of western Canada, especially British Columbia, had Chinese people as a main contributing force; Chinatowns have since become a "traditional brand" of Canadian communities. Therefore, it is not just a simple Chinese enclave that is excluded from the history of Canadian communities.

The best-preserved old Chinatown today was the largest Chinatown during the Canadian Gold Rush, Barkerville. The town's origin comes from a Scottish miner, William (Billy) Barker, who dug up over 30, 000 ounces of gold in William Creek, which attracted hordes of people with their dreams of riches. The place became a lively town in a very short period of time. There were about seven to eight thousand Chinese miners in this area at its population peak, who formed a Chinatown in the eastern part of Barkerville. Besides the miners, other Chinese people who resided there included workers in lumberyards, delivery people who used carts, general labourers in convenience stores, chefs in Chinese restaurants, owners and operators of laundries, and errand boys hired by the rich in the region. A huge number of jobs were taken by Chinese workers, covering a variety of fields and professions. These jobs similarly helped form and sustain the earliest Chinese community in Canada.

Of course, this town that rose with the start of the Gold Rush, fell with the end of the Gold Rush. By the early 20th century, Chinese people were mostly gone from Barkerville, leaving only about 150 people and a few stores. The remains of Chinese buildings, daily necessities, newspapers and calendars that were glued on the walls, all became treasured historical documentation of that era. There are still over 100 buildings in Barkerville today; they currently serve as museums and exhibition halls. Historical remains are divided into categories; objects are on display in almost every room, with even remnants of decorations used in Gold Rush times. What is truly praiseworthy is that the "Chinatown" still remains intact; the tribunal halls, Chinese museums, residences for Chinese miners, Sheng's Herbs and Pharmacy, and the graveyard for the Chinese all remain intact. Barkerville later toured its historical exhibition to the Chinese Cultural Centre of Greater Vancouver, as well as to the homeland of the Chinese workers, Guangdong, with the expectation of communicating with China and the descendants of the nameless workers from China. This serves to connect history with modernity and helps the descendants of those workers to honour their ancestors.

This piece of history has been manifested in English narratives, thanks to the efforts of many Chinese and Euro-Canadian historians.

The Chinese and the Railway

If we say that the Fraser River Gold Rush brought the first stir in building up western Canada, then the construction of the Canadian Pacific Railway set up the foundation that kept British Columbia from withdrawing from Canada's Confederation. Chinese people were among the main forces and key contributors of that railway construction. This is a vital chapter in Canada's historical narrative, which should not be understated and especially not be willfully ignored.

In Canada's history of development, building the railway was the most important national construction project during the early days of Canada's founding. Reasons for this are crystal clear. In order for the Confederation to gain support from all directions and share the benefits of becoming a part of the Canadian Confederation, it had to address the shortcomings in communication and transportation between western and eastern Canada. The CPR would effectively connect the western and eastern provinces as the transportation hub and form a transportation system that goes from one side of Canada to the other. Moreover, this would speed up the immigration from eastern to central and western Canada, and with that increase in population would bring economic development in the west. Trade between the people of eastern and western Canada would increase, and access to the Pacific Ocean on the West Coast would allow Canada to boost its fur trade with Asia. Naturally, the most important function of the CPR extension at that time was to keep British Columbia in the Confederation and prevent it from leaning towards the expanding United States. After the War of Independence, the United States was hastening its expansion towards the west. The original vision of the U.S. at its founding was to incorporate all of

North America into its territory.

Between the end of the 19th century and the start of the First World War, Canada completed three cross-country railway systems. The first was the Canadian Pacific Railway (CPR), completed during the term of Prime Minister Sir John Alexander Macdonald. The second was the Canadian Northern Railway, and the third was the Grand Trunk Railway of Canada, built during the term of the first French Canadian Prime Minister, Sir Wilfrid Laurier. The CPR that reached all the way to Vancouver was by far the most important; this railway was indeed a lifeline, a thousand miles longer than the first transnational railway of the United States. This posed a tremendous challenge to Canada at the time, because Canada had a population of only 3.5 million. It is no wonder that Macdonald once said, "As soon as this railway is built, we will become a truly unified country with common interests and inter-provincial trade."

For building this railway that linked the future of Canadian Confederation and determined the territory of modern Canada, the Chinese workers did as much hard work and sacrificed no fewer lives than any other ethnic group. A word of justice: the CPR would not have been completed before the originally planned date if it were not for the sacrifices and contributions the Chinese people made—they "laid down the tracks at the cost of their lives" over the most dangerous sections of this railway.

In order to convince Alberta and Saskatchewan to join the Confederation, and B.C. to stay in the Confederation, Prime Minister Macdonald, who led the Conservative government, promised to build the railway that would connect the east and the west without additional taxes. This policy essentially doomed the funding for the railway construction from the very beginning. Thus, Chinese workers were recruited to take up the heavy burden that others, especially white workers, would never have taken, to build the most dangerous section of the railway while accepting the lowest of wages. This 10-year construction plan was attacked politically, and Macdonald lost his position as Prime Minister in 1873 due to a scandal when acquiring funds for building the railway. The plan was temporarily put on hold.

The Liberals had little interest in building the CPR. The second Prime Minister of Canada and the first Liberal Prime Minister, Alexander Mackenzie was in no rush to incorporate the western territories into the Canadian Confederation, despite his other great achievements in establishing the Supreme Court, the Royal Military College of Canada, and the Auditor General's office. In the five years of his term, only a few hundred kilometres of railway were put in place in Ontario and Manitoba, and the railway was connected to that of the United States. Later, Macdonald returned to power in 1878. He fought against opposition from the Liberals and began to work on the CPR project again due to pressure from the B.C. government. With his help, Canadian Pacific Railway was incorporated on October 21, 1880 by railway financiers from the United Kingdom, France, and the United States, under the leadership of bankers and investors including Donald Smith (Director of CPR), George Stephen (the first president of CPR and the president of the BMO), and William Van Horne (General manager and President of CPR, one of the founders of Banff National Park) to undertake the construction of the portion that goes from central Canada to the Pacific Coast. This western Canada portion of the railway was not terribly long considering the nearly 3000 miles of CPR. However, this part of the railway required crossing the Rocky Mountains to reach the Pacific Coast, and its harsh working conditions and technical requirements were extreme. These factors turned it into a task that attracted the most attention. This was the reason that Macdonald's plan to build the railway was called "Canada's craziest dream". It became a "Mission Impossible" as soon as construction reached the Rockies. The railway workers were unable even to find spaces between the mountains through which to build a railway. There are endless mountain ranges along the border between Alberta and British Columbia, so many that even trekking across the region would be "harder than climbing up to heaven". Building a whole railway was even more of a pipe dream. Andrew Onderdonk, the contractor for the construction project, estimated that it would take 10, 000 workers to build the 615 kilometres of railway from Fort Moody to Eagle Pass.

Where could one find so many workers? He suggested hiring Chinese workers. This was a very realistic suggestion. First, the funding was very limited, so it would be impossible to complete the project with white workers who required high wages and worker's rights; second, he knew well that Chinese workers were able to endure the hardships for meager wages through his ten years of experience as a railway contractor in America. Chinese workers were the best choice for this dangerous task. However, at the time B.C. had a population of only 35,000, and the entrance of 10,000 Chinese workers would create a large impact. Looking back in history, Onderdonk not only hired Chinese railway workers from the United States, but also hired thousands of workers from Guangdong and Hong Kong. The final number of workers should have been well over ten thousand.

Many people believe that those in charge simply wanted to hire cheap Chinese workers to build the railway in Canada, but that was not the case. White workers were against using "Mongol labour" from the very beginning. They were concerned that these Chinese workers would steal their jobs and undercut their benefit claims to the investors. They also righteously attacked the plan, claiming that Chinese people would not take root in B.C. and in Canada, and only white immigrants would stay and make use of its resources, build businesses, and allow communities to flourish. Only they could help make this region prosperous. Chinese workers would be passersby who would not settle and contribute to the society but would leave as soon as they earned the money. The most typical example of these ideas was that Noah Shakespeare, the chairman of the Workingman's Protection Association, firmly insisted on during one of the workers' gatherings: he would rather have the construction of the CPR fail than to have Chinese workers joining the workforce.[2] In other words, white workers would prefer having western Canada not join, and having B.C. withdraw from the Confederation over having Chinese workers hired in the construction. Shakespeare's speech earned cheers throughout the meeting, but he never expected that his extremist words would mirror the words of Prime Minister Macdonald: "It is simply a question of alternatives: either you must have this (Chinese) labour or you can't have the railway." This proved that the Chinese railway workers were pivotal to the formation and maintenance of Canadian Confederation from another angle, and that Chinese workers were, in fact, builders of today's Canada.

Taking the portion between Fort Moody to Eagle Pass as an example, the construction took 15,000 workers, and 9,000 of them were Chinese. That portion of the railway was full of high mountain ranges and horrific working conditions. Along with wild animals in primeval forests, waters

---

2   Refer to *History of Chinese Migration to Canada*, 1858-1966 by David Chuenyan Lai, Guo Ding, Baoheng Jia. People's Publishing House, 2013.

infested with bacteria, and a lack of medical and sanitary care, many of the Chinese workers had no access to timely medical treatment after falling ill or becoming injured. Accidents in dynamite explosions, collapsing of tunnels, and various other mishaps led to a huge number of deaths and countless injuries. The dead had no autopsy, not even a grave. Many were buried among the rocks, their souls left to roam aimlessly without a headstone. Andrew Onderdonk estimated that there were five to six hundred Chinese workers who died during the construction. In other words, three Chinese souls were lost for every kilometre of the railway. Another unofficial set of statistics shows that out of the 17,000 Chinese workers, about three to four thousand died on this alien land.

Errors in Historical Evaluation

From the evidence presented above, we can see that many Chinese people participated in the construction of the CPR. Although they had only taken part in the construction of the portion in British Columbia, and did not make up the majority of workers, their participation in the final phase of the construction was crucial to the timely completion of the CPR. The CPR of course, was a decisive factor that ensured B.C.'s commitment to stay within Confederation, forming the territory of Canada as a political entity today. In fact, once the CPR became operational, it took only five days to go from Montreal in eastern Canada to the Pacific Coast of B.C. in the west. Canada's economic development accelerated rapidly, and the country was stabilized. What is more noteworthy is that despite the hatred from white workers and the unsympathetic reactions from some money-crazed Chinese business people towards the loss of lives, the Chinese workers undertook the most excruciating parts of the construction of the CPR, and in so doing lost the highest number of lives. They deserve to be named rightfully as national heroes in the building of Canada during her early days.

Canada has had no dynastic changes or regime changes, but only alternation between political parties in the same regime. Overall, the 150 years of history has been one filled with optimism. That being said, in the thick history book of national development, parts of the earliest chapters still are shrouded in darkness. There is little praise for the Chinese workers and their contribution in building the railways. The mainstream historical narratives did not give the Chinese workers the medals they deserved, but appear to have written them off, with or without intent. Despite Prime Minister Macdonald and CPR contractor Onderdonk having given praise to the Chinese workers as key to the timely completion of the CPR, these words of praise were only at the level of recognizing the hard work and cost-efficiency, and not at the level of national heroes who contributed to the building of Canada in the early days of her founding. Likewise, no Chinese representatives were invited to the completion ceremony of the CPR on November 7, 1885, where Donald Smith drove the last spike of the railway in Craigellachie, B.C.. For a long time afterwards, Chinese people made few appearances in mainstream English works on the heroic achievements of the CPR's construction. This means that the mainstream historical narrative of Canada's founding, and of CPR's construction have been incomplete in the last hundred and some years, to which we finally add these pages today.

Chinatown, a Stage and Also a Fortress

Even today, Canadian Chinatowns remain as tourist attractions full of cultural features. Many Europeans, Americans, or even other Asians enter Chinatowns in search of an Asian oasis in the sea of white people; or an ancient historical atmosphere within a young country.

The Encyclopedia of Global Human Migration wrote about the origins of Chinatowns around the world: "A Chinatown is a neighborhood outside mainland China, Hong Kong, and Taiwan that has historically been a place of residence for overseas Chinese and a center of distinctly Chinese business, social, and cultural activities." The appearance of Chinatowns is a product of mass migration of Chinese people abroad. Especially after the 19th century, Chinatowns appeared in Southeast Asia, North America, Australia, Europe, and even Africa and Latin America following the footsteps of the early Chinese pioneers. At the same time, Chinatowns appeared as a result of anti-Chinese actions. Chinese immigrants faced cultural differences with local society, and due to a surge of nationalism at the time, Chinese culture-centered economies emerged. The masses of Chinese migrants abroad had limited knowledge of the new lands. Having no families and being unable to communicate effectively, they were forced to live amongst themselves due to psychological, social and economic needs. They formed relatively safe, cheap, convenient buffer zones between themselves and other cultural communities." [3]

Indeed, Canada's Chinatowns functioned as fortresses in the beginning, giving these explorers far away from home a relatively safe nest; a place

---

3   Kang Qing Zhang, "Chinatowns," The Encyclopedia of Global Human Migration, edited by Immanuel Ness, Blackwell Publishing, 2013.

of mother tongues, a place with some comfort, a place of messages from home, and a place with friends that would lend a hand when needed. Consequently, regionally-based guilds, gangs, and meeting halls arose quickly in Chinatowns as mutual support groups for their members.

Chinatowns not only provided a place for young people who travelled to Canada in search of prosperity, they also become the spiritual support for the times when North America experienced its anti-Chinese movements. As things changed with time, the Chinatowns have gone through continuous cycles of flourishing and downfall together with history. Their cultural significance has also accumulated day by day. For second and third generation Chinese immigrants, their goals were to flee Chinatowns, "from Chinatown to Vancouver's west side" became a road of tears, sweat and struggle. Those Chinese who were able to make it outside even thought that those who stayed in Chinatowns were worthless and inauthentic "bananas", yellow only on the outside, white on the inside. On the opposite end of the attitudinal spectrum, the close-minded and xenophobic "Chinatown consciousness" slowly turned into a new "mental fortress" that inhibited positive interactions between Chinese people and the surrounding society at large. It also served to encourage pitting the Chinese people to scheme against one another within their limited society. Those Chinese who made it in terms of material wealth became wanderers in terms of spirituality, living as strays on the fringes of culture.

As a matter of fact, the earliest Chinatown in Canada was not in Vancouver, but in Victoria, where the earliest Chinese settlers landed on Canadian soil. As stated before, Chinese workers and other Chinese people flooded into Canada along with the Gold Rush and railway construction. These two waves of immigration became the earliest two times when

Chinese people participated in the building of Canada, but they also turned into the beginning of Canada's history of racial discrimination against Chinese people in Canada. The early Chinese workers came to Canada to engage in hard labour; they dreamed of becoming wealthy in the "gold mountains", and returning home dressed up in fine clothing one day. They were travelers away from home, full of hope to return one day. This "temporary resident" mentality is a true reflection of what many overseas Chinese thought for a long time, and it is unnecessary for anyone to conceal or frame it in some other fashion.

However, this is not the same as what many white workers claimed, that the Chinese people had no intention of staying in Canada. As their homeland in China was in turmoil and experiencing massive poverty, many Chinese workers actually intended to stay in Canada over the long term. However, during the early days of Canada's development, the so-called mainstream society had a "utilitarian" attitude when dealing with the Chinese. Their minds were filled with prejudiced and discriminatory ideas of the Chinese following the Opium Wars, making it impossible for them to treat Chinese people with the same equal and just principles they used for themselves, to the point that they "burned the bridges" after the railway was completed.

After the completion of the CPR in November 1885, a surge of unemployment struck the Chinese workers in western Canada. The Chinese business brokers were so unconcerned with the plight of their own brethren that they refused to pay Chinese workers money for their return trip back to their homeland. Aside from a few workers who came from and returned to the United States, many were held up in B.C.. Adding insult to injury, many municipal governments had racially discriminatory laws on employment, and at the same time the Chinese workers had limited English. These workers were forced to continue doing hard labour in coal mines and lumberyards, or in the homes of rich white families as servants. A few ended up farming or selling vegetables. However, most had to return to Chinatown in Victoria or New Westminster. Those who had some money saved up opened restaurants, convenience stores or laundries, and those without capital ended up laboring in Chinatowns. They added new lifeblood into the Chinatowns that had developed along with the Gold Rush and the railway construction.

Looking at the history of Chinatowns from a Chinese person's perspective, they were places where Chinese people gathered, resided, huddled, and survived in the darkest of times. Whether it be the Chinatown in Victoria or the Chinatown in Vancouver, they were areas with a radius of less than 300 metres. But it was in such small neighborhoods that many Chinese followed their thorny paths of life during the period of over a hundred years of Canadian history.

In the late 19th century, Chinese people crossed the Pacific in search of the gold mountains during the Gold Rush period, then starting in 1881, when construction of the CPR began, 17, 000 Chinese workers from China and the United States were hired by Canadian contractors. More than 3, 000 of them lost their lives.

In 1885, the railway was completed, and the federal government passed a new immigration act targeting Chinese people, stating that starting in January 1886, every Chinese immigrant would be charged a head-tax of 50 Canadian dollars. The head-tax rose to 100 dollars in July 1900, reflecting the growth of anti-Chinese sentiment in Canada. Parliament increased the head-tax yet again after amending the immigration laws, and the price became 500 dollars in July 1903. This amount was equal to two years of salary for a Chinese worker at the time. Finally, in 1923, the federal government altogether banned Chinese people from entering Canada with a new Chinese Immigration Act (commonly referred to as the Chinese Exclusion Act), which replaced the head-tax. It was not until May 17, 1947 that the Act was abolished. This simple historical record tells of the countless tears shed by the many broken Chinese families, and Chinatowns are the silent witnesses to this period in history. At the beginning of the 20th century, the anti-Chinese movement dealt a strong blow to Chinatowns. Chinese people were ridiculed, their homes destroyed, and in a great blaze, Chinatowns turned into a ruin of bloodshed.

That was a time which no Chinese Canadian wants to think back on. Logically speaking, the Chinese people should have been vindicated right after World War II, yet it took another half a century after the abolishment of the Chinese Exclusion Act. On June 22, 2006, 3:15 PM EST, the official status of the Chinese people made a critical turn in history. On Parliament Hill in Ottawa, Prime Minister Stephen Harper offered "a full apology to Chinese Canadians" for the 1885 head-tax on Chinese immigrants and for the *1923 Chinese Exclusion Act*. Harper said in his speech: "While Canadian courts have ruled that the head tax and immigration prohibition were legally authorized at the time, we fully accept the responsibility to acknowledge the shameful policies of our past," because "for over six decades these race-based financial measures aimed solely at the Chinese were implemented with deliberation by the Canadian state...this was a grave injustice and one we are morally obligated to acknowledge."

It was a 100-year-long wait for Canadian Chinese and Chinatowns to finally reach this moment. However, despite the fact that the federal government has officially apologized through parliament and is currently paying 20, 000 dollars to each of the 20 surviving victims and the 200 family members of the victims of the head-tax, together with funding a Community Historical Recognition Program with 24 million dollars for educating and memorializing the history of wartime contributions and immigration restrictions of Canada, how could money possibly make up for the hardships that Canadian Chinese and Chinatowns have endured over the last hundred years?

The Department of Canadian Heritage (responsible for national policies and programs in communal history and multiculturalism) organized a rectifying journey for the victims of the head-tax and their families to get together in western Vancouver as an act to show sincerity and profoundness of the official apology. The tour started from Vancouver's Chinatown, then headed towards Ottawa, making stopovers in Winnipeg and Toronto on the Canadian National Railway train. This train named "Rectification" by some Chinese and English media took its trip on the CPR, the railway that was constructed using thousands of lives of young Chinese workers. Harper wrote in his apology regarding the Chinese workers on the railway: "From the shores of the St. Lawrence, across the seemingly endless expanses of shield and prairie, climbing the majestic Rockies, and cutting through the rugged terrain of British Columbia, this transcontinental link was the ribbon of steel that bound our fledgling country together. It was an engineering feat—one for which the back-breaking toil of Chinese labourers was largely responsible." Who would have thought that the Canadian government not only did not bestow rewards based on merit, but rather burned the bridges for the Chinese people, and began its racially discriminatory actions by first collecting head-taxes, then constantly increasing the amount to prevent Chinese people from arriving, and finally passing the *Chinese Exclusion Act* that left many families broken, parents and children separated, husbands and wives apart. It was a great tragedy of humanity. This ride on the "Rectification" train summarized the hardships and sufferings of the Chinese people in Canada over the past hundred years. Yet, how was this tragedy exclusive to Chinese in Canada? The same was done to the Chinese people in the United States at the time. The historical justification on June 22 did not fall out of the sky, nor was it granted by a superior power. It was earned through the hard work and peaceful protest by generation after generation of Chinese Canadians.

During the Second World War, Chinese Canadians actively volunteered to join the Canadian army to show their love and compassion for Canada. They performed great military feats in the bloody war against fascism. After the war, the Canadian government finally abolished the *Chinese Exclusion Act* in 1947, and finally the families who were separated by an ocean for decades were able to reunite, but the painful wounds caused by the head-tax and the *Chinese Exclusion Act* would not heal easily. By the 80s of the 20th century, Chinese people and social justice groups began taking action towards getting compensation for the head-tax. There were almost ten thousand victims alive at the time. However, the path towards justice was not a smooth ride. The road was filled with bumps and twists that almost turned the movement into a complete failure. In the last couple of decades, victims of the head-tax continued to pass away disappointed. Such was the cold hard end created by a century of injustice. As times continued to change, Chinese communities kept growing stronger, and the historical opportunity finally came for head-tax compensation. Through this example we can see that Chinese communities are no longer just a herd of sheep.

They would no longer cower in the government's shadows, nor act as slaves to the system; they would be gentle and civil citizens, but not to be stepped on. Chinese communities began to display significant political power.

Chinatown was a great fortress, but it has become even more of an open stage. As Canada established policies on multiculturalism in 1971, culturally brilliant Chinatowns slowly turned into archetypes of traditional Asian cultures and were celebrated as such by local communities. In 1971, Vancouver's Chinatown was designated by the B.C. provincial government as a Provincial Historic Site, and later in 2011, it was designated by the federal government as one of 956 National Historic Sites.

Five Key Characteristics of Chinatown Value

The historical injustice suffered by the Chinese communities has been rectified, but the position of Chinatowns in the history of Canadian community development is still lacking clarity. This is a matter of great importance. As a part of Canada's historical remains, the position of Chinatowns is no different from any other community; their vital communal contributions to the development of Canada as a nation still go under-recognized; their level of importance still does not match that of European communities.

The reasons that Chinatowns are communities that made a great contribution to the development of Canada and have become examples for other communities, especially communities of new immigrants in their developmental stage, are as follows: First, Chinatown communities are loyal to Canada. Having existed for over a century, Chinatowns still survive in various large cities. They never backed down even when facing discrimination, and they worked hard to meet the challenges that confronted them. They adapted to the times and shined brightly with youthful vigour. They are exemplary among the various ethnic communities of Canada. When Canada was facing the challenges of war, people in Chinatowns fought hatred with kindness, and volunteered to join the army, even though they were treated as second-class residents. They fought for Canada's democracy and freedom, loyally and strongly. Such characters are rare in Canadian history.

With constant striving for improvement, and great loyalty to their country of residence, Chinatowns and their residents are a manifestation of Canadian spirit at her founding and are prime examples of outstanding Canadian communities.

Second, Chinatowns are self-sufficient communities. They do not occupy an excessive sum of tax-payer resources, but rather keep their residents well-fed and its community constantly developing through hard work and lower-than-average wages. In the hundred and some years of their history, Chinatowns were criticized for being dirty, but this was not entirely the Chinese people's doing. Discrimination from mainstream society alone limited Chinese people's merging into mainstream society. At the same time, Chinese people occupied underprivileged positions in society; they were limited in their English and had inherited different customs. Combined with their low income, they could only afford cheap housing in and around Chinatowns, "harbouring" places to some degree, from all the various forms of discrimination by a different culture—the Anglo-Saxon culture. Closed-off Chinatowns had no reliance on government or outside resources; they started as economic and residential centres for Chinese people, then later turned into self-sufficient communities with all kinds of services, including groceries, restaurants, churches, travel agencies, clinics, pharmacies, schools, education centres, media, clan societies, and funeral homes. They became miniature societies of their own.

Not only were the Chinese self-sufficient, they also made notable contributions to the country. Just the discriminatory head-taxes alone accounted for at least 23 million dollars from 1886 to 1923, paid by 82,371 Chinese immigrants. This amount almost equals the 25 million dollars the federal government spent on building the CPR. The British Columbia Parliament Buildings located in Victoria were financed by federal funds collected from the head taxes. From the Gold Rush to building the railway, to running the Chinatowns, the taxes paid by Chinese residents for maintaining their Chinese communities and employment were fairly significant and were used to fund the development of western Canada. An incomplete set of statistics showed that in the ten years between 1874 and 1884, the tariffs collected from goods imported from Guangdong to British Columbia reached 410,000 dollars; during the period 1879-1883, almost 40,000 dollars were collected from Chinese people by the Victoria Municipal Government for business licenses, water bills, road maintenance levies, and property taxes.

In 1883, there were 276 Chinese businesses in British Columbia; each year they paid 160 dollars in tariffs, 2,300 dollars for tobacco taxes, 7,560 dollars for business licenses, 500 dollars for property taxes, 1,100 for municipal taxes, 27, 000 dollars in rent, 6,180 dollars in farmland leases, and 8,400 dollars for interests on loans. The total amount was over 21,600 dollars. This shows that Chinese people were not just participants in building the Canadian nation, they were also among the earliest tax payers.

Third, the survival and development of Chinatowns was driven by both economic and cultural forces. They showed a healthy and balanced development trend for communities, and thus are considered highly meritorious in all Canadian communities. As mentioned, Chinatowns remained unshakable through a hundred years even when faced with systemic discrimination from the country, and isolation from mainstream society. The key support that helped Chinatowns pull through was economic power. Chinatowns by themselves have been centres of production, sales, and living. Countless shops and free-flowing trade made Chinatowns fully independent as a communal economy. Moreover, the "healthcare system" formed by traditional Chinese doctors, herbal shops, and community hospitals were able to help the sick and injured; the Chinese Benevolent Associations and various societies based on regions of origin or based on clan membership formed a "system of social organizations". This system helped the Chinese people to stay organized and close-knit, while also serving as links to the outside. During the turbulent times of the Chinese Exclusion Act, Chinese Benevolent Associations also took on leadership roles in negotiations with government.

Aside from their economic and social organizations, Chinatowns were never written off in history (despite a few troughs in development), and the most important factor was the cultural power which served as the backbone of their communities. A community with a cultural backbone is a community with a foundation for continuous development. During their hundred years of history, Chinese residents needed comfort from their homesickness as well as methods to maintain Chinese cultural traditions. Thus, Chinese newspapers, schools, operas (Cantonese Opera in the beginning, then later stage plays), literature, and religion appeared in these communities. Supported by their culture, Chinese souls were empowered and had what it took to maintain Chinese communities. Chinese culture, which started from Chinatowns, eventually became an integral part of Canada's multicultural wealth.

Nonetheless, Chinese communities have had their down sides. For example, gambling, prostitution (due to the sexual needs of single male workers), opium dens, and fighting with weapons were the four greatest threats during the early days, and became an excuse for racism directed against the Chinese; the persistent "corrupting environment" within their culture featuring internal fighting and disunity kept Chinese communities from participating in mainstream politics and societies for a long time. Chinese communities to this day are reflecting on such problems and reforming them.

Fourth, Chinatowns are open and independent communities. Many would mistakenly assume that Chinese people isolate themselves due to cultural and language barriers; discrimination on the part of government and mainstream society furthered their isolation. On what appears in the history of Canada's development, Chinese communities were isolated groups and had little influence on the country and society. Such a claim is not at all true! Chinese communities, as represented by Chinatowns, are open communities despite their being independent. This is a very important characteristic in Canadian communities. Even during the days of the Gold Rush and railway building, Chinese workers had very close relationships with the earliest land owners of North America, the First Nations.

Since all of the Chinese workers during the Gold Rush and railway construction were men, they built relationships with the local First Nations people through work. From misunderstanding each other, to second guessing, to recognizing, to mutual understanding, the Chinese and First Nations became bosom friends, as they were both placed at the very bottom of Canadian society. The law passed in British Columbia during the first legislative assembly in 1872 stripped voting rights from both the First Nations and the Chinese, condemning both groups as second-class races. This made their relationships grow even closer. After the Gold Rush and the railway construction, white people "burned their bridges" and left many Chinese workers unemployed. Many of the workers went to eastern Canada to find a new life; some wandered in the west, and reached the Indian Reserves, where they married and had children with local people. Their children were called "half breeds". There are Chinese surnames still flowing in some First Nation Tribes. For example, Senator Lillian Eva Dyck's father was from Kaiping of Guangdong and her mother was a First Nation member. Her mother lost all her privileges and social benefits from the reservation as soon as she got married.

Although many white people were discriminatory towards the Chinese, there were some who had good relationships with Chinese people, and even helped Chinese workers to claim their rights. During the period of Chinese exclusion, Chinese people undertook to find conscientious supporters to help. Chinese were also very active in joining the army to fight for Canada during the Second World War.

It was the open-minded attitude of Chinese communities that helped the Chinese to survive during adversity. No hatred was spread, no revenge was sought. They received help from all sources when times changed and won respect and support from many other ethnic groups, and thus were able to change their fate.

Fifth, Chinatowns are communities that developed through growth and openness. A misunderstanding that lasted over a hundred years about Chinese communities represented by Chinatowns was that Chinatowns were closed and segregated communities. This historical observation is a close-minded, horizontal, and narrow view of the development of Chinatowns; a more holistic and vertical view should be used to understand the development of Chinatowns. The truth is that the DNA programming of Chinatowns are pro-openness; Chinese communities have developed through inclusive growth.

Another characteristic of Chinatowns is that although they have been a last line of defense for Chinese people seeking refuge and shelter from racism, and to unite against the same oppression, Chinese people were never satisfied with being left to sink or swim in their tiny strip of land. They moved out of Chinatowns whenever an opportunity arose, and they joined mainstream society looking towards a broader world. They displayed the life energy of a tree growing leaves and branches. This is an exemplary case of community development for all ethnic groups around the world, and therefore has international significance.

For example, the family of Mr. Yip, a Cantonese who settled in British Columbia in 1881, has been here through five generations. The family has now spread across the globe with over 800 members, many of whom married across ethnicities and cultures, have become high-end professionals, and have made extraordinary contributions in different countries and professions. They were not forced to wander the world as Jewish people have been. Most of them went out in pursuit of their own dreams. This branching type of spread by the Yip family happens to be precisely the way of internationalization. This is proof that Chinese communities are communities that have a life force with a future.

While we celebrate the 150th birthday of Canada and review the history of Canada from its founding, we should acknowledge the "founding genes" of the Chinese people and admit that Chinese "genes" have always been and continue to be a part of Canada's historical "bloodline".

Chapter 2

How 700 Soldiers Changed the Status of an Ethnic Group

If we point out that the contributions made to Canada by Chinese people during the Gold Rush and railway construction were not purposeful because they migrated to Canada to work for their own fortune, then their participation in the two world wars derived from totally different motives. The former had an objective premise of historical circumstance that turned the Chinese people into one of the founders of Canada; the latter, however, was the first time that Chinese community members joined the Canadian forces of their own accord under the guidance of Canadian national consciousness. They fought and contributed just as much for this country as any other ethnic group in Canada. Only a small number of Chinese actively participated in battle during the First World War, but during the Second World War, this participation became a collective consciousness of the community, and the number who joined the Canadian armed forces reached a record high.

Chinese Canadian participation in the Second World War was unique in the history of warfare. They were seen as "second class residents" of Canada and were not rightfully respected even though they were born in Canada. They were discriminated against in society. Some parents of Chinese Canadians were unable to come to Canada and join their families because of the *1923 Chinese Exclusion Act*, leaving many families disbanded and broken. Even under such circumstances, hundreds of young Chinese Canadians broke through the barriers that prevented them from joining the forces, and actively sought battle. They did not fear injury or death, and only wanted to fight for Canada, for the Commonwealth, and for the anti-fascist Allies. This "true patriot love" filled a precious chapter in the history of Canadian armed forces; their actions moved an entire nation. Besides being recognized for their valiance and glory in battle, their actions became a key factor in abolishing the Chinese Exclusion Act. It could even be said that participation in the war by the 700 Chinese soldiers completely changed the status of the entire ethnic group in Canada.

"Head-tax" and Chinese Exclusion — a "Democratic" Decision

The reasons for Chinese people actively seeking to join the fight for Canada goes back to a period of history that people can hardly bear looking upon. As previously mentioned, the reasons Chinese people traveled across the ocean to Canada to mine for gold and build the railway, even if it cost them hefty loans, were first to make a living, and second to flee from endless warfare at home. Little did they know that the "gold mountains" had no shred of kindness, but only the exploitation of ruthless capitalism. After the CPR was completed, the Canadian government burned the bridges. Not only were the Chinese workers not rewarded for their contribution, they were left with nowhere to settle and had to face economic hardships, unemployment, and rampant discrimination from white ethnic groups. Many Chinese people ended up homeless on the streets. On the other hand, Aboriginal people made a world of difference by kindly taking Chinese in.

The next steps of the unemployed Chinese became a matter of life or death under such horrible social conditions. Some Chinese workers chose to go back to the U.S., some travelled back home across the Pacific, and those who could not afford a ticket back migrated to central and eastern Canada to find opportunities for survival. The majority, however, ended up staying in British Columbia in places such as Vancouver and New Westminster. Many of the unemployed Chinese workers ended up "stuck here" because they were unable to travel back to China. Besides, as the governing power of the Qing Dynasty was declining day by day, domestic conflict was constantly increasing in China, there was risk in returning to any part of Guangdong and Fujian, and it was extremely difficult to obtain accurate information. All these things forced more and more impoverished Chinese people to move to Canada's "gold mountain" to search for ways of survival.

At the same time, Canadian mainstream society's detesting of Chinese workers grew stronger by the day, and word was constantly spread of "the Chinese threat". Some publications even spoke openly about this topic, "If no measures are taken to suppress the Chinese from entering our land, the number of Chinese swarming into Canada will be ten times the number of Canadians." (Manitoba Free Press). The so-called mainstream public opinion became much more widespread, with various media playing an important role in furthering that agenda. Representatives from all levels of the public began condemning the Chinese and moved further and further away from the spirit of the Canadian Constitution onto a path of Chinese exclusion.

As the CPR had just been completed, the Federal Government was in no place to turn its back on the Chinese immediately. Therefore, the Royal Commission on Chinese Immigration was founded in July 1884 to conduct interviews and investigations in San Francisco and British Columbia. These actions were done entirely focusing on one specific ethnic group—the Chinese; the investigation included every aspect imaginable: the living conditions, ideas, actions, population, sex-ratio, occupations, income, criminal and other forms of misbehavior, taxation status, and social activities. There were two testimonies from Chinese officials among the testimonies from 51 people; only a few employers of Chinese workers spoke positively for the Chinese, and most other testimonies from white Canadians were full of prejudice, discrimination, or even hatred towards the Chinese.

According to the *History of Chinese Migration to Canada, 1858–1966* [1], there were three typical standpoints in the testimonies found by the Commission. One was from John A. Bradly, on the morality of the Chinese people. He believed that the Chinese conducted acts of smuggling, disregarded health regulations, used opium, brought leprosy

---

[1] *History of Chinese Migration to Canada*, 1858-1966, pages 139-130. David Chuenyan Lai, Guo Ding, Baoheng Jia; published by the People's Publishing House of the PRC in 2013.

to the West Coast, and used opium to poison young people. Another was from Gilbert Malcolm Sproat, who spoke about the unfair competition from Chinese workers in the job market. He said, "Chinese labourers only need ten cents a day to survive because they are completely separated from mainstream society. They are cold and without feeling like lower animals." Last was from the former Attorney-General of British Columbia, Alexander Edmund Batson Davie, who believed that the Chinese had difficulty integrating into society. He believed that the Chinese people were "deviants", and no white people would want to have them integrate into their society, nor did they themselves even want to integrate at all.

There was some factual evidence that supported these arguments, of course. However, as the whole purpose of investigation was based on justifying discrimination against the Chinese, it is obvious that the conclusion would be tilted towards Chinese exclusion. The person responsible for the federal investigation at the time was Dr. Joseph Adolphe Chapleau. He suggested that a "head-tax" of five Canadian dollars should be charged for every Chinese person who entered Canada as a means of compromise and submitted this proposal to the Parliament on April 10, 1885.

This miniscule head-tax apparently did not appease the intense public opinion and was repelled by anti-Chinese groups. By early 1885, the anti-Chinese forces were already a part of the national atmosphere. The federal government had little motivation or capacity to resist public opposition to imposing heavy taxes on Chinese people who would enter Canada, and thus let the opposition take its natural course. On July 29, 1885, Parliament passed the despicable and racially discriminatory "head-tax" as a part of the Chinese Immigration Act of 1885. A fifty-Canadian-dollar tax was charged to every Chinese person who entered Canada (excluding diplomats, travelers, scientists, students, merchants, and those with exit permits). 15 years later, the head-tax was raised to 100 dollars.

However, this failed to stop Chinese people from entering Canada, and this caused stronger and stronger protests from the anti-Chinese groups. A second round of investigation was conducted by the Royal Commission on Chinese Immigration, as a form of so-called "verification". Chinese exclusion was already a landslide favorite attitude at the time. Not a single person with social influence would stand up and advocate justice for the Chinese. Thus, by 1904, the head-tax was raised to 500 dollars. An entire year's income was about 300 dollars for Chinese labourers in Canada. The 500-dollar head-tax was almost equivalent to two years of work income for Chinese workers, truly a heavy burden. These acts clearly showed the strong resolve of society to exclude Chinese people.

"Head-tax"—Massive Contributions to Canada through Injustice

The two reports from the Royal Commission on Chinese Immigration revealed a few factual problems that existed within Chinatowns, however these problems, such as gambling, prostitution, opium use, and fighting, were not exclusive to Chinese communities, but existed in other communities including white communities as well. Overall, these investigation reports and society in general focused solely on the problems that existed within Chinese communities while turning a blind eye towards the contributions made by Chinese people. If we are to claim that tax contributions from its residents set up the foundation for Canada's national development, then the early Chinese settlers should also be acclaimed for their tax contributions.

From the implementation of the head-tax in 1885, to the complete exclusion of Chinese people in 1923, about 80,000 Chinese paid almost 24 million dollars in head-taxes during the three stages of head-tax collection. According to the Canadian annual report of 1924, over 1.43 million dollars was paid by nearly 30,000 Chinese between 1886 and 1900, the 14 years in which the head-tax was 50 dollars; over 1.12 million dollars was paid by more than 11,200 Chinese in 1901-1903, the period in which the head-tax was 100 dollars; 21.22 million dollars was paid by 42,000 Chinese during the 20 years in which the head-tax was 500 dollars, from 1904 to 1924.

A simple comparison can be made to show how much the Chinese "head-tax" was worth to Canadian tax revenue. The funds provided by the federal government for the CPR construction amounted to 25 million; this amount was comparable to the total amount of head-tax paid by Chinese immigrants. These taxes were distributed to various provinces to build schools, roads, parking lots, and other public infrastructures. The city of Victoria in British Columbia received the highest percentage of the tax as it had the highest population of Chinese people at the time. The still-in-use British Columbia Parliament Buildings were built using funds from the head-tax.

Today many Chinese new immigrants have been criticized for their limited contributions to the development of public infrastructure; however, their Chinese Canadian ancestors had already made immense contributions to the urban infrastructure in Canada, especially in British Columbia. These contributions did not simply stop at "head taxes", despite the fact that much of their contributions were forced. Taking the construction of the CPR for example, the low wages of the Chinese workers helped to relieve other Canadians of countless "tax burdens" at the time. The worst part of the inequalities was the hefty head taxes that the Chinese workers had to pay to move to Canada, while the immigrants from Europe, including family-class immigrants, could actually receive financial support and assistance from the government (similar to the welfare offered to refugees today). Judging from these aspects, the tax and economic contributions to Canada from the early Chinese workers were no less than those of European immigrants at the time, however, the treatment they received was horrible by today's standards of equality, not to mention the fact that the Vancouver Chinatown was attacked by anti-Chinese mobs. There were two anti-Chinese riots, one in 1887 and another in 1907 in the city of Vancouver. The riot in 1907 left an especially dark memory for its size, influence, and overall damages. About eight or nine thousand people of western descent holding banners that read "For a White Canada" marched to Vancouver City Hall, and then to Chinatown. They had clubs, wrenches and bottles in their hands, and shouted furiously time after time. The band of people threw rocks at the shops in Chinatown, destroyed any business sign that showed a hint of the Orientals, and attacked the gathering spots of Chinese Canadians in Vancouver. Almost no storefront was spared during the riot. The riot eventually escalated to property destruction, looting, and even arson. During the 100th anniversary of the "anti-Chinese riots", some media wrote the following in commemoration of the catastrophe to describe the impact and influence these riots had on the Chinese community: A fourth-generation resident of the Vancouver Chinatown, Mr. Yip, said that his grandfather told him the day of the riot was a day of true horror; the white people could not bear the sight of any

Asian in this place. Faced with such threats, Chinese Canadians had to arm themselves just in case. A number of shops owned by Chinese Canadians suffered serious losses. Mr. Yip said that the riot had left a huge impact on him and his entire family, like a shadow that followed them throughout their entire lives. He said that there is still a long way to go for people to accept and accommodate each other no matter where they have come from. Many of the participants in the riot were actually first generation European immigrants who had just arrived in Canada or had been here for 20 years at most, which was even shorter than the history of the Chinatown, but they were screaming for the Chinese people to "Go back".

The Chinese Exclusion Act:
Canadian Immigration History's Medal of Dishonour

Due mostly to the social and economic situation of China at the time, the Canadian "head-tax" did not stop Chinese people from coming in. We can see from the statistics already presented that the Federal Government had constantly increased the amount of the "head-tax" in response to public opinion, but Chinese people still continued to come to Canada, and their numbers kept increasing even as the head-tax grew higher. The Chinese who had already settled in British Columbia could sense that the greater the increase of Chinese immigrants, the more anti-Chinese sentiments would grow, which would then force the government to establish even more extreme measures. Thus, the Chinese Consolidated Benevolent Association mailed the four counties in Guangdong where most of the immigrants came from to advise against further immigration.

Similarly, the Republic of China's government proposed to the Canadian government in 1914 that they set a quota on the number of Chinese immigrants into Canada to 1000 people and cancel the head-tax. However, the federal government lacked the courage to displease the provincial governments, knowing that such a treaty with the Chinese government would cause displeasure in certain discriminatory legislatures in places such as British Columbia, so the Chinese proposal was rejected.

Under such circumstances, anti-Chinese sentiments grew more intense by the day in Canada, especially in the west. Thus, the Federal Government finally took the step of going against its own constitution and against its own Canadian spirit of immigration: they passed an act to fully stop Chinese people from coming into Canada. At the end of March 1923, Parliament passed a draft of an all-new "Chinese Immigration Act", and the notorious immigration act was passed on June 30th of the same year. The act came into effect on the symbolic day of July 1st, the 56th birthday of Canadian Confederation. This was the reason Chinese communities stopped celebrating Canada Day in the following twenty-some years, and the reason that this day was celebrated as the "Day of Shame" instead. The new Chinese Exclusion Act that replaced the "head-tax" contained 43 discriminatory articles and was thus called the "Onerous 43 Acts" by the Chinese. The new law not only prohibited new Chinese workers from entering Canada, it also imposed strict rules on Chinese Canadians. For example, the spouses and children of Chinese Canadian citizens would have difficulty entering Canada if they had never come here before; if a Chinese Canadian wished to go visit families in China, the person had to apply for an exit permit with a two-year time limit, and if the person failed to return within the given period, that person would no longer be allowed re-entry into Canada.

The politicians who established the *Chinese Exclusion Act* may have felt that they had done the right thing, and the anti-Chinese activists who forced politicians to push forward anti-Chinese laws at the time may have felt a sense of power in their "democratic politics". However, judged from a modern perspective, the Chinese Exclusion Act was not only in violation of the constitution, it was also extremely inhumane; this act forced countless Chinese families to become battered and scattered. The reason it was against the constitution is simple; a discriminatory immigration policy directed at a single ethnic group is absolutely against the constitutional principles of equality and justice. The reasons for its being inhumane are even more apparent. Here we will look at an example of Mr. Syutong Tam, the father of an older generation Chinese immigrant, Wingdak Tam.

Syutong Tam arrived in Canada in 1912 after paying a 500-dollar head-tax. Like many other Chinese workers, he spent ten years working as a labourer in Canada, then got married after he had saved enough money to return to Guangdong. He would never have thought that the *1923 Chinese Exclusion Act* would forbid his wife from ever entering Canada because she had never been in Canada before, forcing her to wait indefinitely and hopelessly in Guangdong until her death. Syutong Tam eventually married again, and this wife became the mother of Wingdak Tam. Another example would be the parents of Janhong Lee, who each paid the 500-dollar head-tax and entered Canada, then gave birth to two children in Canada. Mrs. Lee took their two children back to Guangzhou while she was pregnant with their third child. It was during the time of the Japanese invasion of China that they went back, as Mrs. Lee decided to take their children back to Canada to seek refuge. However, as their third child Janhong Lee was not born in Canada, he was denied entry. Having had no other options, she let the two older children go back to Canada and stayed with the baby son in war-torn China. Mrs. Lee was killed by Japanese invaders when Janhong Lee was five years old. It was not until the 1950s that he was allowed to join his family in Canada. We can see that the "head-tax" and the Chinese Exclusion Act left indelible stains of shame and darkness in Canada's history of immigration, and in Canada's history as a Western democracy. This shameful chapter of history was only officially rectified and apologized for over half a century later by the Canadian Parliament and government. However, the protests from Chinese communities against anti-Chinese laws, along with Chinese Canadians' active participation in the Canadian armed forces, are linked tightly together.

Chinese Canadian Soldiers—Battling on Two Fronts

It seemed "abnormal" for Chinese Canadians to become soldiers; what was even more unimaginable was that Chinese Canadians proactively asked to join the forces to fight and perhaps die for Canada even during times of anti-Chinese discrimination. War is not romantic drama; it is cruel, bloody and often fatal. In traditional Chinese culture, "good sons don't join the military" is a common belief held by every Chinese family. Besides the search for "gold mountains", survival and dreams, one of the main reasons that the Chinese people risked their lives to come across the ocean to Canada and the United States was to avoid the chaos and despair of war, and help their families and descendants find a peaceful and fulfilling life as average civilians.

Yet when Canada joined in the war against fascism, Chinese Canadians stood up without a hint of regret. This was very true in army enlistment at the time. For example, all four siblings of the longest-surviving Chinese veteran John KoBong joined the army and were put into different units. If we counted his two uncles that participated in the First World War, this family contributed six soldiers. Douglas Jung, who later became the first Chinese Canadian Member of Parliament, also went onto the battlefield along with his two brothers; he was a part of the Pacific Command Security Intelligence, while his brothers served in the air force. When the UK was faced with war, royals and aristocrats were expected to put down their luxurious lives to fight for their country like every other soldier. Putting lives on the line was common during times of national crisis. This was not the case for Chinese Canadians who decided to enlist; not only was it against their traditional culture, it was also unreasonable considering their social status at the time. Three reasons can show clearly why that was the case.

First, the Chinese were viewed as "second class residents" in Canada at the time; in fact, they could be called "untouchables". Many of the Chinese who joined the fight had not been granted Canadian citizenship even though they were born in Canada. They lived in a country that oppressed them, and a society that looked down upon them. Yet they had the desire and the courage to defend this country and created a rare example in the history of Canadian warfare, when they fought for the country of which they were not even citizens. How is one to make sense of a situation like this?

Second, the rules of enlistment prohibited Chinese people from joining the army, or at the very least did not welcome them. Let us take the Second

World War as an example. In 1939, Germany invaded Poland and brought on the beginning of the war. Canada followed suit when the UK declared war on Germany. Under the leadership of the UK, Canada put forward the National Resources Mobilization Act (NRMA) on June 21, 1940, which gave the Federal Government the power to conscript soldiers, while also authorizing it to mobilize the military to places other than Canada. However, the Royal Canadian Air Force and Navy had their own rules of conscription, through which they put ethnic restrictions on enlistment, that is, only "pure-blooded Europeans" and "pure whites" were allowed to enlist, completely excluding Asians and other ethnic groups. The Canadian Army was a bit more "open-minded" and had no restrictions on ethnic background openly listed. However, in actual practice, they did not accept Chinese people into the army. In other words, it was perfectly legal for Chinese people not to be enlisted in the army during the war. It should be noted that during times of war in China, the ancestors of Chinese Canadians were often rounded up and forced into labour for the military, possibly to become cannon fodder. Since it was possible to legally avoid military service in Canada, most would think "why ever not"; but Chinese Canadians insisted on enlisting even though it was "against the law". Some even travelled by horse over the mountains to Alberta to do so. What was the reason behind this?

Third, despite Canada being a young member of the Commonwealth, it still took part in both World Wars. Yet since Canada was far from the battlefront, being located in North America, it had little reason to do so. The flames of war never reached the Canadian border. Normally speaking, anybody, whatever status they might have, would join the fight if the war came to their doorstep because the lives of their own family would be at risk. Since Canada was a whole ocean away from the front, there was no reason for Chinese Canadians to risk their lives and fight at all; so why did they still bravely step forward?

Speaking from individual perspectives, each Chinese Canadian had a different reason for joining the war. Some hoped to receive better treatment in the army, which would change their status from being one of the oppressed in civil society; some wanted their professional skills to become useful in the army; some were motivated by their parents' sentiments and were angered by the Japanese invasion of China, thus they enlisted to fight against the Japanese both to serve Canada and their homeland China; some went forth out of a sense of justice, and fought against the fascists. From a general perspective, since they had been living in Canada, Chinese Canadians were affected by prevalent Canadian values; when a Commonwealth nation was attacked, Chinese Canadians felt the need to defend the country just as much as other young Canadians; at the same time, Chinese Canadians were also clear on this being a historical opportunity to win respect from mainstream society through fighting and vanquishing the enemy. It was a chance for them to win the same social status as white people, and eventually gain citizenship and the right to vote.

A Chinese proverb, "the strength of grass is shown in the face of gales; the strength of loyalty is shown in the test of time." Even though it was to earn respect, Chinese Canadians still actively participated in battle and went in with their lives at stake when Canada was faced with war, even when they had no social or political status. Their loyalty to Canada was unquestionable. They showed through action that mainstream society's discrimination and slander against the Chinese was groundless.

Chinese Canadians had begun participating in the army as early as the First World War, the two uncles of John KoBong being well-known veterans in the Chinese community. However, only a few individuals joined the military then and did not create much influence. The large scale participation from Chinese Canadians began in the Second World War; this group participation had a huge influence on Chinese communities and on Canadian history. It was also one of the most significant contributions made to Canada by the Chinese.

Since Chinese people were discriminated against in Canada, the historical records of Chinese Canadian enlistment were also affected. Even to this day we do not have an accurate recording of the number of Chinese Canadian soldiers who officially joined the fight. The most common belief was between 600 and 800 people in total. It took a long time even for their military achievements and decorations to become clarified. Some of their military achievements took until the end of the 20th century to become verified.

Besides having a small percentage of the population, another reason that Chinese people did not have high enlistment levels was because of discrimination against Chinese people by the Canadian army. As stated earlier, as soon as the call for enlistment was put out in June 1940, some Chinese Canadians responded immediately to join in military training, even though they had to fight hard to break through the systemic barriers to joining the military. This actually caused anti-Chinese sentiments to rise again in society. Three months later in September 1940, the federal government ordered that Chinese and Japanese descendants were prohibited from joining in military training and battles, including those who had already passed physical examinations. In January of 1941, the Cabinet War Committee (CWC) fully implemented the law to prohibit

Chinese and Japanese Canadians from voluntary enlistment. It took until the start of the Pacific War that the gates were finally opened for Chinese Canadians to join the army. Faced with battling on both European and Asian fronts and a heavy loss of personnel, the UK's War Office suggested that Canada increase its recruitment range, especially towards Asians, to fulfill the special needs on the Asian front against the Japanese aggressors. On October 1st, 1942, the Royal Canadian Air Force took the first steps to accept Chinese Canadians for pilot enlistment. In 1943, the Canadian Army began recruiting both naturalized and by-birth Chinese citizens of the Commonwealth.

This showed that despite the wave of desire to enlist that had flooded Chinatowns, only a few Chinese were actually accepted and formally enlisted as professional soldiers. Canada had a population of around 15 million at the time, with about one million soldiers, yet there were only slightly over 700 Chinese Canadian soldiers who were formally enlisted. However, the numbers are unimportant in this case. What was important to the Chinese Canadian fighters, and different from the white soldiers, was that they shouldered two duties instead of one—a situation they were all too familiar with from the very beginning. First, they had to fight to defend their homes as a part of the Anti-fascist Alliance (and not necessarily to defend the system because the system was oppressive to them); second, they wanted to break through their status as second-class residents, for themselves and for their entire community. Chinese Canadians, like the anti-Chinese powers, were clearly aware of the battle on the second front. The facts played out exactly as expected. Chinese Canadian soldiers contributed no less than white soldiers or soldiers of other ethnic background.

No one can deny that all of the Chinese who asked the Service Bureau to become enlisted all shared one thought: since they were responding to the call for voluntary enlistment like "every other normal Canadian citizen", they should be granted citizenship and given the same rights, especially the right to vote, as any other Canadian person. This thought was just as clear to anti-Chinese activists like T. D. Pattullo, Premier of British Columbia, the province with the largest Chinese population and the worst of anti-Chinese sentiments. He openly warned that if Canadian Chinese and Canadian Japanese could enlist, they would further demand the right to vote, which was absolutely not to be allowed in British Columbia. Mackenzie King, Prime Minister at the time, specifically banned Chinese and Japanese descendants from enlisting due to pressure from British Columbia.

All mainstream Canadian history narratives on the Second World War uniformly avoided a highly controversial historical fact. While the Canadian army was determined to fight against German and Japanese fascism and ethnocentrism on the battlefield, they also maintained similar anti-Asian and racist actions in Canada and among its own soldiers. The military still has not reflected on this matter even to this day.

However, the disadvantageous situation in the war, together with the pressure from Chinese Canadians wanting to join the army, motivated the army and the government to change their disgraceful policy before the end of the war. Tight situations on the European front and the start of the Pacific War forced the UK to fight on two fronts, and a greater number of soldiers were needed. Only when the Commonwealth widened its recruitment range to the maximum could they stage a war of attrition and make decisive strikes against the Axis. Despite such pressures, the

Canadian government was stubborn in its insistence on setting up barriers and delayed the opening of enlistment to all Chinese. It was not until the end of 1942 that Chinese people were allowed to enter the air force, navy and army. In August 1944, the Pacific Command that controlled British Columbia, Alberta, Yukon and Northwest Territories finally proposed to establish an independent detachment of Chinese soldiers; it began recruiting Chinese Canadian drill sergeants in September of the same year.

Yet despite having joined the army, Chinese people still faced discrimination and restrictions from the Chinese Exclusion Act. For example, a white pilot would receive 800 dollars per month, while a Chinese pilot only was paid 485 dollars. It was hard for Chinese soldiers to bring their spouses into Canada were they to marry someone abroad, but white soldiers had no problem doing the same. The worst part was that the unique contributions made by Chinese soldiers in war were often deliberately "forgotten" or "left out". Even after half a century later, war stories of heroic achievements by white veterans were dug up, however small, and were recorded in the Canadian Army's history and Canadian war history. Yet much of the same exemplary achievements by Chinese Canadian veterans was forgotten through the passage of time. It could be said that without the Chinese Canadian Military Museum in Vancouver's Chinatown, the exploits of the Chinese Canadian veterans would be just a few random pieces of stories that would never appear in Canada's collective memory, because the Canadian War Museum in Ottawa had no comprehensive display of the contributions made by Chinese Canadian veterans in the Second World War.

In 2013, the documentary film producer Bradley Lee produced the film "Operation Oblivion", which dug up one rarely-heard military operation from the ashes of history 60 years ago. This military operation occurred at the fiercest moment of the Pacific War when the British Secret Service required the Canadian Army to recruit 13 Chinese volunteers for training. These 13 soldiers were parachuted into Japanese occupied territory, where they trekked through the jungle, found Chinese resistance fighters and trained them. After the war, these veterans created their own "Pacific Unit 280" as a part of the Army, Navy and Air Force Veterans of Canada, and celebrated Remembrance Day in their own community.

Since some of the Chinese Canadian soldiers were registered with English names or had other identification issues, the Canadian Army used this as an excuse to disconfirm the "historical accuracy" of some military exploits. But do not forget that the reason these errors existed derived from Canadian discrimination against Chinese people. With any level of effort, it would not be difficult to find the truth behind these Chinese Canadian exploits, especially having had so many years to do so following the war.

The effectiveness and performance of the Chinese Canadian soldiers was not in any way inferior to that of white soldiers. As for the air force, the entire world knows about the "Flying Tigers" led by the American general Claire Lee Chennault and their contributions to the War of Resistance against the Japanese Invasion in China. Canadians also made similar contributions in aerial battles during the war. The Chinese Canadian from Calgary, Gimjeun Mah went back to China in 1932 to join the Guangdong Provincial Air Force and took part in the bombing of Japanese-occupied Yuncheng Airport in 1939. His merits were outstanding; however, he later lost both of his arms during his service. Harold Chinn, born in Vancouver, was responsible for delivering goods "over the Hump" since 1942, after joining the Guangdong Provincial Air Force, and made 600 trips delivering supplies. Albert Mah and Cedric Mah, brothers from British Columbia, both served as instructors of the British Commonwealth Air Training Plan; they later joined the China National Aviation Corporation and flew more than 400 trips "over the Hump". Quon Jil Louie from Vancouver, Jim Gen Lee and Joseph Hong from Winnipeg all consecutively joined the RAF and RCAF and were killed in action on the European front. Within the navy, the most legendary figure would have to be William King Lowd Lore. He was the first Chinese Canadian to join the navy in 1939, though unofficially. In 1943, he officially became a part of Canadian Navy at the request of the Deputy Chief of Naval Staff. He became the first Chinese officer in the navies of the Commonwealth. He served in the Operational Intelligence Centre at Naval Service Headquarters, as well as other vital positions responsible for U.S., UK, and Asian war zones. By the time he retired from service in 1947 he was still just a lieutenant; this is clearly an example of the unequal treatment in promotions based on ethnic background. It took until 1952 before he was promoted to lieutenant commander as a retired member in the RCN. The majority of Chinese Canadian soldiers joined the Canadian Army, and also suffered the highest casualties, most of whom died for their country on the European front.

The facts provided above clearly displayed Chinese Canadian patriotism and sacrifice, and finally forced the Canadian government and military to recognize the ignorance and sheer absurdity behind Chinese exclusion; they also realized that they were not that different from the anti-Semitic spirit of Hitler in their own racial discrimination. Thus, within two years after the war ended, Canada abolished the Chinese Exclusion Act. In this sense, the Chinese Canadian soldiers served Canada, the Canadian army, and the spirit of the constitution through fighting hatred with kindness and fighting enemies by putting their own lives on the line. These soldiers won battles on both fronts, and the more than 700 Chinese Canadian soldiers completely changed the historical status of their entire ethnic group in Canada.

Chapter 3

New Immigrants Bring Fresh Blood to Canada after World War II

With the new era following World War II, Chinese immigrants were able to come to Canada on a new and brighter road but not one without hurdles. There were a few historical breakthroughs which allowed Chinese immigrants to enter Canada using gradually fairer selection criteria that applied to people of all ethnic backgrounds. The new schemes also brought Chinese immigrants to Canada not just as hard-working labourers, but with various skills and talents that could better contribute to this country in nearly every spectrum of the Canadian economy and society.

After the Chinese Exclusion Act was repealed, Chinese immigrants could legally enter Canada. However, restrictions continued which allowed entrance only to the spouse and children of Canadian citizens and permanent residents of Chinese descent. It was not until 1967, when a "Points-Based System" was adopted in Canada's immigration selection, that the last element of racial discrimination was eliminated, and Chinese immigrants could enter this country under the same criteria as people from other ethnic groups. In 1971, Canada became the first country in the world to adopt multiculturalism as an official policy which affirms the value and dignity of all Canadian citizens regardless of their racial or ethnic origins, language, or religious affiliation.

Nevertheless, significant waves of Chinese immigration only started in the 1990s, when Canada opened independent immigration categories to lure more economically desirable immigrants to Canada. On the supply side, the transfer of sovereignty over Hong Kong in 1997, the 1996 Taiwan Strait Crisis, and the "open door" policy in Mainland China become major factors that pushed considerable numbers of Chinese immigrants coming to Canada from those three major sources.

How did these changes over time in Canadian immigration policy shape new pathways for Chinese immigrants to Canada? What were the effects of historical incidents that triggered a large out-flow of immigrants from major Chinese sources? How was the new "blood" of Chinese immigration adopted into the long existing Chinese community "tissues" and "organs", and into Canadian multicultural fibres? In this chapter, we will review multiple streams of ethnic Chinese immigrants coming to Canada and some important characteristics associated with these inflows.

The "Chinese Exclusion Act" Repealed but Restrictions Continued

In 1947, Canada repealed the *Chinese Immigration Act* of 1923, also popularly known as the *Chinese Exclusion Act*, which marked one of the most important turning points on the road to justice for Chinese Canadians. Even after the explicit language of exclusion was removed after the Exclusion Act was repealed, restrictions still continued that allowed entrance to only the spouse and children under the age of 18 of Canadian citizens and permanent residents of Chinese descent. Such restrictions were not applied to other ethnic groups. Men in the Chinese "married bachelor society" who dreamed of bringing their families to Canada remained largely disappointed for another 20 years.

Undoubtedly, the restrictions on Chinese immigration between 1947 and 1962 reflected the racial bias of Canadian immigration policy against Asian and other non-white immigrants. It was even fueled by a new wave of fear of China emerging from the Korean War (1950–1953) and the Cold War of the 1950s and 1960s. This was in part prompted by fear of communist infiltration, which became another convenient pretext to restrict the entry of Chinese who were immediate family members of Canadian citizens (Li, 1998). Regrettably, the fear of China has never gone away even in the later days of Canada-China relations that we will discuss in later sections of this book.

On the supply side, there was an intensified civil war during the period 1945 to 1949 between the Chinese Communist Party (CCP) and the Nationalist Kuomintang (KMT) fighting for legitimacy as the government of China. People suffered badly from the war and poverty. In 1949, the CCP ultimately won the war and became the ruling power of mainland China. Nevertheless, in the early years of the People's Republic of China, there remained widespread poverty, hunger and social instability caused by the war, natural disasters and sociopolitical movements. People and families tried every possibility to find ways to flee the country. Being a son or daughter of a Chinese Canadian became a fortunate thing because it would allow children to reunite with parents in Canada for a journey leading to a more hopeful future.

Nevertheless, things didn't happen as smoothly as expected. Many individuals immigrated to Canada as children by adopting false identities of others and became so-called "paper sons or daughters". While paper sons were common, paper daughters were unusual for the traditional reasons that Chinese families usually favoured sons over daughters. As a result, there was an extreme imbalance in the gender-ratio among immigrant youths. Therefore, it was a common practice in the 1950s and 1960s for both older and young Chinese bachelors to send for "picture brides," who were arranged by marriage brokers in their hometowns. Dr. Vivienne Poy documented "picture brides, paper sons, and paper daughters" phenomena in detail in her book (Poy, 2013). In May 2012, the Chinese Canadian National Council produced a documentary video telling personal stories of "paper sons and daughters" family reunification at a time when Canada had limited Chinese immigration.[1] It was estimated about 11,000 Chinese children came to Canada illegally as "paper sons or daughters". In 1960, the "Chinese Adjustment Statement Program" was established to provide an amnesty to all the "paper children". It is believed that Douglas Jung, the first Chinese Canadian elected as a Member of Parliament in 1957, played a role in pushing for the amnesty.[2]

---

1   Chinese Canadian National Council, 2012

2   The Metro Toronto Chinese & Southeast Asian Legal Clinic (MTCSALC), 2011

The "Points-Based System" Selects Skills, Not Skins

In 1967, Canada's immigration restrictions on the basis of race and national origin were finally removed when a "Points-Based" immigrant selection scheme was introduced. That year, Canada became the first country in the world to introduce a points-based system which was an attempt to overcome fluctuations in the inflow of migrant workers by linking immigration to the needs of the labour market, and to move away from the earlier, transparently racist, "whites only" entry criteria.

To improve objectivity of admissions procedures, a new system was set up in which so-called "independent immigrants" were assessed by giving points in specific categories relating to their human capital factors, including education, occupational skills, employment prospects, age, proficiency in English and French and personal character. Individuals receiving points equaling or exceeding the qualification mark out of a possible 100 were granted entry to Canada, regardless of their race, ethnicity or national origin.

The priority of assigned points and qualification marks have changed over time. Dr. Poy's book (2013: 212) summarized these changes in great detail. In general, prior to 2002, applicants were assessed on a points system that generally required applicants to have a job offer for a position that no Canadian citizen was willing and able to fill. In enacting the Immigration and Refugee Protection Act, 2001 (IRPA), Canada adopted a slightly different philosophy. The system seeks to identify the types of persons who are most likely to integrate into the Canadian workforce based upon their human capital background. According to the Government of Canada, the latest conceptualization of the point system is described as "we choose skilled immigrants as permanent residents based on their ability to settle in Canada and take part in our economy." [3] The ability to become established in Canada is assessed based on six selection criteria and the maximum number of points available for each are as follows:

- Education: A maximum of twenty-five points.
- Language proficiency in English and French: A maximum of twenty-four points.
- Work Experience: A maximum of twenty-one points.
- Age: A maximum of ten points.
- Arranged employment: Ten points.
- Adaptability: Ten additional points for a spouse's education, previous work in Canada, and family relations in Canada.

The points-based system, in combination with other reforms, has led to a shift in immigrants' origin from 70 per cent European in the mid-1960s to around only 12 per cent in 2015, while those from Asia and the Pacific increased from less than 10 per cent to 53 per cent in the same period (Government of Canada, 2017). Chinese immigrants could now apply for entry on equal footing with other applicants, especially those with more education and diversified skills than previous generations of Chinese migrant labourers.

Canada's Multiculturalism Policy Embraces Contributions from All Ethnic Groups

In October 1971, Canada became the first country in the world to

---

3   Government of Canada, 2017

adopt multiculturalism as an official government policy. Multiculturalism was intended to preserve the cultural freedom of individuals and provide recognition of the cultural contributions of diverse ethnic groups to Canadian society. Under the multiculturalism policy, Canada affirms the value and dignity of all Canadian Citizens regardless of their racial or ethnic origins, language, or religious affiliation (Government of Canada, 2012).

The multiculturalism policy allows citizens to practice their religions and keep their identities without fear of official persecution. The government was committed to support multiculturalism in four specific ways: assistance to cultural groups in their development and growth; assistance to members of cultural groups to overcome barriers to full participation in society; promotion of creative exchanges between cultural groups; and assistance to immigrants in learning Canada's official languages, be it French or English.

More importantly, this policy guaranteed equality before the law and for pursuing opportunities whether personal, career-wise, or in any other field. Canadian law, as a result, reflects many of these rights and beliefs as they are guaranteed to all men and women. All of these rights are guaranteed in the Canadian Charter of Rights and Freedoms which is part of the Canadian Constitution.

This policy, along with the Canadian Constitution and other laws, emphasizes mutual respect between ethnicities and also acceptance of one's personal beliefs, and has reshaped the entire Canadian society to become more welcoming and harmonious for all Canadians and immigrants from around the world.

It has been noted by many historians and politicians that the origin of official multiculturalism in Canada had little to do with the ethnic Chinese. It grew out of the federal government's attempt to deal with the separatist movement in Quebec. As an unintended but logical outcome of this policy, a Chinese Canadian identity emerged as quoted by Dr. Poy in her book: "A Chinese Canadian is anyone of Chinese descent who has been in Canada long enough for Canada to affect her or his identity" (Poy, 2013). Dr. Poy further quoted the Reverend Andrew Lam to describe Chinese Canadian identity as such that: "To be proud of our origin and to appreciate it fully is an attitude of mind that is not inconsistent with good citizenship or loyalty to Canada." Since then, more phenomena, events, and activities with Chinese heritage and Chinese elements have been observed in many local communities across the country. Most importantly, Chinese heritage being part of Canada's multicultural society has been gradually embraced by more and more Canadians.

Immigrants Admitted under Three Streams

Since 2001, immigration to Canada has been predominantly regulated by the Immigration and Refugee Protection Act (IRPA), (Government of Canada, 2001). According to the IRPA, Canada accepts mainly three categories of immigrants for permanent residence:

Family reunification: A foreign national may be selected as a member of the family class on the basis of their relationship as the spouse, common-law partner, child, parent or other prescribed family member of a Canadian citizen or permanent resident.

Economic immigration: A foreign national may be selected as a member of the economic class (skilled or business immigrants, including provincial nominees) on the basis of their ability to become economically established in Canada.

Refugees: A foreign national, inside or outside Canada, may be selected as a person who under the IRPA is a Convention refugee or as a person in similar circumstances, taking into account Canada's humanitarian tradition with respect to the displaced and the persecuted.

According to 2015 Citizenship and Immigration Canada (CIC) figures, Canada welcomes about 250,000 permanent residents from all categories each year, with the highest record of 280,000 in 2010. Among all intakes of 3.7 million immigrants during the period from 2002 to first half of 2016, economic immigrants received about over 60 per cent of permanent resident visas, with one quarter given for family reunification, and 10 per cent granted for refugee class, and the rest given to individuals.

The 2011 Canadian census also reported that in that census year, Canada had a foreign-born population of about 6,775,800 people, who represented 20.6% of the total population, the highest proportion among the G8 countries. Between 2006 and 2011, around 1,162,900 foreign-born people immigrated to Canada, of which, Asia (including the Middle East) was Canada's largest source of immigrants during that five-year period. The vast majority of the foreign-born population lived in four provinces: Ontario, British Columbia, Quebec and Alberta, and most lived in the nation's largest urban centres.

Chinese immigration to Canada also experienced a sea change in terms of the growing size and changing composition of all categories. Economic immigrants from the PRC, having been selected based on human capital, financial capital and work experience, made up about one quarter to one third of the total annual number of immigrants from China to Canada in the late 1980s. This quickly increased to 57 percent in 1990 and 63 percent in 1991. By 1998, they accounted for 67 percent of immigrants from China and by 2000, over 80 percent[4].

Changing Sources of Immigrants from Hong Kong, Taiwan and the Mainland

Ethnic Chinese in Canada came from various source countries or regions. According to the 2006 census, nearly half of the Chinese immigrants arrived in Canada from the mainland People's Republic China (49 percent), and 23 percent came from Hong Kong. Others came from the Caribbean and Bermuda, the Philippines, India and other Asian countries.

The major source countries and regions from which ethnic Chinese immigrated to Canada have changed considerably over time. Before formal diplomatic relationship between Canada and PRC was established in 1971, there were no Canadian visa offices in mainland China that could issue visas of any type to Chinese nationals to enter Canada. Even after 1971, the Cold War effects still deterred direct immigration from mainland China to Canada until the mid-1990s. Hong Kong was the primary source of ethnic Chinese immigrants to Canada during that period, and immigrants from Hong Kong to Canada accounted for over two-thirds of combined immigrants from Hong Kong, Taiwan and mainland China to Canada (Li, 1998).

Even as the primary source of immigration to Canada, arrivals from Hong Kong never exceeded 8,000 a year until 1987 when the total number

---

4 Li, Immigrants from China to Canada: Issues of Supply and Demand in Human Capital, 2011

of landed immigrants from Hong Kong jumped to 16,170, a skyrocketed increase from just 6,000 to 7,000 a year in the past three years. From 1987 onwards, annual immigration from Hong Kong continued to rise, reaching a peak of 44,000 in 1994, after which it began to decline. Since the year 2000, less than 2,000 immigrants per year have arrived in Canada from Hong Kong (See Figures below.)

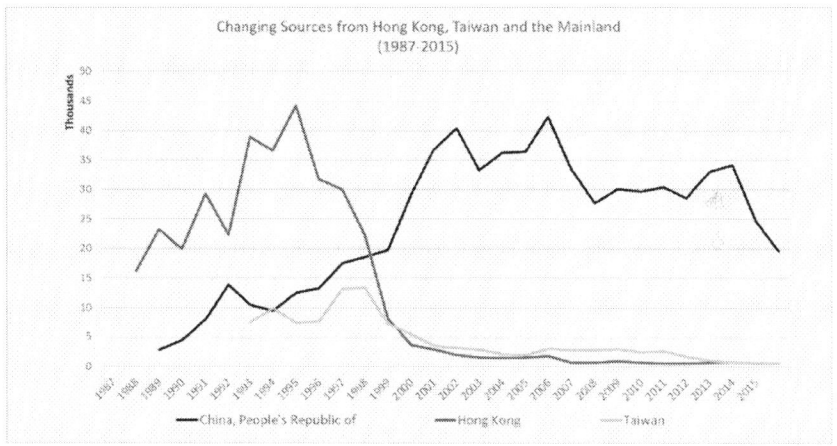

Source: CIC, Facts and Figures, various years.

The dramatic ups-and-downs of arrivals from Hong Kong to Canada from the mid-1980s to 2000 is a classic example of an immigration wave being triggered by a significant political change and associated political uncertainty in the sending region. On December 19, 1984, Premier Zhao Ziyang of the People's Republic of China (PRC) and Prime Minister Margaret Thatcher of the United Kingdom (UK) signed the Sino–British Joint Declaration on the question of Hong Kong. In the Joint Declaration, the PRC Government stated that it had decided to resume the exercise of sovereignty over Hong Kong (including Hong Kong Island, Kowloon, and the New Territories) to take effect from July 1, 1997, and the UK Government declared that it would hand over Hong Kong to the PRC effective on July 1, 1997. The PRC Government also declared its basic policies regarding Hong Kong in the document. The Declaration entered into force with the exchange of instruments of ratification on May 27, 1985 and was registered by the PRC and UK governments at the United Nations on June 12, 1985.

The Joint Declaration provides that the "one country, two systems" principle would be implemented, and Hong Kong's previous capitalist system and its way of life would remain unchanged for a period of 50 years until 2047. Many in Hong Kong still were skeptical about the future after 1997 and started considering out-migration. In 1989, the June 4th incident in Beijing led to more pilgrimage and fear of Hong Kong's prospects after the return to mainland China, and large-scale out-migration from Hong Kong emerged. The historical peak of 44,000 immigrants landed in Canada from Hong Kong in 1994 was a direct reflection of out-migration flows. After July 1, 1997, people in Hong Kong and Canada observed the smooth transferring of sovereignty from the UK to the PRC, and the outcomes were not as bad as many had anticipated. This not only led to a decrease in immigrant arrivals to Canada to as low as 2,000 a year after the year 2000, but also changed the direction of migration. Many Hong Kong Canadians returned to Hong Kong for business, family and other reasons. According to a study by the Asia Pacific Foundation of Canada, there are approximately 300,000 to 500,000 Canadians living in Hong Kong, many of whom are returnees from Canada (Zhang & DeGolyer, 2011).

Similarly, after World War II, massive immigration to Canada from the PRC was also triggered by political uncertainty in 1989. The June 4th

Tiananmen Square incident took place and triggered an increase in the number of immigrants from the PRC to Canada. As shown by Canadian landing statistics, immigration from mainland China did not begin to increase until 1989. The aftermath of the incident was that Canada joined the U.S.A., Australia and many other western countries in allowing Chinese students with visas studying at Canadian universities and schools to remain in Canada as permanent residents. Later, this so-called "June 4th Visa" was extended to nearly all Chinese visitors, workers and asylum seekers who were physically present in Canada at that time. Within two years, the number of landed immigrants from China rose to 14,203 in 1991 before dropping to 9,485 in 1993.

The "June 4th visa" was significant as a pathway for immigration from mainland China to Canada in many ways. First, it led directly to the first wave of contemporary immigration to Canada from China that exceeded 14,000 a year, compared to less than 8,000 a year in recent decades. Secondly, it had a multiplier effect on follow-up intakes. According to Canadian immigration policy, a citizen or permanent resident is able to bring in his or her spouse, children and parents or other legally eligible family members to Canada for family reunification. In other words, every "June 4th visa" issued could possibly bring in 2, 3 or even more family members as permanent residents. Thirdly, it targeted Chinese temporary visitors in Canada during that time period and turned them into the permanent resident category.

From the 1990s onwards, China entered the "emigration phase" (Guo & DeVoretz, 2007). As China's "open door" policy continued, the economic boom, growth of the new middle class, and relaxed passport restrictions led to an increase in annual immigration from China. Furthermore, Canada opened its visa offices and centres in China, which processed immigration applications directly from mainland China. Annual immigrants to Canada quickly reached almost 20,000 in 1998, and over 40,000 in 2001, before pulling back to 33,000 in 2002. The number exceeded 36,000 for 2003 and 2004 and reached an all-time high of over 42,000 in 2005. The annual arrivals remained at the 30,000 level until 2013, then dropped significantly in the following years to under 20,000 in 2015.

This same story repeats in the process of immigration from Taiwan to Canada. Out-migration from Taiwan has always been associated with geopolitical instability in the region since 1949 when the Communist Party established the People's Republic of China and the Kuomintang (KMT) established itself in Taiwan as a Chinese government in exile. Every time their relationship suffers a setback, whether it is from deteriorating Cross-Straits relations, the threat of using military force by the PRC government, the uncertainty of Taiwan's future, the fear that Taiwan might fall under Communist rule, or the discomfort and tension between "mainlanders" and "locals" within Taiwan, the out-flow of migration rises. The big wave of immigration to Canada from Taiwan in the late 1990s was a clear reflection of the Third Taiwan Straits Crisis, or the 1995-1996 Taiwan Straits Crisis. The annual arrivals of immigrants from Taiwan to Canada reached an all-time high over 13,000 in 1996 and 1997 respectively. It was nearly a 70 per cent increase from pre-crisis levels. In 1998 when the crisis was over, the arrivals immediately fell to the previous level at 7,200 and continued to drop to less than 1,000 annually in recent years.

Overall, from 1989 to 2015, nearly 1.1 million ethnic Chinese immigrants arrived in Canada from Hong Kong, Taiwan and mainland China combined, representing one in every six of all the immigrants that Canada welcomed during the period. Among them, over 673,000 from the PRC, 305,000 from Hong Kong and 109,000 from Taiwan landed in Canada, representing 62 per cent, 20 per cent and 10 per cent of total intakes of ethnic Chinese immigrants. Today, mainland China has taken over from Hong Kong as the largest source of Chinese immigration to Canada. It has also taken over from all countries and regions as the country sending the most immigrants to Canada during the period from 1998 to 2009, still remaining on the top three list of source countries in recent years.

Temporary Arrivals on the Rise

Canada offers two types of visa to foreign nationals that allow them to enter this country. One is for permanent residents and the other is for temporary entries, including such categories as visitor, worker and student. Chinese nationals coming to Canada have to have either a permanent resident permit or a valid permit for temporary visit, work or study in Canada.

In conventional immigration discussions, temporary visits are not considered as part of immigration, and therefore are discussed separately. The reasons we include temporary arrivals in this chapter are three-fold. First, once they enter Canada, ethnic Chinese visitors appear quite like local Chinese most of the time other than those occasions when they have to present their entry visa or passport. In fact, many economic and social issues and debates about the Chinese community in Canada are related to ethnic Chinese rather than differentiating types of entry visa. Second, the Canadian immigration system allows many possibilities for temporary visitors to change their entry visa to a permanent resident permit. A temporary visitor today is likely be a landed immigrant tomorrow or soon after. Third, the scale of temporary visits to Canada by Chinese nationals has grown to significant levels. Their degree of interaction among ethnic Chinese and cross-ethnic groups has intensified regardless of their type of entry visa.

The most noticeable growth is Chinese students studying in Canada. In the early 1990s, only a few hundred students a year came to Canada from the PRC. In just 10 years, the number skyrocketed to over 10,000 students a year entering this country in the 2000s. In recent years, the number of international student admissions from the PRC has repeatedly broken previous records almost every year. By 2015, nearly 140,000 Chinese students were registered and studying various subjects at all levels in Canadian universities and schools, a growth of 11 per cent over the year before, and an increase of 3 multiples compared to 10 years ago.

The PRC has become the largest source country of international students in Canada. Students from China are 2.2 times the number of students from the second largest source country (India), and 5 times the number of students from the third largest source country (Korea). The number of Chinese students in Canada is greater than that of all international students from the second to the fifth largest sources (India, Korea, France and Saudi Arabia) combined. Adding students from Hong Kong and Taiwan together, Chinese students represent nearly one third of all 460,000 international students in Canada (IRCC, 2015).

At the provincial level, Ontario is the top destination attracting nearly half of Chinese visa students, followed by British Columbia which attracts one-third. The remaining Chinese visa students are distributed among other provinces or regions. Obviously, this extreme variation of Chinese student visibility on campuses between the provinces and schools will have significantly different impact on the regions in many ways. The most important ones are that growing numbers of Chinese students are increasingly becoming a significant segment of existing Chinese communities, especially in Ontario and B.C.; and Chinese students in Canada are becoming an important reserve pool for immigration under the current immigration policy with the possibility of transitioning from international student to permanent resident.

Chinese nationals entering Canada as temporary foreign workers (TFW) is another category of temporary arrivals. However, their stories are quite different from those of Chinese students coming to Canada. In general, the number of temporary foreign workers in Canada increased considerably from the early 1990s. New entries of temporary foreign workers doubled from the early 1990s to the late 2000s, and most of this increase occurred in the late 2000s. Traditionally, Canada admitted foreign workers from the U.S.A., the Philippines, France, Australia, U.K., India and Mexico, etc. through either the International Mobility Program (IMP) or the Temporary Foreign Worker Program (TFWP), which has included various skill levels.

However, annual arrivals of foreign workers from PRC to Canada did not show the same pattern as the general trend from earlier major source countries. The number of arrivals from China had always remained under 2,000 a year, with an exception of 2,500 and 2,400 in 2007 and 2008 respectively. The share of TFWs from China in Canada's total intake of TFWs from all sources reached the record of 2.2 percent in 2007, while it had remained stable at 1.5 percent annually during the period from the late 1990s to 2015. In terms of the ranking, China has always been ranked below the top 10 source countries, except for once as the number 10 source in 2007. Although still insignificant in number, visa issues for foreign workers from China have always been over-stated in some media or in public opinion when a related story breaks out. In 2013, there was a plan to bring in as many as 200 Chinese miners to work on a proposed project in northeastern British Columbia. A public backlash was directed at the company bringing in non-Canadian employees to take jobs in this country. Two labour unions brought their struggle against the company to the Federal Court (CBC News, 2013). The former Conservative government ended up tightening rules for importing foreign workers.

Chinese tourists make up the third largest group of temporary arrivals in Canada, including those from the PRC, Hong Kong, Taiwan or other sources. Trips to Canada from the PRC grew at an average rate of 14 percent year-over-year between 2001 and 2015, rising from a total of 82,000 to 483,000 a year. (The exception was in 2003, when the outbreak of Severe Acute Respiratory Syndrome or SARS curtailed much international travel.) Currently, Canada is the 2nd most popular destination for Mainland Chinese tourists. In addition to growth of total visits, the total of nights spent and total of expenditure in Canada by tourists from the PRC have also increased significantly. By 2015, PRC had become the third biggest contributor of tourists to Canada, up from 10th place in 2005. In 2015, PRC tourists contributed nearly one billion dollars to the Canadian economy. Adding visitors from Hong Kong and Taiwan together, the total number of Chinese visitors and their spending in Canada is even greater (See Table 3.1).

It is interesting to note that the growth of tourists from PRC to Canada has been strongly associated with bilateral relationships. After over a decade of negotiation between Beijing and Ottawa, the Approved Destination Status (ADS) was granted to Canada in June 2010 and the first direct flights from China to Canada started arriving in August 2010. The total number of tourists from the PRC has continued growing since then. From February 6, 2014, visitors to Canada were automatically considered eligible for multiple-entry visas. These visas allow qualified visitors to enter and exit Canada for up to six months at a time for up to 10 years. In the same year, the fee for the temporary resident visa program was reduced from $150 to $100 for the processing of either a single- or multiple-entry visa. This was intended to make the visa application process easier and to promote tourism and trade by increasing the number of eligible travelers who are able to make multiple visits to Canada. The multiple-entry visa and lower visa fee attracted more Chinese tourists and many frequent visitors became "de facto residents" in Canada.

The growing number of visitors from the PRC to Canada shows no sign of slowing down in the near future. In September 2016, after the back-to-back visits by Prime Minister Justin Trudeau to China and Premier Li Keqiang to Canada, both governments issued a Joint Statement on September 23rd, 2016. Both sides agreed to take further action to open a new chapter in the Canada-China strategic partnership, including announcing the goal of doubling bilateral trade and two-way visits by 2025 based on 2015 statistics (Government of Canada, 2016). In other words, it is foreseeable that in ten years the total number of tourist visits to Canada from the PRC will have reached nearly one million a year by 2025.

Table 3.1 Chinese Tourists to Canada from PRC, Hong Kong and Taiwan

Year	Tourists from PRC			Tourists from Hong Kong			Tourists from Taiwan		
	Trips (1,000)	Nights (1,000)	Spending in Canada (C$M)	Trips (1,000)	Nights (1,000)	Spending in Canada (C$M)	Trips (1,000)	Nights (1,000)	Spending in Canada (C$M)
2001	82	2,781	163	125	2,075	175	n.a.	n.a.	n.a.
2002	95	2,472	185	118	2,015	158	104	1,441	134
2003	77	2,329	143	87	1,623	106	68	1,079	78
2004	95	3,114	171	115	2,168	142	106	1,308	125
2005	113	3,723	219	109	2,161	151	98	1,536	110
2006	139	4,007	257	107	1,707	118	93	1,352	98
2007	151	4,096	258	111	1,781	127	79	1,171	92
2008	159	4,439	263	125	2,022	144	n.a.	n.a.	n.a.
2009	160	4,471	261	105	1,780	119	n.a.	n.a.	n.a.
2010	193	5,401	315	111	1,958	130	n.a.	n.a.	n.a.
2011	237	6,904	407	114	2,132	138	n.a.	n.a.	n.a.
2012	273	8,137	486	114	2,241	140	n.a.	n.a.	n.a.
2013	342	13,240	805	128	2,431	189	n.a.	n.a.	n.a.
2014	448	15,365	1,026	133	1,987	180	n.a.	n.a.	n.a.
2015	483	15,078	993	142	2,164	193	n.a.	n.a.	n.a.

Source: *Statistics Canada*, "Travellers to Canada by country of origin, top 15 countries of origin", http://www.statcan.gc.ca/tables-tableaux/sum-som/l01/cst01/arts38a-eng.htm, accessed 29th August 2017. (Note: "n.a." data is not available in years that Taiwan was not among the top 15 origins.)

Transition from Temporary Visitors to Permanent Residents

Canada's immigration system is shifting towards encouraging immigration by young, bilingual, highly skilled immigrants that can help the country replace its aging labour force. In order to attract migrants with the right skills, Canada is opening its doors to more and more temporary foreign workers and international students. The federal government has granted exclusive eligibility to 29 different occupations under the federal skilled worker program and has devolved responsibility for immigrant selection to the provinces. In 1998, the Provincial Nominee Program (PNP) was introduced to give provinces a mechanism with which to respond to economic development needs at the local level. In September 2008, Canada introduced a new Canadian Experience Class (CEC), which aims to make Canada more competitive in attracting and retaining individuals with the skills the country needs. These programs have paved the way for some immigrants initially classified as temporary workers to shift their status to permanent residents.

A recent *Statistics Canada* report (Lu & Hou, 2017) finds that the considerable increase of temporary foreign workers in Canada since the early 1990s also became an increasingly important source of permanent residents admitted to Canada over this period. From the late 1990s to the late 2000s, proportionately more temporary foreign workers gained permanent residence status. Within five years after receiving their first work permits, about 9% of temporary foreign workers who arrived between 1995 and 1999 became permanent residents. The level increased to 13% for the 2000 to 2004 arrivals, and rose further to 21% for 2005 to 2009 arrivals.

Similarly, another study by the Asia Pacific Foundation of Canada (2012) also finds that the probability of Chinese temporary workers making the transition to permanent residents is also high. Of the 1.4 million foreign workers entering Canada between 2001 and 2010,

17,000 were from China. During the same period, of the 186,000 foreign workers who became permanent residents in Canada, more than 13,000 were from China (see Table 3.2). Indeed, nearly 79 percent of the temporary workers from China were granted permanent residency during that period, compared with just 13 percent for workers of other nationalities. And 90 percent of the Chinese workers who were admitted as permanent residents came through the economic classes, chiefly through the skilled workers program (36 percent). Finally, Chinese temporary workers made up one-third of all the immigrants who entered Canada under the CEC program.

Table 3.2 Transition from Temporary to Permanent Resident Status (2001-2010 Aggregated)

	Entry as International Students			Entry as Temporary Foreign Workers		
	From China	From all sources	Share of Chinese	From China	From all sources	Share of Chinese
Total entries as temporary residents	114,275	768,218	15%	17,480	1,425,330	1%
Total transitions to permanent residents	14,240	83,674	17%	13,845	186,635	7%
Probability of Transition	12%	11%		79%	13%	

Source: Zhang, K., 2012. (https://www.asiapacific.ca/research-report/multi-stream-flows-reshape-chinese-communities-canada-human)

The same pattern of transition also happens to international students from China. From 2001 to 2010, Canada welcomed over 768,000 international students from around the world, of whom over 114,000 were from China. During the same period, more than 83,000 international students made the transition to permanent resident status and 14,000 Chinese students became permanent residents of Canada. The probability of making the leap to permanent resident during that time period was 11 percent for all international student groups and 12 percent for those from the PRC. The majority of the 70 percent of Chinese students succeeded in becoming permanent residents through the economic classes, including the skilled workers program (41 percent). Chinese students made up 58% of all CEC participants during the first two years of the program.

Conclusion: Fresh Blood Injected into Chinese Communities in Canada

During the whole period following World War II, Canada's admitting ethnic Chinese into this country was seen as a significant moving away from the exclusion and restriction policies towards a more open and fair immigration system, which has shaped new paths for Chinese coming to Canada. The new paths brought Chinese immigrants to Canada who are no longer just hard-working labourers, but people with higher skills and talents that can better contribute to the Canadian economy and society. Canada also admitted Chinese from various sources, the PRC, Hong Kong and Taiwan being the major ones due to different historical incidents that triggered large out-flows from those source regions. The fast growing numbers and composition of Chinese immigrants, as well as the transitioning of temporary to permanent residents, has expanded the base of Chinese communities in Canada. Most importantly, a Chinese Canadian identity has emerged under the multiculturalism policy, and the Chinese heritage is becoming an accepted part of Canada's multicultural society, gradually accepted and embraced by more and more Canadians. In closing, let us repeat the words of Rev. Andrew Lam: "To be proud of our origin and to appreciate it fully is an attitude that is not inconsistent with good citizenship or loyalty to Canada."

References

CBC News. (9 April 2013). B.C. mine's temporary foreign workers case in Federal Court. Source: http://www.cbc.ca/news/canada/british-columbia/b-c-mine-s-temporary-foreign-workers-case-in-federal-court-1.1374502

Chinese Canadian National Council. (12 June 2012). "Our Stories-Paper Sons and Daughters". Source: https://ccncourstories.wordpress.com/videos/paper-sons-video/

Gonverment of Canada. (18 July 2017). Immigrate as a skilled worker through Express Entry. Source: http://www.cic.gc.ca/english/immigrate/skilled/index.asp

Government of Canada. (2001). Justice Laws Website. Source: Immigration and Refugee Protection Act (S.C. 2001, c. 27): http://laws-lois.justice.gc.ca/eng/acts/I-2.5/FullText.html

Government of Canada. (2012). Canadian Multiculturalism: An Inclusive

Citizenship. Source: http://www.cic.gc.ca/english/multiculturalism/citizenship.asp

Government of Canada. (23 Sept 2016). News. Source: Joint Statement Between Canada and the People's Republic of China: http://pm.gc.ca/eng/news/2016/09/23/joint-statement-between-canada-and-peoples-republic-china

Government of Canada. (20 June 2017). Statistics and Open Data. Source: http://www.cic.gc.ca/english/resources/statistics/index.asp

Guo, Shibao, & DeVoretz, Don. (Aug 2007). The Changing Face of Chinese Immigrants in Canada. Source: IZA Discussion Paper No. 3018 : http://ftp.iza.org/dp3018.pdf

IRCC. (2015). Facts and Figures 2015. Source: Immigration Overview-Temporary Residents—Annual IRCC Updates: http://open.canada.ca/data/en/dataset/052642bb-3fd9-4828-b608-c81dff7e539c?_ga=2.140835762.1854832651.1502753991-1488428533.1429565837

Li, S. Peter. (1998). Chinese in Canada, second Edition. Oxford University Press.

Li, S. Peter. (2011). Immigrants from China to Canada: Issues of Supply and Demand in Human Capital. Source, Potter, Pitman with Adam Thomas, Issues in Canada-China Relations. Canadian International Council.

Lu, Yuqian, & Hou Feng. (2017). Transition from Temporary Foreign Workers to Permanent Residents, 1990 to 2014. Source: http://www.statcan.gc.ca/pub/11f0019m/11f0019m2017389-eng.pdf

Poy, Vivienne. (2013). Passage to Promise Land. McGill-Queen's University Press.

The Metro Toronto Chinese & Southeast Asian Legal Clinic (MTCSALC). (2011). Road to Justice-The legal struggle for equal rights of Chinese Canadians. Source: http://www.roadtojustice.ca

Zhang, Kenny. (2012). (ReportsResearch, Asia Pacific Foundation of Canada), Source: https://www.asiapacific.ca/research-report/multi-stream-flows-reshape-chinese-communities-canada-human

Zhang, Kenny, & DeGolyer E.Michael. (2011). Hong Kong: Canada's Largest City in Asia-Survey of Canadian Citizens in Hong Kong. Source: Asia Pacific Foundation of Canada: https://www.asiapacific.ca/sites/default/files/filefield/hk_survey_feb2011_v8.pdf

Chapter 4

"Gold Rush" in the 21st Century: New Opportunities and Challenges

It was the mid-19th century "Fraser River Gold Rush" that first brought Chinese pioneer immigrants to Canada. During the 1881-1885 period, thousands of Chinese workers took part in building the trans-Canada Pacific Railway. At that time, nearly all Chinese workers in Canada were low-skilled, hard-working and low-paid labourers hired for those jobs that other workers were reluctant to perform. Gradually, other economic activities emerged with the growth of Chinese worker communities as a so-called "enclave economy" that provided daily services for the Chinese labourers, such as barber shop, restaurant, tailor and laundry store, and grocery and medicine stores. Li's book (1998:24) shows the stated occupations of 4,564 Chinese who entered Canada between 1885 and 1903: 72.5 percent were labourers; merchants and storekeepers accounted for only 5.7 percent; farmers 6.8

percent; laundrymen 5.9 percent; and cooks 3.0 percent, etc.

When the Fraser River Gold Rush was over, and the last spike of the Pacific Railway was hammered in, some Chinese labourers stayed, and many moved on to find other jobs or businesses in Canada. The most long-lasting one is perhaps the Chinese restaurant business. There is a saying in Chinese that states where there is sunshine there are Chinese, where there are Chinese there will be Chinese restaurants. The early Chinese restaurants in Canada were called "Tang Restaurant," which partially reflected the memory within Chinese communities about their identity as descendants of the Tang Dynasty, and partially related to the common location that these restaurants were operated in Chinatown—"Tang Ren Jie" in Mandarin or "Tong Yun Gai" in Cantonese. Today, Chinese restaurants can be found in places across Canada, particularly in Montreal, Toronto and Vancouver (MTV). People are always full of praise that Canada's Chinese restaurants are among the top quality, apart from those in mainland China, Hong Kong and Taiwan.

The long thriving of Chinese restaurants in Canada has been a clear sign of the importance of the restaurant business in Chinese communities in this country. In fact, after 150 years of evolution, the Canadian Chinese community's economic and business participation in this country has undergone a sea change that can no longer be represented by just the restaurant industry. In this chapter, we will discuss a new round of "Gold Rush"—people and capital from China to Canada in search of better opportunities—this is a diversified process of economic activities, professional development and business progress of Chinese communities in Canada, and new challenges faced by these communities.

Multitalented Chinese Communities Contribute to Canadian Society

The importance of Chinese communities in Canada has been underestimated for a long time. As a country of immigrants, Canada has been accustomed to looking at immigrants from an economic perspective, particularly from labour market needs. Chinese immigrants, like all immigrants, have traditionally been seen as suppliers of needed manpower. Too often when people try to measure the contribution of Chinese to Canada, they tend to talk about higher unemployment numbers, lower earnings, therefore lower income tax contributions, etc.

This is apparently outdated. The image of today's Chinese Canadian is vastly different than it was one and a half centuries ago when Chinese immigrants were stereotyped as railway coolies, laundrymen or restaurant waiters. Hollywood exaggerated the stereotype with movies about opium dens, celestials in pig-tails with knives hidden up their silk sleeves, slant-eyed beauties with bound feet and ancient love potions (Lee, 1984). What the Chinese Canadian communities look like today is as diversified as Canadian society as a whole, and they have made a variety of contributions to Canadian society with their multitalented skills.

Firstly, inflows of skilled immigrants fill skill shortages in Canada, and therefore keep Canada on the leading edge of innovation and technology development. China constitutes an important source of international brain flow to meet Canada's human resource needs. According to Citizenship and Immigration Canada (CIC, 2011), between 2001 and 2011, China supplied Canada with a total of 196,220 immigrants with post-secondary education, of whom, 5,435 immigrants had doctoral degrees, 34,750 people had Master's degrees and nearly 100,000 people had undergraduate degrees. An early study (Qiang, 2013) found that Chinese immigrants have dominated the increase of foreign-born PhDs in Canada, outnumbering the U.S. and U.K., the two dominant sources prior to 1981. The U.S. share went from a high of 24 percent during the 1971-1980 period to a low of 6 percent over the 1991-2000 period, while China's share went up from a low of 2 percent to a high of 25 percent. Over the past decade, China supplied nearly 70,000 professionals from all occupations; 25,000 managers including 2,400 senior ones; and 14,000 skilled workers and technicians (CIC, 2011).

Secondly, diversified Chinese communities play a crucial role in the accumulation of human capital for Canada and will continue to do so for many future generations. This is particularly true in terms of teachers at Canadian schools and universities. On the one hand, faculty and staff of Chinese origin represented the largest minority group, 28.2 percent of all minority faculty or 4.2 percent of the total Canadian university staff as of 2006. And as of September 2010, of the 1,845 Canada Research Chair positions, nearly 100 or 5 percent are identified as Chinese, including those from the PRC, Hong Kong and Taiwan (Qiang, 2013).

On the other hand, the Canadian census (2006) shows children from Chinese families have the highest university completion rate (62 percent) among 25-to-34-year-olds in 2006, compared to 24 percent of children of Canadian born families. Like other Canadian kids, Chinese children typically select four areas as their major fields of study in post-secondary education: business, management and public administration; architecture, engineering and related technologies; health, parks, recreation and fitness; social and behavioral sciences and law. The various skills that Chinese immigrants, students and temporary workers contribute to the Canadian economy are well documented. For example, the 2006 census reported that

Chinese are more likely to work in occupations related to applied sciences and business, such as natural and applied sciences and related occupations; processing, manufacturing and utilities; business, finance and administrative occupations and sales and service. Perhaps not surprisingly, Chinese are more visible than average Canadians in accommodation and food services (restaurant jobs); professional, scientific and technical services (accountants and lawyers); finance and insurance (bank jobs); manufacturing (general labour) and wholesale trade (import and export). However, Chinese are less likely than average Canadians to work in construction, agriculture, forestry, fishing and hunting; health care, social assistance, and public administration. Similarly, it is often reported in the Chinese media that Chinese immigrant communities have experienced significant upward skill mobility from the traditional "Three Blades" (kitchen knives, tailor scissors, razor blades) to the more modern professions of lawyers, engineers, doctors, accountants, senior technicians and university professors.

Thirdly, human capital flows from China to Canada saved billions of Canadian public investment in education. Li's study (2011) finds that Canada saved about 2.2 billion dollars in education-related expenses by accepting immigrants from China with university degrees between 1991 and 2000. In other words, Canada saved nearly 200 million dollars annually in public expenses on education by accepting highly-skilled immigrants from China.

Fourthly, business immigrants from China brought with them financial funds, entrepreneurship and international business skills to Canada. There are many other contributions that Chinese communities have made to our society, however, that are less well-known. It was estimated that there were 120,000 business immigrants landed in the Vancouver metropolitan area between 1980 and 2001, who brought in a total of 35-40 billion dollars in financial capital to the region (Ley, 2011). In addition to financial funds that business immigrants contribute upon admission to Canada, they also bring their entrepreneurship and international business skills, but these have seemed to be less appreciated. From 2001 to 2010, over 52,000 business immigrants from China arrived in Canada.

Finally, the Chinese diaspora's "bamboo network" effects have brought great business benefits for Canada. The transnational networks of immigrants can have the same effects for the host societies. As an essay in The Economist (2010) pointed out, in the case of the U.S., immigration provides legions of unofficial ambassadors, deal-brokers, recruiters and boosters. Immigrants not only bring the best ideas from around the world to North American shores, they are also a conduit for spreading American ideas and ideals in their homelands, thus increasing the "soft power" of their adoptive country. The same holds true for Canada. Transnational links also take place in knowledge sharing and innovation. As The Economist also pointed out, in Silicon Valley more than half of all Chinese and Indian scientists and engineers reported having shared information about technology and business opportunities with people in their native countries. At the same time, as people in emerging markets continue to innovate, North America will find it ever more useful to have so many citizens who can tap into the latest information from cities like Mumbai and Shanghai (The Economist, 2011). Another study (Lin, Guan, & Nicholson, 2008) identifies specific roles of internationally educated Chinese transnational entrepreneurs in linking Canada and China in innovation activities. Their study finds that the innovation links established and maintained by Chinese transnational entrepreneurs who concurrently engage in business in

Canada and China, but keep Canada as home base. Furthermore, the local knowledge immigrants bring from their home countries reduces the cost of doing business for the U.S. and Canadian firms.

In fact, there are countless examples of Canadian individuals with Chinese heritage making great contributions domestically and internationally for this country. Here we will just name a few to highlight how these individuals have served Canada in their professions, making Canada more prominent on the world stage and stronger at home.

Hok Yat Louie (1875-1934) and his family established some of the most recognized companies in British Columbia, and the family's holdings now employ over 8,000 and include the London Drugs chain. Hok Yat Louie paid the 50-dollar head tax to enter Canada from Zhongshan, China in 1896, at age 21. After toiling at a variety of manual labour jobs, he began to farm on a plot that he leased. He eventually ventured into opening his first retail store in 1903, the Kwong Chong Company, selling seeds, fertilizer and wholesale groceries in Vancouver's Chinatown. In 1927, Mr. Louie renamed and incorporated the company as H.Y. Louie Company Limited. Building community in his adopted country was so important to Mr. Louie, he became a leader in this burgeoning Chinese community, as a mentor and trusted advisor. His belief in being a full member of the community was imprinted on his children and each contributed a great deal in time, expertise or tangible philanthropy. He considered service to his community at large to be his duty; a passion and core value that has acted as a legacy for succeeding generations of his family and their employees. After his death, his four sons managed the family business guided by the principles and values of their father. Eventually, Tong Louie took over and in 1955 his company acquired the IGA franchise for B.C. and in 1976 purchased London Drugs.

The family holdings now own some of the most recognized companies in the province. Despite its diverse interests, it is still very much a family business with the fourth generation now in place. The entire group of companies is still driven by the same values its founder practiced and expressed so eloquently. It is quite unique and remarkable that names of three generations of Mr. Louie's family have been included in the Business Laureates of British Columbia Hall of Fame, Mr. Hok Yat Louie, and his son and grandson, Dr. Tong Louie (1914-1998) and Dr. Brandt Louie (1943-) (JA British Columbia, 2017). In 2012, Dr. Tong Louie was subsequently inducted into the Canadian Business Hall of Fame with his son Dr. Brandt Louie.

Joanne Liu (1965 -) is a Canadian pediatric doctor, Associate Professor of Medicine at the University of Montreal, Professor of Practice of Medicine at McGill University, and the current International President of Doctors Without Borders (MSF). Liu was born and raised in Québec City to a Chinese immigrant Liu family from Taishan, Guangdong. Her family ran a Chinese restaurant called China Garden. Liu graduated from the McGill University Faculty of Medicine with the M.D., C.M. degree. Liu has worked in Kenya, the Democratic Republic of Congo, Honduras, Haiti, Ethiopia, Nigeria, Indonesia, the Palestinian Territories, Uganda, Sudan and Sri Lanka. In 2015, she was named one of TIME's 100 most influential people, for her leadership of MSF during its response to the Ebola crisis in West Africa.

Carol Huynh (1980-) is a Canadian freestyle wrestler. Huynh was the first gold medalist for Canada in women's wrestling and was the first gold medalist for Canada at the 2008 Beijing Olympics. She is also the current reigning Commonwealth Games and two-time Pan American Games champion. Success was also achieved at the world championships where Huynh has totaled one silver and three bronze medals. Huynh is also an eleven-time national champion. Huynh was born in British Columbia to parents who were ethnic Chinese refugees from northern Vietnam. She started her studies at Simon Fraser University in 1998, then moved to the University of Calgary in 2007. In 2013, she was appointed as Chairwoman to the International Wrestling Federation.

Milton Wong (1940-2011) was a Canadian businessman, financier, and philanthropist. Born to Chinese immigrant parents, Wong was raised in Vancouver's Chinatown. His father was a tailor. Wong became one of Canada's most prolific money managers and was the Chairman of HSBC. In addition to being active in the world of Canadian finance, he was on the boards of a myriad organizations and served as Chancellor of Simon Fraser University. He won the Freedom of the City Award of Vancouver for his outstanding contributions to the city. He was honoured with numerous awards such as the Order of Canada and the Order of British Columbia.

Bing Wing Thom (1940-2016) was a Canadian architect and urban designer. Born in Hong Kong, he immigrated to Vancouver, British Columbia with his family in 1950. Thom received a Bachelor of Architecture degree in 1966 from the University of British Columbia and a Master of Architecture in 1970 from the University of California, Berkeley. Thom specialized in urban planning and complex building types for international and domestic projects. His representative works include the Chan Centre for the Performing Arts at UBC and Aberdeen Centre in Richmond, BC. In 1995, Thom was made a Member of the Order of Canada and was a recipient of the Golden Jubilee Medal for outstanding service to his country. He was a Fellow of the Royal Architectural Institute of Canada. In 2011 he was awarded the RAIC's highest honour, the RAIC Gold Medal.

Chan-hon Goh (1969-) is a Chinese-born Canadian ballet dancer. She was Principal Dancer with the National Ballet of Canada. Born in Beijing to parents who were principal dancers in the National Ballet of China, Goh and her parents left China for Vancouver in 1976. She began her career in 1978 at the Goh Ballet Academy. She entered the National Ballet of Canada in 1988 and was appointed Second Soloist in 1990 and First Soloist in 1992. She became a Principal Dancer in 1994. Goh is a winner of the Prix de Lausanne (1986) and a silver medalist in the Genée International Ballet Competition (1988).

Jim Chu (1959-) is former Chief Constable of the Vancouver Police Department (VPD) from 2007 to 2015. Chu is the first non-white Chief Constable in Vancouver. Born in Shanghai, Chu grew up in East Vancouver after his family immigrated to B.C. He graduated from Sir Charles Tupper Secondary School where he played on the rugby team. Joining the VPD a year after his high school graduation, he continued his education at the same time, going on to earn a Bachelor of Business Administration from SFU, and an MBA from the UBC. In May 2007, the Governor General of Canada awarded Chu the Order of Merit of Police Forces, for service beyond the call of duty. In 2015, he was promoted to the rank of Commander of the Order of Merit. He was named one of 25 Canadians chosen to receive the Transformation Award by the Globe and Mail/La Presse (2010) and became the first municipal police senior officer in B.C. to be granted a Commission (2015).

The list goes on and on, and 1.5 million Canadians with Chinese ethnic origin would have 1.5 million stories to tell about their individual contributions to the community. One thing is obvious: today's Chinese Canadians have upgraded their skills and professional expertise to levels that are incomparable with those of the earlier generations of coolies or labourers.

This allows them to be more capable of participating in and contributing to Canadian society at levels that are not measurable merely by income tax contribution.

Businesses Extend beyond the "Chinatown Economy"

In the early days, Chinese immigrants in Canada and other host societies suffered painfully from anti-Chinese racism and cultural barriers between them and local societies. Racism, hatred, and violence against Chinese immigrants resulted in residential segregation. In addition to physical abuse and intimidation, white or local indigenous landlords would often sell or lease properties to Chinese immigrants only in areas that were unattractive to the local residents. In hostile environments, Chinese immigrants felt safer in relative isolation from local communities. As one of their survival strategies, many Chinese had to choose living together in the same neighborhood where they could speak their own dialects, eat their own customary foods, and worship their own gods as they had done in China (Zhang K. Q., 2013).

A typical Chinatown originally functioned as a place of residence and a neighborhood community for Chinese immigrants who could not readily afford, or were not welcomed, to live outside of Chinatown. When new Chinese immigrants joined their relatives, friends, or fellow villagers in Canada, they tended to live in the place where their sponsors were living and shared the cost of room and board. Gradually, enclave businesses also shaped the birth and growth of a Chinatown. To serve the needs of Chinatown residents, Chinese grocery stores, tailors, laundrymen, barbers, restaurant workers, Asian goods importers, labourer brokers, and other businesses were set up, and theaters, schools, and various types of associations were also established in the neighborhood. In the periods when Chinese immigrants were less discriminated against, some Chinese immigrants scattered throughout a city but often came back to Chinatown for shopping and social gatherings. Thus, Chinatown became a nexus for communication with home and places of business and work.

After World War II, Canada's economy experienced rapid recovery, and Chinese businesses in Canada grew correspondingly. According to some estimates, there were over 4,600 stores, firms or companies that were owned and operated by Chinese immigrants in the late 1960s. The total value of real estate, farms, factories and all industries at that time was about 280 million dollars, representing a wide range of industries, including Chinese and Western restaurants, nightclubs, motels, grocery stores, flower shops, factories, farms, import and export companies, laundry shops, etc. (Wu, 1987).

Entering the 21st century, the economic strength, professionalism and hard-working tradition of Chinese communities became even more impressive. Compared with the situation in the early postwar period, Chinese immigrant-invested and operated businesses in Canada have established many more firms and injected greater capital in a much wider range of industry sectors that are important for Canadian economy. For example, in July 2016, Canada's first Chinese-immigrant-owned bank, Wealth One Bank of Canada, was officially opened with a focus on providing services to Chinese-Canadians. As a Canadian Schedule I bank headquartered in Toronto, it provides banking services online and through retail offices in Toronto and Markham, ON and in Vancouver, B.C. Although the economic status of Chinese Canadians has greatly improved with overall economic strength significantly more enhanced than before, many Chinese businesses are still characterized by their noticeable enclave economy performance. The difference is that they are no longer subject to the geographical restrictions within a "Chinatown".

Regardless of whether the location of a business is in Chinatown or elsewhere, the flourishing of Chinese immigrant-operated businesses is mainly fueled by both Chinese and non-Chinese customers, especially with the rapidly growing number of new arrivals of Chinese immigrants, students, tourists and other visitors. Some representative businesses include, but are not limited to, examples discussed below.

Chinese restaurant businesses have a long history in Canada. Although its popularity among non-Chinese communities has improved, daily clients and consumers are still mainly Chinese. The owners and employees are mostly ethnic Chinese, and its supplies are also sourced from local farms or importers operated by ethnic Chinese. In the past two decades, immigrants, students and tourists from China, Hong Kong and Taiwan or elsewhere have dramatically increased the demand for Chinese food. On the supply side, the industry has been fueled to a higher level by new capital, management, and work force that recent Chinese immigrants have brought into this country. This was the reason why some people argue that Canada, especially in Vancouver, Montreal and Toronto, offers some of the best Chinese food in the world—Canada has a multitude of Chinese restaurants that serve culinary creations from different regions of China, and it keeps growing. Therefore, in addition to traditionally famous Cantonese cuisine, more and more types of Chinese cuisine and flavors have been added to the culinary industry in Canada. Even many well-known Chinese cuisines and brands in the PRC, Hong Kong and Taiwan have become a part of Canada's restaurant scene, such as "Old Beijing Roast Duck," "Flower and Horse in Spring" serving Yunnan's "crossing the bridge rice noodles", "Wang's Taiwan Beef Noodles," "Little Sheep Mongolian Hot Pot," etc. In 2016, two Toronto-based Chinese restaurants, Dailo Restaurant (#15) and Lai Wah Heen (#79) were named on 2016 list of Canada's 100 Best Restaurants (Canada's 100 Best Restaurants, 2016).

Groceries and imports are other business areas that have successful traditions in Canada. This industry was able to grow steadily based on increasing Chinese and other Asian populations, as well as the rising Chinese and other Asian restaurant businesses. It basically supplies raw materials and ingredients for Asian restaurants and provides daily living supplies for Asian families. The businesses have taken various forms, including grocery stores, convenience stores, gift shops, boutiques, antique shops, pharmacies, bookstores, import firms, supermarkets, household appliances, bakeries, hardware stores, car and tire dealers, and many other shops. As taste and consumption of Asian products has grown in recent years, some immigrants from the PRC, Hong Kong and Taiwan are transforming this industry into a supply chain including "import-wholesale-retail" by drawing upon their original business relationships established in Asia. In turn, this has further accelerated the development of the industry in Canada which has created jobs and generated taxes for the economy.

Over the past decades, real estate has become perhaps the most profitable and controversial industry that has attracted attention from investors, policy makers and the general public across the country. The booming industry that has been fueled by soaring demand for both residential and commercial buildings, low interest rates for long periods, and global excess liquidity, etc., has generated investment interest from Chinese immigrant communities. Due to the convenience of language, culture and access to local Chinese community networks, the first stage was that mainstream real estate companies hired a large number of Chinese real estate agents to sell properties to newly arrived Chinese immigrants. Then the profitable opportunities were soon addressed by sensitive Chinese entrepreneurs who opened real estate brokerage firms and real estate development companies. Despite the debate on housing affordability and foreign buyers, the real estate industry as a whole contributed roughly 12 percent of Canada's GDP and real estate and construction together now represent roughly 25 percent of B.C.'s GDP. The sector and related business also recently have generated 75 percent of newly added jobs in the Canadian economy (CREA, 2016). Chinese immigrant real estate investors and developers have made their share of this important contribution to the entire Canadian economy.

There are many Chinese immigrant-operated businesses in the service industry focusing mainly on Chinese clients. Their areas of service cover almost everything from the cradle to the grave, such as the postpartum care facilities, daycare centres, senior homes and funeral services. It also provides the basic necessities of life and daily consumption, such as family hotels, apartment rentals, cinemas, travel agencies, beauty salons, medical clinics, laundries, video rentals, private schools, driving schools, and so on. Recently, with the increase of high net worth Chinese immigrant families arriving in Canada, financial services related to business investment, wealth management, banking and insurance brokerage have become popular and are flourishing. However, as the Chinese saying goes, "there are many kinds of birds in a large forest", which means "it takes all sorts" in English— businesses may turn out to be good, bad or ugly. For example, financial investment fraud targeting new immigrants and new versions of the "Ponzi scheme" are sometimes reported by newspapers or social media.

Chinese ethnic media such as book publishing and newspapers, radio, television, online media etc. have been growing vigorously and also play an important role into promotinge the entire Chinese community's businesses development. In addition, the cultural industry is also booming in Chinese communities. Chinese or Asian thematic arts exhibitions, cultural festivals, and musical and drama performances, etc., have mushroomed across the larger communities in Canada where there are abundant audiences. In Vancouver, for example, it was estimated by local Chinese media that there were more than 30 Spring Festival Evening Gala performances, large or small, during the Chinese New Year (Spring Festival) period in 2015. Some were organized by local Chinese communities, and others hosted incoming Chinese performance groups. In recent years, Canadian audiences in Vancouver, Montreal, Toronto and other cities have had the fortune to enjoy top performances by the world renowned ethnic Chinese superstar artists and groups from China or around the world, such as the renowned pianist Lang Lang, cellist Yo-Yo Ma, the China Philharmonic Orchestra, and countless Chinese traditional folk artists. Many of these outstanding artists were even able to perform for audiences in China itself. Canada has truly become a place where eastern cultures meet western ones.

Manufacturing has never been a major business sector for Chinese immigrants in Canada. In the early days, they were involved in some small scale food seasoning processing facilities, garment factories, butcher and meat processing, skin care cosmetics production, and other processing industries. Most of these were brought in and operated by business immigrants from Hong Kong. In recent years, some business immigrants from the PRC have turned their attention to wineries, bottled drinking water production, and jade processing, etc. Others have been involved in advanced manufacturing, such as solar panel manufacturing, etc.

Farming was one of the major areas of economic activity for Chinese immigrants in Canada in the early years. They grew vegetables, fruits and flowers to supply the Chinese community and local markets. Unfortunately, the farming sector is diminishing within the Chinese community because the second or third generation of farming operators have received higher education and professional training in Canadian schools and are reluctant to take over the family farming business, preferring to move on to professional jobs.

The High-tech industry is booming in Chinese communities as well. With the global advancement of science and technology and arrivals of highly skilled professional immigrants from mainland China, Hong Kong and Taiwan, the Chinese Canadian community has seen the convergence of a large number of scientific and technological professionals. With strong high-tech professional backgrounds, some scientists or technicians have turned themselves into entrepreneurs to begin start-ups in various areas such as VR/AR, clean energy, shared economy, e-commerce, intelligence, new media, O2O and internet applications, etc. When innovation meets entrepreneurship backed by venture capital, the high-tech industry is able to grow, and Chinese scientist-turned entrepreneurs are giving full play to their talents as naturally as ducks in a pond.

Mr. James Zahn, founding CEO and President at Cantronic Systems Inc., is one of many such examples of scientist-turned entrepreneur. Mr. Zahn attended universities in both China and Canada. He earned a Master of Science Degree from the University of British Columbia in 1989. He earned a B.Sc. in Mechanical Engineering and a master's degree in Mechanical

Engineering from Zhejiang University in 1984 and 1987 respectively. Mr. Zahn founded the Cantronic System Inc. which has become a global technology leader in infrared thermal imaging and night vision systems. It manufactures and distributes active and passive infrared imaging and night vision cameras. These complex camera systems are used for monitoring, protecting and managing facilities and people. Cantronic has supplied systems responding to high demand for military, public health, homeland security, and industrial applications. In 2003 Mr. Zahn was a recipient of the Queen's Golden Jubilee Medal for his company's innovative fever scanner that assisted in controlling the spread of SARS in Canada and many Asian countries.

In fact, such cases of ethnic Chinese successfully running high-tech companies are numerous in Canada. Each year, many organizations such as chambers of commerce, business associations or media organize various achievement awards in recognition of all types of successful enterprises and entrepreneurs in the Chinese business community, and many of the winners are high-tech companies. The annual Mandarin Profile Awards presented by Fairchild TV, featuring stories of successes and hardships of Chinese immigrants to Canada, have been continually presented since 2008 (Fairchild TV, 2017). Over the 10 years, there were 6 years when top achievement awards were presented to entrepreneurs managing high-tech innovative companies, including those with outstanding accomplishments in the fields of pharmaceuticals, cancer treatment, solar energy, hybrid auto engines, etc.

Overall, Chinese Canadians and their business activities in Canada retain, to some extent, the features of a traditional enclave economy. Nevertheless, the scope of businesses has gone far beyond "Chinatown," with the expansion of the Chinese immigrant population into communities that have smaller Chinese populations. From the perspective of social integration, these Chinese-founded enterprises are no longer confined to serving the Chinese community and clients, but rather provide products and services to local markets and the general public. Judging by their ways of doing business such as commercial approaches, customer targets, and corporate structures, ethnic Chinese operated businesses are no different from other Canadian enterprises managed by other ethnic groups, despite the retention of some Chinese management styles. The expansion of industry sectors that Chinese businesses are involved in is clear evidence that the Chinese business community should not be labelled by the perception that they are only interested in real estate speculation, but they do all types of business, and do them well. This is illustrated well by the traditional Chinese Taoist folk adage: "The Eight Immortals cross the sea, each displaying his/her unique endowment."

Contemporary Hong Kong Investments Boost the Canadian Economy

The role of Chinese immigrants in the Canadian economy has traditionally been seen as a means of alleviating Canada's labour shortage, whether it was in early gold mining and the construction of the Pacific Railway, or as modern independent skilled immigrants. Even those flourishing Chinese ethnic businesses that started from "Chinatown" were still considered as a survival strategy being self-employed to offset the lack of job opportunities in industries where Chinese immigrants were not welcome or were not capable due to constraints of language capability, skills, experience or professional qualification. It was not noticeable nor recognized until the 1980s when modern corporate investments and business management gradually started to emerge among ethnic Chinese in Canada.

The early waves of investment to Canada came from Hong Kong. At that time, Hong Kong was known as one of the Four Asian Tigers that had experienced fast industrialization and rapid economic growth between the early 1960s and 1990s. As a newly industrialized economy, Hong Kong accumulated strong financial capital that was ready for international business expansion, and additionally they had a highly educated and productive work force with strong entrepreneurship. When flows of immigrants, especially business immigrants, from Hong Kong to Canada started to rise in the 1980s and 1990s, they brought both financial and human capital to reshape and upgrade Chinese ethnic business activities in Canada. Since then, Hong Kong immigrants have gradually played a leading role in local Chinese business communities. It can be said that the money and talent from Hong Kong were the driving forces in the development of contemporary Chinese economic activity in Canada and laid a strong economic foundation for Hong Kong immigrants who dominated Chinese political participation in three levels of Canadian politics.

In addition to immigration related investment, there was also foreign direct investment (FDI) from large corporations or groups from Hong Kong, Taiwan and other Southeast Asian economies to Canada. In the 1980s, those Asian companies started their internationalization process when the globalization trend was just accelerating, and the largest trade block was just taking shape under the North American Free Trade Agreement (NAFTA). Some brilliant Asian business leaders understood that the NAFTA would include Canada, the United States and Mexico with the purpose of reducing trading costs, increasing business investment and helping North America be more competitive in the global marketplace. They decided that their Asian-based businesses should be part of the new North American game. Since the late 1980s, Hong Kong and Taiwan Chinese business consortiums began to enter Canada. They made joint investments with Canadian partners (including both local Chinese capital and non-Chinese capital), and have made remarkable achievements in real estate, manufacturing, hotel and department store businesses.

Among many investment stories, the names of Li Ka-shing and his family are among the most frequently heard for their substantial, successful and sometimes controversial investment deals and generous philanthropic donations in Canada. Born in Chaozhou China, Sir Li Ka-shing (1928 –) is a Hong Kong business tycoon, investor, and philanthropist. According to Forbes, Li is one of the richest persons in Asia, with an estimated net worth of 34 billion US dollars. He is currently the chairman of the board for CK Hutchison Holdings, through which he is the world's leading port investor, developer, and operator, and is the largest health and beauty retailer in Asia and Europe.

Li's family has invested extensively in diversified sectors in Canada, such as ports, energy, banking, real estate, etc. Li started investing in Husky Energy, one of Canada's largest integrated energy companies headquartered in Alberta, in the late 1980s when the global oil price was so low after the two energy crises in the 1970s. In 1991, Li and Hutchison Whampoa became the major shareholder, and Husky became a publicly-listed company on the Toronto Stock Exchange in 2000 (Husky Energy, 2017), and Li is still a driving force of Husky's global businesses.

Mr. Li was also the single largest shareholder of Canadian Imperial Bank of Commerce (CIBC), the fifth largest bank in Canada, until the sale of his stake for 1.2 billion dollars in 2005. All proceeds went to private charitable foundations established by Li, including the Li Ka-shing Foundation in Hong Kong and the Li Ka-shing (Canada) Foundation (LKSF) based in Toronto. From 1993 to 2011, LKSF and Li's group of companies donated generously in Canada to support Canadian education, media and community welfare organizations across this country, totaling 75,525,442 dollars. Some latest examples include:

• In September 2013, Montreal-based McGill University received a generous gift of 6.635 million dollars from the LKSF, to support McGill's ties to a Chinese university. The donation allows the university to create three important new initiatives promoting scholarship and exchange between McGill and Shantou University in the Chinese province of Guangdong: the Li Ka-shing Initiative for Innovation in Legal Education, the Li Ka-shing Liberal Arts Exchange Initiative and the Li Ka-shing Program in International Business.

• In October 2011, the Li Ka-shing Knowledge Institute, established with a generous donation of 25 million dollars by the LKSF, was opened at St. Michael's Hospital in Toronto. This transformative gift has created a world-class institute in downtown Toronto that will benefit people around the world by combining ground breaking medical research, education and patient care.

• In April 2010, LKSF donated 28 million dollars to the Edmonton-based University of Alberta, the largest cash gift in the university's history, to help establish the Li Ka-shing Institute of Virology and add the U of A to an elite global health science research network facilitated by the LKSF.

In 1988, Li's investment of 320 million dollars in Vancouver's Expo 86 land development transformed the industrial lands to False Creek residential condominium community in the heart of the City of Vancouver. The Expo 86 land development project can be said to be classic business case that has been discussed and debated by many business scholars, practitioners as well as the general public. For example, in his 2001 book, Globalization and Urban Change: Capital, Culture and Pacific Rim Megaprojects, Kris Olds dedicated a chapter as a case study of Li Ka-shing and his development of the Expo lands (Olds, 2001). Olds points out that Li's involvement sent a key message at a time when Hong Kong families were looking for a safe place to land, and to store their money, in the event of a takeover by PRC. Others argued that sale of Expo 86 land to international buyers was really a message that the government was deliberately sending that it was open for business on the Pacific Rim, says Gordon Price, former Vancouver city councillor (CBCNews, 2016). Even at time of the 30th anniversary of the Expo 86, Canadian media helplessly sighed that False Creek land development was a deal of the century. It was controversial but set the stage for Asian investment and growth in the city of Vancouver down the path to becoming one of the world's most liveable—and expensive—cities (CBCNews, 2016).

From the commercial real estate development perspective, Hong Kong investors not only brought capital, but also brought innovative development models to Canada. Condominium shopping centres had never been seen in Canada until they were introduced from Hong Kong to Toronto and Vancouver regions in the 1990s when a large number of Hong Kong residents were looking for immigration paths to Canada. It became so popular in Canada's urban development at that time for many reasons. Firstly, developers benefit from a much lighter financial burden and lower risk for the property development as it is diversified and shared among all investors who bought one or more commercial units in the condominium structure. Secondly, owners of commercial units can operate their own business free of worry about lease increase. Their business can benefit from an operation that is more predictable and manageable in terms of business expenditures. When the property price rises, the owner can even make extra gain by selling units to others. Thirdly, buying a commercial unit at 250,000 dollars to 500,000 dollars, which is affordable to many Hong Kong residents at that time, would qualify a family to apply for business immigration to Canada. Many Hong Kong families came to Canada under this arrangement and became self-employed operating businesses in these shopping centres or collecting rentals as the landlord of units in the shopping centres.

In many cases these shopping centres were developed by local Canadian business groups with strong input from Hong Kong. For example, the Torgan Group is also known for the construction of the Pacific Mall in Markham, Ontario. At over 270,000 sq. feet and over 500 retails stores, Pacific Mall is the largest Chinese mall in the western world and a recognized tourist destination. Designed by Wallman Clewes Bergman Architects, Pacific Mall incorporates a traditional Hong Kong-style market place design. Pacific Mall first opened its doors for business in 1997. Its Cantonese name, " 太 古 广 场 " (Tai Gu Gwong Cheung), is derived from Pacific Place in Hong Kong. The corridors of the main floor are named after streets in Hong Kong. As the largest developer and owner of medical centres in Ontario, Torgan was founded in the early 1980's by Eli Swirsky and Sam Cohen, both experienced businessmen who came from Israel to Canada. Torgan quickly established itself in the forefront of commercial real estate in the Greater Toronto Area and other parts of Ontario. Torgan has been involved in the development, ownership and management of over 70 commercial projects totalling over 3.5 million square feet (Torgan Group, 2017).

Another example is Market Village (城市广场) which has been an iconic symbol to the Asian community in Markham. Opened in 1990, most stores in Market Village are family-run stores, but there are a few non-Chinese retailers and some stores with links to Hong Kong have been opened. This growing Asian community in the region has made Market Village their daily destination for Asian food, groceries, gifts and more for decades since its opening. Many other people come to Market Village simply for a unique experience—one that embraces both Asian culture and Canadian lifestyle. Market Village has taken on a new life and become a world-class Asian retail destination. It is likely the largest Asian retail complex outside of Asia—The Remington Centre. With its unique architectural design, excellent facilities and the grand vision of creating a community of its own, the Remington Centre becomes a new landmark of Markham. The developer and investor of the original Market Village who later transformed it into the new Remington Centre is Mr. Rudy Bratty, named one of the richest Canadians by Canadian Business magazine with a personal net worth of almost 1.3 billion dollars (Toronto Star, 2009).

Over 60 Asian themed shopping centres have been developed in Toronto, Vancouver and other major cities across Canada since the 1990s, including such well-known examples as Market Village, Pacific Mall, First Markham Place in the Toronto region and Public Market, Crystal Mall and Aberdeen Centre in greater Vancouver. In recent years, the trend of developing condominium shopping centres has slowed down due to declining demand for commercial units, partially because of fewer customers physically visiting stores as online shopping has become popular, and partially because of less demand for commercial units for immigration purposes following the cancelation of Canada's Investor Immigration Program in 2014. Instead, mixed-use of commercial complex is becoming a new fashion for commercial property development.

The importance of contemporary Hong Kong investment to Canada should not be underestimated. Whether it is a corporate FDI or immigration-related family investment, tens of billions of US dollars from industrialized Hong Kong have been invested in all types of business activity in Canada so that the Canadian economy could resist the global recessions of the 1990s and 2000s. Through partnerships with local Canadian business and capital from Taiwan or other Asian partners, Hong Kong investment in large joint projects has made considerable contributions as part of the Canadian economy. At the same time, these investments upgraded the Chinese ethnic economy in Canada, promoted exchange and cooperation between Chinese Canadian and Asian businesses, and boosted local economic growth in Canada. More specifically, these investments not only met consumer needs of Asian communities, they also generated a considerable number of jobs, and paid more business taxes. Furthermore, many successful Hong Kong Canadian business people also set role models of philanthropy for the entire Chinese community by repaying Canadian society through their generous donations.

China Inc. "Going Global" vs. Mainland Business Immigrants

Similar to investments from Hong Kong, investment capital flow from the PRC to Canada has added another layer to the Chinese Canadian business landscape. There are also quite remarkable stories in Canada about FDIs from China Inc., as well as about investments by business immigrations from mainland.

Since the open door policy and economic reforms in China began in the late 1970s, companies from the PRC have gradually mounted the global stage. With accelerated corporate internationalization as encouraged by the governmental "going global" strategy, global FDI by Chinese enterprises has seen impressive growth for nearly 15 consecutive years. In 2016, Chinese investors made a direct non-financial investment of RMB1.1 trillion (equivalent to 170 billion US dollars), up 44 percent year on year, in global markets. As of the end of 2015, China's foreign investment enterprises reached 30,800, distributed among 188 countries and regions around the world. Total assets of Chinese overseas enterprises were recorded as 4.37 trillion US dollars (Ministry of Commerce of the PRC, 2016). This impressive growth has transformed China from a top FDI recipient but small-scale investor into the world's largest exporter of foreign direct investment, accounting for nearly 10 percent of global FDI and overtaking the USA for the first time.

Canada is one of the main recipients of Chinese outbound FDI. Chinese FDI to Canada has risen from virtually nil in the early 1980s to a record high of 21 billion dollars in 2016 (*Statistics Canada*, accessed: 2017). The especially sharp increase of Chinese FDI to Canada in the late 2000s has invited both policy-makers and the public to engage in a lively discussion about Chinese companies' investment coming into Canada, but a meaningful discussion requires a better understanding of three main features of Chinese investment to Canada.

Growing fast but remaining small. Chinese FDI to Canada experienced a sharp rise in the late 2000s but remained as a small share in total FDIs to Canada. In the early 2000s, Chinese FDI stock in Canada was only at 200 million dollars. In just a decade, China's investment to Canada continually accomplished historic milestones. In 2008, China's FDI in Canada grew to 5 billion dollars, surpassing Canada's total investment in China for the first time. In 2009, China's investment in Canada exceeded 10 billion dollars. In 2013, China's State-owned giant energy company CNOOC Ltd. successfully completed takeover of the Canadian oil and gas company Nexen Inc. for 15.1 billion US dollars, which became the largest single overseas M&A deal made by Chinese companies, also triggering national security concerns over Chinese SOE investments among Canadian citizens, political leaders, and business communities. In 2014, China's FDI exceeded 20 billion dollars. It currently stands at the 8th spot of the top 10 sources of global FDIs to Canada in 2016 (Shown Figure below).

Top 10 Sources of FDI to Canada in 2016 (C$ Billion)

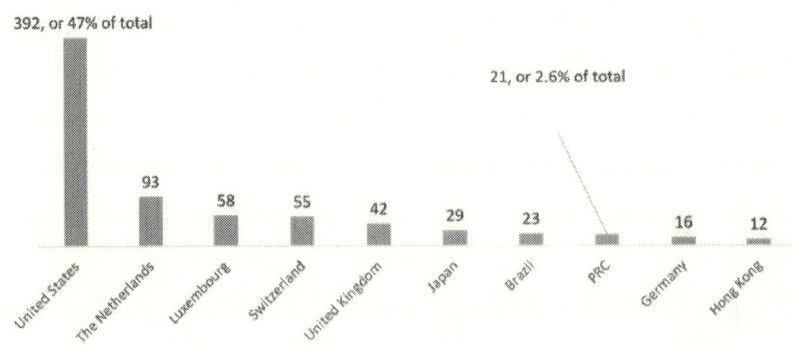

Source: Statistics Canada, CANSIM 376-0051.

Nevertheless, it might be surprising to many that the share of China's FDI to Canada remains tiny, close to 3 percent of total global FDIs to Canada, while FDI from the United States takes the top position at 392 billion dollars, accounting for 47 percent of total FDIs to Canada. This fact has been largely exaggerated by many Canadians as the result of public misperception. A recent APF Canada survey on Asian investment in Canada found that Canadians estimated that FDI from China made up 25 percent of Canada's total inward direct investment. The APF Canada's President and CEO, Stewart Beck, points out rightly that this type of misperception is directly tied to negative opinions on FDI—opinions exacerbated by a lack of information and corresponding trust (APF Canada, 2017).

Targeting resources but diversifying interest. FDI from Chinese firms, as with FDI from many other countries, has shown diversified interest in seeking markets, resources, assets and efficiencies. As the global manufacturing power house, China's appetite for overseas assets continues to grow, with energy and natural resources as key targets. Branded by former Prime Minister Stephen Harper as a new "emerging energy superpower" (Globe and Mail, 2006), Canada seems like a natural fit for Chinese investors. From 2003 to 2016, investment from China into Canada has been overwhelmingly focused on the energy and natural resource sectors. Recently, with price crashes of oil and other commodities on the global market, Chinese firms are recalibrating their strategy in Canada. Chinese direct investment has begun to expand into industries other than conventional resources, industries such as services, technology, aviation, advanced manufacturing, food, consumer goods, cultural entertainment, high value added sectors, as well as in assets providing high and stable returns (see graph below).

Investment from China into Canada by Industry, 2003-2016

Source: APF Canada Investment Monitor and fDi Markets, accessed March 9, 2017

Over the past several years, Chinese firms investing in industries other than resources include examples in manufacturing, banking, and technology sectors (Zhang & Chen, 2011) such as,

• In June 2001, China's Worldbest invested 45 million dollars to set up a knit dyeing plant in Drummondville, Quebec. At the time, it was China's largest investment in Canada.

• In June 2009, the Industrial Commercial Bank of China (a large wholesale and retail bank) acquired a 70% stake in the Bank of East Asia's Canadian assets, for 80.25 million dollars, and started making footprints in Canada.

• In April 2010, Shenzhen-based Huawei, a global leading telecom solutions provider and one of the world's Fortune 500 companies, opened its first R&D Centre in Ottawa, creating 70 jobs.

• In November 2010, the Chinese manufacturing firm Daqo Group contributed 3.5 million dollars to build a 5 million-dollar solar panel assembly plant in a joint venture with a Hamilton-based engineering company JNE Consulting.

More recently, there have been deals that have demonstrated new strategies and new approaches to diversifying Chinese investment in Canada. By investing in innovative partnerships, Chinese FDI will not only serve China's soaring demands of the growing middle class for cultural and entertainment consumption, safe and high quality food products, and various tourism activities, but also assist Canadian partners in capacity building to elevate the scale of supplies or bases in Canada.

• In 2015, Shanghai-based Fosun International acquired a 25 percent stake in the Canadian national treasure "Cirque du Soleil", which became China's largest investment of that year. Different from previous SOE-led investment focusing on energy and resource industries, Fosun targets the entertainment industry, keeping their eyes on China's middle class of more than 300 million, nearly 10 times Canada's entire population, for their cultural consumption needs.

• In 2017, Heilongjiang-based Feihe International invested 225 million dollars to build an infant formula plant in Kingston, Ontario, in which roughly 85 per cent of the powdered formula output could be shipped back to China. In 2008, Chinese domestic dairy products such as baby formula were discovered to be tainted with melamine. Hundreds of thousands became sick, and at least six children died. Since then, many Chinese distrust domestic dairy products and prefer foreign brands.

• In 2017, the Shanghai-headquartered China Minsheng Investment Group with a 40 percent stake and Vancouver-based CM (Canada) with a 60 percent of stake, created a joint venture, "GM Resorts Limited Partnership", to take control of popular North Vancouver landmark ski and hiking trails, Grouse Mountain Resorts, for an undisclosed amount.

One policy but many players with uneven outcomes. China's "Go Global" policy and related incentive measures have remained strong influences on Chinese companies' outbound FDI decisions. The policy encouraged Chinese companies to establish a larger global presence and boost international competitiveness by seeking international markets, resources, assets and efficiencies, ultimately seeking good returns from their investments.

Addressing these objectives, many players have jumped into the game. The most prominent player is obviously the China Investment Corporation (CIC). Headquartered in Beijing, CIC was founded in 2007 as a wholly state-owned sovereign wealth fund backed by over 3 trillion US dollars in foreign-exchange reserves. The company was established as a vehicle to diversify China's foreign exchange holdings and seek maximum returns for its shareholders within acceptable risk tolerance. CIC has many special connections with Canada. In 2011, CIC established its first foreign office in Toronto, choosing it over global financial centres such as New York or London. Among many considerations, an individual played a significant role. Mr. Felix Chee is a Canadian of Chinese origin and a veteran of the financial services industry, who previously worked at Ontario Hydro, Manulife Financial, and the University of Toronto's asset management fund. In 2008, Mr. Chee was invited by CIC to move from Canada to Beijing to help set up the CIC. In 2009, Mr. Chee facilitated the big CIC investment of 1.74 billion dollars for 17 percent stake of Tech Resources, a Vancouver-based diversified miner. When CIC opened its first overseas office in Toronto, CIC recruited Mr. Chee as its Chief Representative in Toronto (2011-2014) to find good investment opportunities in Canada and to dispel Western fears about the CIC being a geopolitical tool of the Communist Party (Institutional Investor, 2012). Two other individuals representing Canada have served on CIC's International Advisory Council, of whom, Hon. David Emerson (2009-2012) is a former Minister of Foreign Affairs, former Minister of International Trade and former Minister of Industry, and David Denison, Chairman of Hydro One Limited and former CEO of the Canada Pension Plan Investment Board. After five years of operation, CIC decided to close its Toronto office in December 2015 when the global commodity market was weak. As media have reported, CIC's exit from Canada is a symbolic act that underscores the fading fortunes of Canada's battered resources sector (Globe and Mail, 2015).

Alongside the CIC is the second group of players, i.e., other SOEs, including oil giants PetroChina, Sinopec and CNOOC. The latter holds China's highest record in Canada for a single deal of 15.1 billion US dollars taking over Canadian Nexen. All of China's big-four banks—Bank of China, Agricultural Bank of China, Industrial and Commercial Bank of China and China Construction Bank—have set up presences in Canada. Seven of China's airlines have been operating direct flights between major Chinese cities and Vancouver or Toronto, including Air China, China Southern Airlines, China Eastern Airlines, Sichuan Airlines, Xiamen Airlines, Beijing Capital Airlines, and Hainan Airlines. On April 18, 2012, with its head office located in Toronto, the Canada China Chamber of Commerce was established as a business association for Chinese enterprises established in Canada. Its members cover such sectors as finance, ICT, transportation, import & export, energy, resources, minerals, pharmaceuticals, health food, real estate, equipment and machinery, etc.

The players corresponding to SOEs are Chinese privately owned enterprises (POEs), which are playing a more aggressive role in China's OFDI. This is because POEs are active in many of the new sectors where Chinese companies are investing, and because from the perspective of many overseas countries, there is typically less sensitivity around investments by POEs compared to SOEs. In recent years, it has been observed from the global perspective that more deals were announced by POEs, accounting for 75.9 percent of the total number of deals in 2015, which was up from 68.0 percent in 2014 and 55.1 percent in 2010. Nevertheless, SOEs are still doing the majority of the largest deals (KPMG, 2016). In Canada, the most notable active POEs include Huawei Technologies, Anbang Insurance Group, China Minsheng Investment Corporation (Grouse Mountain Resorts deal) and Fosun International ("Cirque du Soleil" deal).

• Shenzhen-based Huawei has been operating in Canada since 2008, and now employs over 700 Canadians. Huawei's innovative wireless products and services support many of Canada's leading telecommunications companies, and Huawei's Canada Research Centre is a global leader in advanced communications technologies, including 5G. Huawei has been integrated to become a key part of Canada's ICT Ecosystem.

• Headquartered in Beijing, the Anbang Insurance Group is a holding company whose subsidiaries mainly deal with insurance, banking, and financial services. In 2016, Anbang purchased four office towers of the Bentall Centre in Vancouver for over 1 Billion dollars. The same year, Anbang invested 1 billion dollars to purchase Retirement Concepts, a Canadian company with 24 retirement homes in British Columbia, Calgary and Montreal.

There are many other well-known POEs or brands in China but less well-known in Canada who have become active in Canada, such as "Old Beijing Roast Duck," "Little Sheep Mongolian Hot Pot," etc. "Little Sheep" is a restaurant chain specializing in a traditional Inner Mongolian hot pot cuisine featuring tabletop cooking served in a metal pot with a variety of herbs and spices in its stock. Since the first North American franchise opened in Toronto in 2005, "Little Sheep" has grown quickly to become a restaurant chain with over 30 locations in Canada and the USA with headquarters based in Vancouver B.C., introducing Mongolian culture and food into North American markets.

The last group of players that fit into the China-Canada investment game is the class of investor and entrepreneur immigrants. The Immigrant Investor Program (IIP), which began in 1986, was a federal program aiming to attract experienced business people to contribute to Canada's growth and long-term prosperity by investing in Canada's economy. To qualify for the IIP, foreign investors must show that they have business experience; have a net worth of at least 1,600,000 dollars that was gained legally and would invest 800,000 dollars into a legitimate business in Canada. On June 19, 2014, the IIP was finally terminated by the Canadian government (CIC, 2014).

In the 28-year history of the IIP, a total of 190,000 immigrants from around the world were admitted to Canada, of which nearly 50,000 were the principle investors and about 14,000 were their spouses and children. Many of them were from mainland China, and later became important parts of Chinese Canadian communities. There is no doubt that they must complete investment transactions and participate in business operations in order to meet the requirements of IIP. Furthermore, perhaps due to their "business gene," many investors and entrepreneurs who came to Canada are naturally in the new market to find a variety of business and investment opportunities. They often keep their contacts and relationships with the business ecosystem back in China, so that their personal investment behavior sometimes leads to a larger SOE or POE investment down the road.

To sum up, regardless of the types of investor or areas of investment, China's investment in Canada is increasingly showing a full range of diversification, which reflects the ways and abilities of Chinese investment gradually becoming mature. Chinese SOE, POE or individual investors have experienced a significant transition from the initial inclination to obtain physical assets, such as energy, resources, sales markets and channels, to acquiring intangible assets including brands, technology, human capital and management systems. There has also been a rise of investor interest in consumption-related goods, safe and healthy food products, and other high-demand products to feed the increasingly mature Chinese market. In addition, the Chinese investment style has also become more diverse, including Greenfield or Brownfield investment; joint venture or partnership, as well as the establishment of science and technology parks and incubators, etc. Investment clubs, business associations and alumni organizations have emerged within Chinese communities that bring like-minded individuals and businesses together to invest collectively in various projects in Canada and globally.

New Challenges Facing the Chinese Community

As the new "Gold Rush" at the turning of the 21st century has diversified economic activities, professional development and business growth in

Canada's Chinese communities, it has also created many new challenges facing them in a variety of domains.

Skills made-in-China are discounted in Canada. As previously mentioned, between 2001 and 2011, Canada admitted a total of 196,220 immigrants with post-secondary education received in China, and over 110,000 professionals, managers and technicians in all occupations. When a Chinese immigrant comes to Canada with certain skills, there is no guarantee that he or she will be able to use those skills as they were trained. Many end up in occupations far below their educational level. They end up driving taxis, mopping floors, bagging groceries, guarding office buildings, delivering pizzas, waiting tables and working at call centers. Reitz calls the problem "brain waste" and estimated that altogether immigrant skill underutilization costs the economy 3.1 billion dollars a year (Reitz, 2011).

Among many reasons for "brain waste", the major challenge is the lack of foreign qualification recognition (FQR) which is becoming a global issue as expanding numbers of skilled professionals seek to migrate from one country to another. In Canada, FQR refers to the verification process by which the education, training and work experience obtained outside Canada are deemed equivalent to the standards established for Canadian workers. It usually includes foreign credential recognition (FCR) and foreign professional qualification recognition.

Canada's FQR system is extremely complex. There are two types of occupations in Canada: non-regulated and regulated. Non-regulated occupations do not require certificates or licenses. Employers are responsible for assessing and recognizing the education, skills and work experience of a prospective employee. Regulated occupations are governed by regulatory bodies and apprenticeship authorities. They require certificates or licenses since they impact the public safety of Canadians. While provinces and territories have jurisdiction over FCR for regulated occupations, the responsibility for credential recognition and licensing is delegated to regulatory bodies. There are close to 500 regulatory bodies across Canada governing 55 professions, and 13 provincial and territorial apprenticeship authorities governing approximately 50 trades. These bodies are responsible for establishing the provincial and territorial standards and practices that are associated with regulated occupations, including nurses, doctors, engineers, teachers and accountants. In addition, there are provincially mandated agencies that evaluate educational qualifications for both academic placement and workforce entry (Foreign Credentials Referral Office, 2012).

An early survey of skilled Chinese immigrants to Canada found six major barriers to finding work in their field of study or in their recognized professions after coming to Canada (APF Canada, 2013):

- Lack of Canadian work experience
- Foreign work experience not recognized
- No Canadian education credentials
- Foreign education credentials not recognized
- Limited language skills in workplace
- Need to upgrade courses to meet Canadian certification requirements

Discounting made-in-China skills not only wastes "brains," but also undermines the capacity, value and importance that today's multitalented Chinese communities are contributing to the whole of Canadian society.

Chinese home-buyers' names misinterpreted as "foreigners". Canadian housing prices have risen crazily, especially in Vancouver and Toronto. A benchmark home in Vancouver is priced beyond one million Canadian dollars, while an average house price has reached 750,000 dollars in Toronto. The rising house prices triggered social controversy—not only being a hot topic of public conversation embraced by mainstream journalists, politicians, academics, and commentators, but also being a top election issue that have caused political parties to make campaign promises for affordable housing to attract voters.

In a free market economy, the ups and downs of housing prices are a function of a number of mixed factors, notably the balance of demand and supply. High prices always reflect the intersection of strong demand and limited supply. If demand in a market is weak, then prices cannot be high, no matter what the supply. And, if supply is unrestricted, then prices cannot be much higher than production costs, no matter what the demand. In practice, growing population, rising income and living standards, low mortgage interest rates, attractiveness to international buyers, expectation of future housing prices vs. inflation, etc., all add to the demand side of equation and tend to push real estate prices up. On the other hand, local building regulations and zoning codes, overall production costs, availability of investment, etc. determine the level of restriction on local supply.

Unfortunately, in such a complex picture, public attention has been overwhelmingly attracted to the role of foreign buyers who are believed to have made Vancouver and Toronto housing prices skyrocket. Even worse, some commentaries have misled the discussion on affordable housing by singling out the names of Chinese buyers', such as, Li, Lee, Lim, and Chan etc., leading to the conclusion that these buyers are all "non-resident Chinese", "buyers from China", and so on. Public policy has responded. On August 2, 2016, B.C. introduced a new foreign buyer's tax (FBT) which is an additional 15 percent property transfer tax that foreign nationals, corporations or taxable trustees pay in addition to the general property transfer tax on transfers of residential property located in the Greater Vancouver Regional District (GVRD). Followed by Ontario, the Non Resident Speculation Tax (NRST) was introduced on April 21, 2017. The NRST is a 15 percent tax on the purchase or acquisition of an interest in residential property located in the Greater Golden Horseshoe Region (GGH) by individuals who are not citizens or permanent residents of Canada or by foreign corporations (foreign entities) and taxable trustees.

Blaming foreign buyers, especially singling out a specific ethnicity of buyers, is not only misguided and unhelpful, but also a dangerous path down the slippery slope of narrow-minded nativism. By most accounts, determination of the role of Chinese buyers does not distinguish between non-residents and residents, or indeed between Canadian citizens, landed immigrants and foreign nationals. The vast majority of homes owned by Chinese people in the Lower Mainland belong to people who have residency status in Canada—in other words, they are Canadians, not foreigners. There are hundreds of thousands of people with last names spelled in the fashion of mainland Chinese who are actually Canadian citizens or landed immigrants. In fact, Li, Lee, Lim, and Chan are among top 20 surnames in Canada according to Canadian telephone books.

One year after B.C.'s implementation of FBT, some commentators have started asking why the foreign buyers tax isn't making Vancouver more affordable (Dugan, 2017). The answer is clear—FBT is irrelevant to housing affordability.

"Fear of Dragons" fuels sinophobia in Canada. There is a Chinese fable saying that long ago, there was a person named Shen Zhuliang who addressed himself as "Duke of Ye." He was a general and Prime Minister of the Kingdom of Chu during the Spring and Autumn period of ancient China. It was said that this Duke of Ye was very fond of dragons. The walls of his house had dragons painted on them, while the beams, pillars, doors, and windows were all had carvings of these creatures. As a result, word of his love for dragons became widespread. When a real celestial dragon heard of this Duke of Ye, he was deeply moved, and decided to visit the duke to thank him for his devotion. You might think the Duke of Ye was very happy to see a real dragon. But, actually, at the very sight of the creature, he was scared out of his wits and ran away as fast as he could. From then on, people knew that the Duke of Ye only loved pictures or carvings that looked like dragons, but not the real thing.

This story may reflect the exact sentiments and stances of many Canadians toward Chinese investment. An early report by The Conference Board of Canada was entitled "Fear the Dragon? Chinese Foreign Direct Investment in Canada," which analyzes both opportunities and challenges associated with Chinese FDI in Canada (Grant, 2012). The report points out correctly that there are two issues facing Chinese investment. One relates to the underlying governance of SOEs, especially from a Communist state. The second is the emphasis on resource investments. Both of these characteristics mean that Chinese investment are among the most politically sensitive and make the public nervous in Canada.

Political sensitivity and public nervousness are directly queried and measured by APF Canada, which has been conducting regular nation-wide surveys to assess Canadians' attitudes toward countries in the Asia Pacific region, and their perceptions of Canada-Asia relations since 2004. According to the findings of the APF Canada's 2017 National Opinion Poll, which focuses on Canada-China relations, Canadians are not only recognizing the importance of closer economic relations between the two countries for creating opportunities for business today and in the future, but they are also warming up to the prospect of a possible free trade agreement with China. A majority is even acknowledging that China has the potential to become a global leader on economic issues. Notwithstanding overall public support for Canada's greater economic engagement with China, Canadians continue to have concerns that engagement will make Canada more vulnerable to economic and political pressures from China and will lead to an influx of cheap Chinese goods in domestic markets (APF Canada, 2017).

This sinophobia or "fear of the dragons", specifically regarding foreign investment from Asia, is clearly shown as a recent APF Canada survey finds (APF Canada, 2015):

• Canadians are generally supportive of investment from Asia. A majority expressed positive views of investment from Japan (78 percent), South Korea (67 percent) and India (59 percent). This is comparable to Canadians' favourable views on investment from the United States (77 percent), Canada's largest source of foreign direct investment.

• Canadians' views on China are more mixed, with two-fifths (42 percent) being favourable to Chinese investment and half (49 percent) expressing opposition.

• Canadians worry that investment from global powers like China and the United States will lead to a loss of control over our natural resources.

• Canadians mistakenly estimate that companies from China own one-quarter (25 percent) of all foreign direct investment in Canada, while official statistics show that it is under 3 percent.

- Canadians do not always disentangle their attitudes about foreign investment from their attitudes toward particular countries, particularly towards China. Although most Canadians recognize that foreign companies operating in Canada abide by domestic laws and practices, they still associate investments from China with terms like "environmental damage" and "poor labour standards."

This perception-based sinophobia presents a serious challenge for Chinese companies, both SOEs and POEs, operating in Canada. Significant investment in Canada by Chinese companies is a relatively recent phenomenon. Chinese investors in Canada do not yet have a visible and established track record of contributing to the country that could be used to counter the skeptical attitudes many Canadians have toward China in general. Barring significant socio-political change in China, Canadians are only likely to warm up to Chinese investment if they see Chinese companies making a positive contribution to Canada (APF Canada, 2015).

China Inc. needs to adapt to the Canadian ecosystem. It sounds easy if China Inc.'s "going global" only refers to making investments outside of the country. Nevertheless, it is quite a challenge when China Inc. wants to be really successful in local marketplaces. In Canada, Chinese firms have to work harder to overcome barriers to adapt local ecosystems and to establish a good track record of contributing to the country.

The first barrier that China Inc. faces is lack of understanding of investment opportunity in Canada. There are popular views among Chinese investors. Some believe that Canada has such a small and mature market that there is no room for new players to enter and grow. Others see only rich energy and resources in Canada, and underestimate opportunities in other sectors.

In fact, Canada is the best country in the G20 for business according to both Forbes and Bloomberg. Canada ranks second in the G20 for doing business over the five-year period 2017-2021, as reported by the Economist Intelligence Unit (EIU). The World Bank ranks Canada as the easiest place to start a business in the G20. Canada's economy is one of the most resilient in the world, as it consistently outranks its G7 peers in long-term economic growth and boasts the fastest-growing economy in the G7. Therefore, Canada is a favourite destination for foreign direct investment, having been the second-largest recipient of FDI inflows per capita in the G20 over the five-year period 2011–2015.

International FDI in Canada has experienced continual growth for over a decade, the stock of foreign direct investment having increased by 4.7 percent to 825.7 billion dollars. Unlike past FDI from China, which was dominated by energy and mining, manufacturing has remained the top industry for global FDI in Canada with a 22.8 percent share at the end of 2016, just ahead of mining and oil and gas extraction with 22.7 percent. The annual growth in the value of foreign direct investment in Canada was spread among most industries in 2016, led by wholesale and retail trade (+10.1 percent), manufacturing (+5.0 percent) and mining and oil and gas extraction (+3.2 percent) (*Statistics Canada*, 2017).

It can be seen that having such a large-scale and wider spread of FDI, investment in Canada has great potential to grow, especially in the service and manufacturing industries. The key is how Chinese entrepreneurs or Chinese companies understand and grasp these opportunities.

Related to identifying investment opportunities, the second barrier for China Inc. is often unclearly defined investment objectives. When it comes to FDI, the common objectives are often classified as resource-seeking, market-seeking, asset-seeking or efficiency seeking. Chinese companies, especially large scale corporations with multiple-lines of business, typically have diversified investment interests which has created difficulties for Canadian counterparts to understand and deal with. Even though it is good to stay flexible in finding investment targets, Chinese firms still need to keep in mind that a clear objective will help them identify strong industry clusters, regions with great potential, and particular growing industries in Canada, so that their investment will grow with the Canadian economy and receive a sound return over the long term.

The third barrier is being unfamiliar with Canadian ways of doing business. Rule of law is the most fundamental principle in Canada, and people uphold belief in the free market economy. In Canada, all business activities are regulated by all kinds of legal provisions, government regulations and bylaws etc., from issues as big as business setup, mergers and acquisitions, listing, and bankruptcy, to matters as small as company signs, language used on restaurant menus, and coffee break time, and so on. Some Chinese companies have only grown accustomed to operating processes in their home ecosystem and will have to redouble their efforts to learn and follow Canadian laws and regulations related to their businesses.

Respecting laws and regulations and following market rules are far from enough. Chinese companies will also need to familiarize themselves with issues like corporate social responsibility (CSR) and social licences to operate (SLO) that are becoming more and more important for Canadian companies and society. Winning trust and acceptance by local communities and stakeholders, such as indigenous groups, labour unions, community organizations, environmental protection agencies, and media is crucial to the management and success of China Inc.'s operations in Canada.

The fourth barrier for many Chinese companies is not taking full advantage of local knowledge. Many Chinese companies have experienced a steep learning curve when they first arrive in Canada. Some have benefited from local professional advice, whether in understanding current investment opportunities, defining investment objectives and entry strategy, learning the Canadian way of doing business, or building reputation and trust among stakeholders. Although there is no guarantee that the quality of professional service will remain the same, the crucial point for Chinese companies is to perform enough due diligence and gain more local knowledge before investing in Canada.

Entrepreneurship of business immigrants is underutilized. Canada has tried through various immigration programs to attract both international investment capital and entrepreneurial skills to contribute to Canada's growth and long-term prosperity by investing in Canada's economy. Tens of thousands of Chinese immigrants have been admitted through programs from the federal Immigrant Investor Program (IIP) and Immigrant Investor Venture Capital (IIVC) Pilot Program both of which have since been terminated, to Start-up Visa Program and Self-employed category, as well as through Entrepreneur Immigration stream of the Provincial Nominee Program such as the BC PNP.

When the IIP was terminated in 2014, many criticized the program, with or without intention to single out Chinese business immigrants, as a way for rich foreigners essentially to buy citizenship and live abroad without creating jobs or economic growth in Canada. Referring to the Chinese business community in Vancouver and Toronto, some described the program as often appearing to help wealthy mainland people gain Canadian citizenship, buy property and then move their family here, while living and doing most of their business in Asia (Globe and Mail, 2014). Did these commentators ask themselves why these entrepreneur immigrants cannot enjoy full play in business as they were supposed to enjoy in Canada?

Our analysis points to problems that actually stem from both lack of preparation by immigrant individuals and systemic failure of programs like the Canadian IIP. Viewed from the investor immigrants' perspective, many Chinese entrepreneurs have insufficient English or French language skills to conduct business in Canada. At the same time, they have little knowledge about Canadian history, culture, economy, legal and political systems, all of which are important for making business decisions in Canada. When they prepared for immigration to Canada, they were likely only immersed in information related to housing, school, tourism, or tax avoidance and the welfare system. Their preparation for starting up a business in Canada were either close to zero, or entirely based on their successful Chinese business experience that may not work at all in Canada most of the time.

They can hardly communicate nor develop business relations with non-Chinese in Canada, which limits their access to financial capital, human capital and social capital through extensive personal and social networks, sources of market information, and trust from local business communities. Needless to say, it is inconvenient when Canadian laws and regulations are new to Chinese entrepreneur immigrants, and it gets even worse when they are misguided or hoodwinked by undisciplined investment advisers and real estate consultants or the like. Negative experiences in early days of doing business in Canada stifles their enthusiasm and willingness and to further invest in Canada.

Systemic failures of Canadian business immigrant programs cannot be overlooked. The first failure is the program's requirement of an investment amount of 800,000 dollars or so does not seem to reflect the program objective of achieving business growth and job creation. An investment of 800,000 dollars was meant to create a typical Canadian small and medium enterprise (SME) with a few employees. Canada has 1.1 million SMEs, accounting for 99.8 percent of the total number of companies, of which 55 percent are small business with fewer than 4 employees. To meet IPP requirements, an applicant for investment immigration was asked to invest 800,000 dollars or so to create a number of jobs in Canada. As a result, a typical SME is cloned when an investor immigrant is admitted to Canada.

Apart from the difficulty of competing in the international market, such a small business will find it even harder to survive in the Canadian domestic market. Statistics show that current survival rates for SME businesses in Canada are declining over time. About 85 per cent of businesses that enter the marketplace survive one full year, 70 per cent survive for two years and 51 per cent survive for five years (Start Up Canada, 2012). It is no wonder that SMEs created by investor immigrants from China have to struggle for survival.

The second systemic failure is the fact that the IIP only focused on checking the boxes to assess whether the program's requirements were met. No business support nor assistance was provided to investor immigrants apart from conventional settlement services and labour market assistance that are less relevant to their business development needs. The success or failure of their SME was totally dependent on their luck with an average 50/50 chance of failing within five years. When investor immigrant businesses failed, they were greeted with booing and jeering from media and the public.

The third systemic failure reflects the challenge of the resident requirement for landed immigrants effectively limiting their access to international markets to carry out their global business activities. According to current rules, to maintain immigrant status as a permanent resident, one must live in Canada for at least two years within a five-year period. During this time the individual must be physically in Canada. The unique competitive advantage of Chinese investors and their businesses is obviously not in the Canadian market, but in the international market, particularly in a massive Chinese market where Canada has tried very hard to push our market share up beyond the current 4.3 percent of Canadian total exports to China, or just 1.1 percent of China's total imports from Canada. Their potential roles to facilitate business and trade between Canada and China are constrained by the two-year resident requirement.

The fourth systemic failure is in the area of policy, wherein the roles of overseas Canadians are not fully recognized. According to APF Canada's studies (APF Canada, 2011), it is estimated that 2.8 million Canadians live abroad, representing 9 percent of Canada's population. With a variety of out-migration rates of Canadians born in Taiwan (30 percent), Hong Kong (24 percent) and mainland China (3 percent) during the period from 1996 to 2006, an interesting phenomenon has emerged in which Chinese Canadian communities exist both at home in Canada and abroad. In Hong Kong, for instance, there are over 300,000 Canadians in the city, which makes it the largest Canadian city in Asia. The challenge for Canada is how to foster these overseas citizens' attachment to this country so as to derive benefits from all perspectives-economic, social, to cultural and international relations, etc.

Conclusion: Opportunities and Challenges

The new round of "Gold Rush"—people and capital flowing from China to Canada in search of better opportunities—as a diversified process of economic activities, professional development and business progress of Chinese in Canada, brings new opportunities and new challenges as well. Today's Chinese have upgraded their skills and professional expertise so much that they cannot be compared with their previous generations of coolies or labourers. Multitalented backgrounds allow them to be more capable of participating in and contributing to Canada at levels that are not measurable by income tax contributions alone. When the scope of businesses has gone beyond "Chinatown," these Chinese-founded enterprises are no longer confined to serving the local Chinese community and clients but are providing products and services to both local markets and the general public. Investments from Hong Kong, Taiwan and lately from the PRC have made considerable contributions to the Canadian economy and have elevated the economic capacity of Chinese in general, while enhancing economic ties between Canada and major emerging markets in Asia. Even though we are still facing a number of challenges associated with new trends emerging within Chinese communities, such as misunderstanding, misperception, and mistrust, one thing can be concluded with certainty: more multitalented and economically capable Chinese in Canada have made Canada better at home and abroad.

References

APF Canada. (2011). Canadians Abroad: Canada's Global Assets. Retrieved from http://www.asiapacific.ca/sites/default/files/canadians_abroad_final.pdf

APF Canada. (2013). Barriers to Recognition of Foreign Qualifications-Survey of Skilled Chinese Immigrants in Canada. Vancouver: Asia Pacific Foundation of Canada.

APF Canada. (2015). 2015 National Opinion Poll. Vancouver: Asia Pacific Foundation of Canada.

APF Canada. (2017). 2017 National Opinion Poll-Canadian Views on Engagement with China. Vancouver: Asia Pacific Foundation of Canada.

APF Canada. (2017). Investment Monitor 2017—Report on Foreign Direct Investment from the Asia Pacific into Canada. Vancouver: Asia Pacific Foundation of Canada.

Canada's 100 Best Restaurants. (2016). Retrieved from http://canadas100best.com/canadas-100-best-restaurants-2016/#1466432694478-4a0f1050-4cf8

CBC News. (2013, April 9). B.C. mine's temporary foreign workers case in Federal Court. Retrieved from http://www.cbc.ca/news/canada/british-columbia/b-c-mine-s-temporary-foreign-workers-case-in-federal-court-1.1374502

CBCNews. (2016, 5 4). Deal of the century: Expo 86 land purchase changed Vancouver. Retrieved from http://www.cbc.ca/news/canada/british-columbia/expo-86-china-business-vancouver-1.3560255

Chinese Canadian National Council. (2012, June 12). Our Stories-Paper Sons and Daughters. Retrieved from https://ccncourstories.wordpress.com/videos/paper-sons-video/

CIC. (2011). Facts and Figures.

CIC. (2014, 7 11). Terminated programs: Federal Immigrant Investor and Entrepreneurs. Retrieved from http://www.cic.gc.ca/english/immigrate/business/investors/index.asp

CREA. (2016). Real Estate in Canada-A Toolkit for Parliamentarians. Retrieved from http://www.crea.ca/wp-content/uploads/2016/02/CREA_MP_toolkit.pdf

Dugan, B. (2017, August 17). Macleans. Retrieved from Why the foreign buyers tax isn't making Vancouver more affordable: http://www.macleans.ca/opinion/why-the-foreign-buyers-tax-isnt-making-vancouver-more-affordable/

Economist, T. (2011, Nov 19). The Magic of Diasporas. Retrieved from http://www.economist.com/node/17797134

Fairchild TV. (2017). Mandarin Profile Awards Presentation. Retrieved from http://

www.fairchildtv.com/shows/mpa/index.php

Foreign Credentials Referral Office. (2012). Strengthening Canada's Economy: Government of Canada Progress Report 2011 on Foreign Credential Recognition. Ottawa.

Globe and Mail. (2006, 7 15). PM brands Canada an "energy superpower". Retrieved from https://beta.theglobeandmail.com/news/world/pm-brands-canada-an-energy-superpower/article1105875/?ref=http://www.theglobeandmail.com&

Globe and Mail. (2014, 2 11). Investor road to Canada hits a dead end with immigrant program's closing. Retrieved from https://beta.theglobeandmail.com/news/politics/investor-road-to-canada-hits-a-dead-end-with-immigrant-programs-closure/article16821623/?ref=http://www.theglobeandmail.com&

Globe and Mail. (2015, 12 31). China Investment Corp. closes Toronto office in wake of commodity rout. Retrieved from https://www.theglobeandmail.com/report-on-business/industry-news/energy-and-resources/commodity-rout-forces-china-investment-corp-to-shutter-canadian-office/article27972618/?arc404=true

Gluszynski, T., & Peters, V. (2005). Survey of Earned Doctorates: A Profile of Doctoral Degre.

Gonverment of Canada. (2017, July 18). Immigrate as a skilled worker through Express Entry. Retrieved from http://www.cic.gc.ca/english/immigrate/skilled/index.asp

Government of Canada. (2001). Justice Laws Website. Retrieved from Immigration and Refugee Protection Act (S.C. 2001, c. 27): http://laws-lois.justice.gc.ca/eng/acts/I-2.5/FullText.html

Government of Canada. (2012). Canadian Multiculturalism: An Inclusive Citizenship. Retrieved from http://www.cic.gc.ca/english/multiculturalism/citizenship.asp

Government of Canada. (2017, 6 20). Statistics and Open Data. Retrieved from http://www.cic.gc.ca/english/resources/statistics/index.asp

Grant, M. (2012). Fear the Dragon? Chinese Foreign Direct Investment in Canada. Ottawa: The Conference Board of Canada.

Guo, S., & DeVoretz, D. (2007, August). The Changing Face of Chinese Immigrants in Canada. Retrieved from IZA Discussion Paper No. 3018 : http://ftp.iza.org/dp3018.pdf

Husky Energy. (2017). History. Retrieved from http://www.huskyenergy.ca/about/history.asp

Institutional Investor. (2012, 1 30). The CIC and Felix Chee. Retrieved from http://www.institutionalinvestor.com/blogarticle/2970178/blog/the-cic-and-felix-chee.html#.WbiieMiGMyU

IRCC. (2015). Facts and Figures 2015. Retrieved from Immigration Overview-Temporary

Residents—Annual IRCC Updates: http://open.canada.ca/data/en/dataset/052642bb-3fd9-4828-b608-c81dff7e539c?_ga=2.140835762.1854832651.1502753991-1488428533.1429565837

JA British Columbia. (2017). Business Laureates: Hok Yat Louie. Retrieved from http://www.businesslaureatesbc.org/laureate/hok-yat-louie/

KPMG. (2016). China Outlook 2016. Retrieved from https://assets.kpmg.com/content/dam/kpmg/pdf/2016/03/china-outlook-2016.pdf

Lee, W.-m. (1984). Portraits of a Challenge: An Illustrated History of the Chinese Canadian. Toronto: The Council of Chinese Canadians in Ontario.

Ley, D. (2011). Millionaire Migrants: Lessons for Immigration Policy Today. Vancouver: Presentation at 2011 Metropolis Conference.

Li Ka-shing Foundation. (2017). Canada. Retrieved from https://www.lksf.org/locations/canada/

Li, P. S. (1998). Chinese in Canada second Edition. Oxford University Press.

Li, P. S. (2011). Immigrants from China to Canada: Issues of Supply and Demand in Human Capital. In P. B. Adams, Issues in Canada-China Relations. Canadian International Council.

Lin, X., Guan, J., & Nicholson, M. (2008, Dec). Transnational Entrepreneurs as Agents of International Innovation Linkages. Retrieved from Asia Pacific Foundation of Canada: Research Report: http://www.asiapacific.ca/sites/default/files/filefield/ImmigEntrepreneurs.pdf

Ministry of Commerce of the PRC. (2016). REPORT ON DEVELOPMENT OF CHINA'S OUTWARD INVESTMENT AND ECONOMIC COOPERATION. Beijing: MINISTRY OF COMMERCE OF THE PEOPLE'S REPUBLIC OF CHINA.

Olds, K. (2001). Globalization and Urban Change: Capital, Culture, and Pacific Rim Mega-Projects. Oxford: Oxford University Press.

Poy, V. (2013). In V. Poy, Passange to Promise Land. McGill-Queen's University Press.

Qiang, Z. (2013). CANADA'S "THOUSAND TALENT PROGRAM" HOW CANADA RESEARCH CHAIR PROGRAM ATTRACTS CHINESE ACADEMICS. Retrieved from https://www.asiapacific.ca/sites/default/files/filefield/researchreport_qiang_zha_0.pdf

Reitz, J. G. (2011, March). Literary Review of Canada. Retrieved from Taxi Driver Syndrome: Behind-the-scenes immigration changes are creating new problems on top of old ones: http://reviewcanada.ca/essays/2011/02/01/taxi-driver-syndrome/

Start Up Canada. (2012). Statistics on Small Business in Canada. Retrieved from https://

www.startupcan.ca/wp-content/uploads/2012/01/Statistics-on-Small-Business-in-Canada_
StartupCanada.pdf

Statistics Canada. (2017). Table 376-0052. Retrieved from International investment
position, Canadian direct investment abroad and foreign direct investment in Canada, by
North American Industry Classification System (NAICS) and region: http://www5.statcan.
gc.ca/cansim/a26?lang=eng&retrLang=eng&id=3760052&&pattern=&stByVal=1&p1=1&p
2=31&tabMode=dataTable&csid=

Statistics Canada. (accessed: 2017, 9 10). Table 376-0051. Retrieved from International
investment position, Canadian direct investment abroad and foreign direct investment in
Canada, by country, annual (dollars), CANSIM (database).: http://www5.statcan.gc.ca/
cansim/a26?lang=eng&id=3760051

The Metro Toronto Chinese & Southeast Asian Legal Clinic (MTCSALC). (2011). Road
to Justice-The legal struggle for equal rights of Chinese Canadians. Retrieved from http://
www.roadtojustice.ca

Torgan Group. (2017). About Us. Retrieved from http://www.torgan.com/About-
Us.8.0.html

Toronto Star. (2009, 6 19). A huge gamble on Markham Asian mall. Retrieved from
https://www.thestar.com/business/2009/06/19/a_huge_gamble_on_markham_asian_mall.
html

Wu, X. (1987). 第二次世界大战后加拿大华侨华人情况的变化 (Major Changes
in Chinese Community after World War II). 中山大学学报 (Journal of Sun Yat-Sen
University), Vol. 1, P.79-86.

Zhang, K. Q. (2013). Chinatowns. In I. N. (Ed), The Encyclopedia of Global Human
Migration. Blackwell Publishing Ltd.

Zhang, K., & Chen, V. (2011). Growing and Diversifying Chinese Investment in Canada:
2000-2010. Asia Pacific And Globalization Review, 1(1), 37-54. Retrieved from https://
journals.macewan.ca/apgr/article/view/33/42

Zhang, K., & DeGolyer, M. E. (2011). Hong Kong: Canada's Largest City in Asia-Survey of
Canadian Citizens in Hong Kong. Retrieved from Asia Pacific Foundation of Canada: https://
www.asiapacific.ca/sites/default/files/filefield/hk_survey_feb2011_v8.pdf

Chapter 5

The Long and Arduous Journey to Participate in Politics

It is common knowledge that democracy as a political system is about the distribution of political power and social resources. Having a voice in political affairs cannot only earn respect from society but can also benefit from a preferential shift in the distribution of resources. The resources in any society are far from sufficient to be distributed according to everyone's need; therefore, an ethnic group's social status and obtaining of resources from government are strongly related to the group's political standing in the given country. This was exactly the case for Chinese Canadians who would take part in political affairs in Canada. Chinese people have experienced many twists and turns in this aspect of Canadian history.

Two Major Challenges Chinese Canadians Face in Political Participation

There are usually two standards for measuring an immigrant group's political status in Western countries with a representative political system. One is the immigrant group's level of contribution to the country of residence and general level of acceptance and recognition from society; the other is how much the immigrant group actively participates in the country's political affairs. As for the status of Chinese Canadians, the early contributions made during the Gold Rush and the building of the railway have already earned Chinese Canadians a position as one of the groups that built the foundation for modern Canada. Regardless of how much discrimination Chinese Canadians have faced historically, no one would be able to deny the contributions Chinese people have made to Canada. However, when it comes to Chinese Canadians participating in politics, the level of growth has lagged far behind the growth of the Chinese population, their economic strength, and their need for development along with the times.

Chinese Canadians have faced two severe challenges when taking part in politics in Canada. First has been the constraint of Chinese culture and traditions, that is: "don't discuss politics". But in Confucian political philosophy, we find Mencius' teaching that "the people take precedence over the rulers". That is, the interests of the common people are not negligible; rather, they demand the constant attention of rulers to the needs of the people which must be kept in mind at all times. Similarly, Fan Zhongyan said: "Worry for the world before the world begins to worry; celebrate success only after the world can celebrate". This again means that people should participate in the events of the world, and in today's terms, participate in political affairs.

However, moving forward in time to Ming and Qing dynasties and the modern era, people became fearful of speaking out due to political persecution. People started to disbelieve politics, and no longer wished to get involved. A famous Chinese couplet written in Ming Dynasty by Gu Xiancheng: "the sounds of wind, rain, and learning reach my ears; I concern myself with family, national, and world affairs" became "Wind and rain are inaudible, and I will be this way to the end; not asking questions about major events or national affairs, I'll stay safe". Social development in China has affected the patterns of thinking and behavior of overseas Chinese like a shadow. This couplet tells exactly how Chinese Canadians have felt about engaging in political affairs in Canada. Nearly one hundred years in ignorance and fear of politics has created difficulties for Chinese adaptation to Canadian social life.

The second challenge was the Canadian political system which blocked Chinese Canadians from participating. If we were to say that traditional Chinese cultural influence has had a negative effect on Chinese Canadians engaging in politics, the banning of Chinese people's participating in politics by all three levels of Canadian government was the root cause of Chinese Canadians lagging in political participation. The worst discrimination was refusing to grant citizenship to Chinese Canadians at first, which turned them into second class Canadians. What was puzzling is that the older generation of Chinese immigrants did not actively participate in politics even after receiving citizenship, despite how hard they fought back and challenged the government for restoring their citizenship in the first place. Looking at the federal government level, the first Chinese Canadian Member of Parliament, Douglas Jung, only came into play in the late 50s of the 20th century; the second one, Art Lee, came in the 60s. The first MP that entered Federal Cabinet only happened in the 90s, Raymond Chan; the first female Chinese Canadian MP, Sophia Leung, also joined in the 90s. It took until the 21st century for a person of mixed blood, Michael David Chong, to become a senior Cabinet Minister, and for a Chinese Canadian woman, Alice Wong, to enter Cabinet for the first time. It took 150 years for Chinese Canadians to reach this level of participation.

Citizenship was a symbol of political status for the older generation of immigrants, thus they had to fight for it no matter what. As economies in Asia and in China soared, new immigrants "split operations" and used "one family, two systems" tactics to take advantage of the development in Asia, and to utilize the opportunities brought by China's economic growth. Business people let their spouses and children obtain Canadian citizenship but would not do so themselves; they would rather go through the arduous process of renewing the permanent resident card. To avoid taxes, they even applied for non-resident status. Such choices suggested a problem: they are not interested in politics, and don't care whether they have the right to vote.

It might truly bring pain to those second and third generation Chinese Canadians who fought for citizenship status offering their lives in battlefields, to see the new immigrants being so indifferent towards citizenship and the right to vote.

Stripping of Citizenship Prompted Zealous Political Participation

The earliest Chinese workers were given the right to vote despite not knowing English; they voted in accordance with whatever their employers wished. As the number of Chinese workers increased day by day, so did criticism of Chinese people, especially since the railway workers flooded in. White society believed that the Chinese people working for low wages took jobs away from Caucasian workers and kept them and their worker organizations from negotiating for better pay and benefits. Under the influence of English media, anti-Chinese voices gave voice to anti-Chinese sentiment that was prevalent in the whole society. The three levels of Canadian government had to step back under the impact of such sentiments. First municipal governments stripped voting rights from the Chinese, followed by provincial and federal governments. Slowly the Chinese people became de facto "second class Canadians" as they were no longer given citizenship.

During this period the federal government organized two Royal Commissions on Chinese Immigration investigations to find out if Chinese people should be allowed to stay in Canada. The results were of course disheartening. They claimed that Chinese Canadians did not consume, pay taxes, conduct social service, or contribute to the local economy. In other words, they believed the Chinese had no loyalty to Canada, and would not become useful citizens. Thus, the government finally banned Chinese people from entering Canada in 1923, having progressed from increasingly heavy head-taxes and stripping of citizenship and citizens' rights. The greatest offence to the spirit of the Canadian constitution was made through this historic act of racial discrimination. This vile act remained in effect until 1947, after the end of the Second World War. What brought about this new change, besides the post-war global environment, was mostly the active participation in the Second World War by young Chinese Canadians, even when they were "second class Canadians", volunteering to fight and die to protect their country.

Looking back into the history of Canada, the Chinese were the group that was systemically discriminated against for the longest period with the highest severity besides the First Nations. With this as the background, Chinese Canadians should actively engage in politics because they have every right to do so, and because they need to remember the lessons of history.

The success of Douglas Jung taking part in politics was one of the most important pages in the history of Chinese immigration to Canada. The event showed that the Chinese people had moved on from being silently abused and entered a stage of having a voice in determining their own fate after a long period of peaceful protest. In terms of social status, the Chinese moved from laborers during the early stages of immigration to that of "second class Canadians" in the middle stages, to conscientiously becoming a part of mainstream society in the final stages after the war.

The social status, personal character and fame of Douglas Jung, the Chinese Canadian pioneer in politics, were not less significant than his white peers. He never thought of himself as just a "token minority" but worked with other politicians as a part of the mainstream norm. He voiced his ideas on policy making and actively spoke of his beliefs in politics. For example, his great foresight led him to propose that

Canada establish a normal relationship with "Red China" during a time of McCarthyism, because he believed that it would bring the greatest benefit to Canada. His view obviously faced challenges from both the ruling and opposition parties. Similarly, Douglas Jung spoke on behalf of the Chinese communities. He proposed to pardon the offenders of illegal immigration using "false papers" (Chinese people used the birth certificates and identification documents of others to immigrate to Canada; the total number exceeded ten thousand between the end of the 50s and the early 60s of the 20th century) during a time of great controversy. He also spoke on behalf of Chinese immigrants who did not receive equal treatment with their European or American counterparts, who were allowed to apply for their relatives to come to Canada. This also became the premise for great changes to immigration policy in 1967.

Unfortunately, Jung's pioneering work as a quality citizen did not become commonplace for other Chinese Canadian candidates, to the point that during times of heated political participation from Chinese Canadians, candidates had varying levels of political skills, and this delayed the overall "quality involvement" of Chinese Canadian politicians.

If we take Douglas Jung as the prelude to Chinese Canadian engagement in politics, then subsequent Chinese participants in politics were second, third, or fourth generation immigrants who were born in Canada. Not only that, at the federal level, Chinese Canadians still received very few votes overall, since neither the Liberals nor the Conservatives were passionate about endorsing Chinese Canadian politicians. Therefore, participation by Chinese people in federal government was "scattered" and not continuous. It was 17 years after Douglas Jung became an MP for the Conservatives that Art Lee became an MP for the Liberals in 1974 after winning the vote in the Vancouver East Electoral District of British Columbia. Then it took another 19 years for Raymond Chan, an immigrant from Hong Kong, to win the election in Richmond, B.C. in 1993. After Chan's successful election, the era where both old and new generations of Chinese Canadians taking part in political affairs took hold. At the same time Chinese Canadians started participating in politics in provinces other than B.C., finally bringing an end to that period in history.

In the 1997 federal election, Raymond Chan and Sophia Leung won the elections for the Liberals in their districts; Inky Mark of Manitoba and Michael David Chong of Toronto won for the Conservatives in the same year. In the 2000 federal election, Chan failed to win his re-election bid, but Leung, Mark, and Chong succeeded; in 2004, Chan, Chong and Mark were elected again; in 2006, Olivia Chow won for the New Democratic Party, and Meili Faille won for the Bloc Quebecois; Chan, Mark and Chong were again re-elected. It was at this point that Chinese Canadians finally had representatives in all of the major parties of the federal government.

This goes to show that there is great diversity within Chinese Canadian participation in politics; rather than putting all their eggs in one basket, they worked with all the major parties. Having representatives in all political parties meant that Chinese Canadians did not have to become a "surefire" vote for any particular party, with the risk of losing out when the party in power changes.

One thing was slightly different between Chinese Canadian participation in provincial and municipal elections versus federal elections: involvement in federal elections started in western Canada, while involvement in provincial and municipal elections showed greater geographical diversity. Chinese Canadian city counselors were spread across British Columbia, Alberta, Saskatchewan, Manitoba and Ontario. Vancouver, where Douglas Jung was the first Chinese Canadian politician to be elected in the 1950s, did not see its first Chinese Canadian city counselor, Peter Yu, until 1982.

The Role of Chinese Canadian Politicians in Federal Government

There are a few notable characteristics in the process of Chinese Canadians participating in politics. Personal involvement in political affairs is the highest for Chinese Canadian candidates at the municipal level, the most basic of democratic elections. This is because municipal election candidates face the greatest level of challenge but offer a much lower level of political glory compared with provincial and federal counterparts. Another reason municipal governance has limited appeal to Chinese politicians is because it has little connection with the Asian homeland and is mostly confined to the day-to-day lives of local citizens. Inversely, provincial and federal levels offer quite a number of opportunities to cooperate with the Asian homeland due to economic and political factors, and thus the positions, competitiveness and exposure of these politicians are much greater in Chinese Canadian communities.

Using the federal government as an example, Raymond Chan defeated his Conservative challenger in Richmond in spite of the general trend to vote for Conservatives in the 1993 federal election. He then became a member of Cabinet under Prime Minister Jean Chrétien, holding the position of a junior Minister of Asian-Pacific Affairs. This was the first time for a Chinese Canadian MP to enter Cabinet. Later on, Chan was appointed as Minister of Multiculturalism. Despite having been criticized for being unable to convince the ruling party to apologize and compensate for the historical problem of the head tax, Chan's entrance into Cabinet still turned a new page in the history of Chinese Canadian participation in federal politics.

In 2006, Michael David Chong, a politician with Chinese ancestry, was selected to enter Cabinet by Conservative Prime Minister Harper and held the positions of President of The Queen's Privy Council, Minister of Intergovernmental Affairs, and Minister of Sport. He was the first person of Chinese ancestry to attain the position of senior minister and was the youngest minister of Chinese ancestry (only 34 years old). Being a firm believer in Confederation, he gave up all of his positions in Cabinet due to his disapproval of Harper proposing Quebec as a distinct nation within a united Canada and became the first Cabinet Minister in Canadian history to proactively resign from Cabinet. This act changed the image of "token minority" for a Chinese Canadian minister and marked a new level of moral principle for Chinese politicians. Despite Chong having become a backseat MP, he still initiated the bill to limit the power of the ruling party and to strengthen the democratic power of general MPs—the C-586 Reform Bill. After several amendments, the bill was finally passed as an act in 2015. This was one of the most successful bills of Parliament proposed by a private member in recent years; the bill had a strong and meaningful impact on Canadian political parties and reform in Parliament. In 2017, Chong took part in the Conservative leadership election; he proposed to balance budgets, lower taxes, boost efficiency of government services, boost the free market economy, free trade, and sustainable environmental policies. He was the first candidate of Chinese ancestry to enter the leadership election of a major political party.

After Chong, Alice Wong, another Canadian of Chinese descent was brought into Cabinet by Prime Minister Harper in 2011; taking up the position of Minister of Senior Affairs, she became a Minister of State, as well as the first Chinese Canadian woman to be selected into Cabinet.

It is interesting to note that while Chinese Canadians get elected, credit has almost always been given to the "power of the party" and "political trends", and not entirely to their own merit and efforts. The same cannot be said for Chinese Canadian MPs in the New Democratic Party though. The NDP, as the "opposition party of the century" has many of its representatives fighting as "lone wolves", working hard by themselves to become elected. Olivia Chow, widow of the late NDP leader Jack Layton, has been re-elected several times as an MP in Toronto. She is a true powerhouse among Chinese Canadian candidates and has even challenged the seat of Toronto's mayor. Despite being a part of the opposition party, Chow has interacted greatly with the ruling parties in Parliament, and made significant contributions to obtain the official apology for the head tax, the apology and compensation from Japan for comfort women in 2007, amendments to the Citizen's Arrest and Self Defense Act (brought about when the Chinese shop-owner David Chen was arrested for having captured a robber in his shop).

As for Jenny Kwan in the Vancouver East Electoral District, she was always the ever-victorious candidate in Vancouver's municipal and provincial elections. She was also the first Chinese Canadian woman to hold a provincial minister's office. She took a detour from her provincial level career, participated in the 2015 federal election and still won her bid for membership in Parliament despite the NDP's clear disadvantage as a "third party". To date, she has maintained an impressive record as she has never lost a single election.

Yet speaking from a broad perspective, aside from Douglas Jung and Michael David Chong having had great influence on federal government policies, Inky Mark having raised the private member's bill for head-tax compensation, and Olivia Chow and a few others having tabled proposals to amend important acts, most Chinese MPs worked only as a bridge between Chinese communities and government, with little influence on governmental lawmaking or policymaking. This is a problem that Chinese Canadian politicians still need to address.

It is hard to foresee notable breakthroughs for Chinese politicians' increased involvement in government when looking at the future trends. This is mainly because of low turnouts by Chinese voters, insufficient involvement of Chinese in political parties, and the small number of Chinese talents engaging in politics overall. If we look at the political map of Canadian minorities, Chinese politicians in Federal government has a much smaller representation and influence than South Asians (mainly of Punjabi Indian descent), which is remarkably disproportionate to the Chinese population ratio in Canada.

Here we look at the 2015 federal elections as an example. There was a total of 28 Chinese Canadian candidates, and 24 of whom were a part of the four dominant parties (Conservatives, Liberals, NDP, and Green Party), which was a record high. However, only 6 of these candidates won their bids: 3 Liberals, 2 Conservatives, and 1 NDP; all of whom were in Toronto or in metropolitan areas of B.C.; 4 from the former, 2 from the latter. Compared with the last federal election, Chinese Canadians had two fewer MPs. However, the total number of seats in the House of Commons increased by 30, from 308 to 338. This shows that Chinese Canadian progress in federal politics is sagging, and their election results are highly affected by larger political trends. If we look at the names of those elected, Alice Wong and Michael David Chong from the Conservatives, and Arnold Chan from the Liberals were re-elected; Jenny Kwan from the NDP, Shaun Chen and Geng Tan from the Liberals were newly elected; Tan was the first and only MP who was originally from Mainland China. No Chinese Canadian was selected into Cabinet by Prime Minister Justin Trudeau; Arnold Chan later became the Deputy Leader of the Government in the House of Commons.

Looking at the South Asian Canadians: 22 were elected MPs in the same federal election, accounting for 6.5% of the total, the majority being of Sikh ancestry. However, the total percentage of South Asians in Canada's population is only 4.8%. This shows that the political power of South Asians in the federal government has exceeded their population ratio. By comparison, Chinese Canadians accounted for 1.8% of MPs, much lower than their 4% population ratio. Looking at the composition of the federal government, the number of Sikh ministers has reached 4, including vital offices such as Minister of National Defense. There were no Chinese MPs in the Cabinet. Looking at the ratio of minorities and vulnerable groups in Trudeau's government: besides the four Sikh ministers, there were two of Aboriginal background, one Afghanistan, two with disabilities, and one with homosexual orientation. Looking at this list of ministers in Cabinet, "poor" is the perfect word to describe the current strength of Chinese Canadians in the federal government.

Voter Turnout Still Low in Chinese Communities

Indeed the wide gap in political power between Chinese and South Asian Canadians has to do with cultural traditions, but more so with voter turnout. Some Chinese Canadians believe that participating in Canadian politics conflicts with maintaining traditional Chinese cultural values; more involvement would mean losing more Chinese traditions. That however is not the case. According to *Statistics Canada*'s 2002 survey, 88% of South Asian Canadians felt a sense of belonging to Canada, and 67% felt strong sense of belonging to their own ethnic or cultural communities. This shows that the two are not necessarily in conflict.

Moreover, there are three significant groups of Canadian Chinese in terms of places of origin: mainland China, Hong Kong, and Taiwan. Their votes may become split between their own groups, failing to generate a synergy, thus causing some candidates to lose even though they may have received a good number of votes. This condition has existed ever since Douglas Jung's time, and hasn't changed much since then. The most fundamental and greatest reason of all, however, is that Chinese Canadians do not have a high level of political involvement or commitment, and thus few come out to vote.

Low voter turnout is a common problem in the Canadian democratic process; the 2015 federal election only brought 68.3% of the registered voter population. And that was the highest out of the 7 elections since

1993. Among all of the federal elections in Canada since 1867, the highest turnout achieved was in 1958, at 79.4%. The lowest was 58.8% in 2008. The turnout usually fluctuates around 70%. An analysis from *Statistics Canada* showed that age, education, home ownership and employment are positively correlated with voter turnout.

In terms of ethnic background, they found that there are dramatic differences between ethnic groups. Overall, first generation immigrants vote less often than those born in Canada, but their turnout increases with the number of years spent living in Canada. The groups of immigrants who have the highest turnout are from the Nordic countries, Western Europe, the US, Australia and New Zealand. The lowest are from East Asia, Western-central Asia and the Middle East. Looking at just South Asian (including Indian) and East Asian (including Chinese) Canadians, the voter turnouts are 68% and 54%, respectively. This shows that Chinese Canadians have the lowest voter turnout of all the visible minorities, and Indo-Canadians have the highest. This factor becomes decisive in their political influence on the federal government.

Our conclusion is that, if we only focus on the historical development of political involvement of Chinese Canadians, we can see an optimistic trend in that voter turnout is increasing, and people are participating more and more in politics. However, when we view things in comparison with other ethnic groups in the same period, Chinese Canadians still lag far behind in political involvement and political influence. There is still a long way to go, and plenty of challenges that must be faced.

Chinese Canadian Lieutenant Governors and Heads-of-State

Despite the fact that Chinese Canadians have been unable to reach the top in the three levels of democratic elections, they have still risen in social status and made contributions to Canada that do not pale in comparison to other ethnic groups. This tradition has lasted since the building of the CPR. The affirmation of Chinese Canadian contributions to this society was shown in the appointment of a Chinese Canadian Governor General and several Lieutenant Governors. These outstanding Canadians have also used their honourable positions to bring a greater level of visibility to Chinese Canadians—an irreplaceable contribution to the group image. They established a crucial foundation in inheriting and modifying the "Chinese gene" in Canada.

Lieutenant Governor David See-chai Lam

On September 9, 1988, David Lam, an immigrant from Hong Kong, was appointed Lieutenant Governor of British Columbia, the Queen's highest representative in the province, by Conservative Prime Minister Brian Mulroney. Lam became the second non-white Lieutenant Governor and the first Chinese Canadian Lieutenant Governor in Canada. He was appointed because of his massive contributions to society after achieving great success in his property development ventures. In 1982, he founded the David and Dorothy Lam Family Foundation, and since then donated millions of dollars to University of British Columbia, University of Victoria, Simon Fraser University and

Regent College. He has also funded the construction of Vancouver's Dr. Sun Yat-Sen Classical Chinese Garden and the Vancouver World Expo's Canada Pavilion. These unique contributions to society had won him membership in the Order of Canada.

Although he was Lieutenant Governor by appointment, his great wisdom and his devotion to service under religious guidance left a political heritage of generous contributions. This was not typical of Chinese Canadian MPs, MPPs, or city councilors. In his 7 years of service as Lieutenant Governor, he gave receptions for over eighty thousand people from all fields and professions and made over a thousand speeches. He established the Order of British Columbia based on suggestions made by British Columbia's Premier Bill Vander Zalm to honour and encourage those who have made great contributions to society. But his sense of justice was not swayed by personal relationships. When Vander Zalm refused to resign after revelation of his involvement in a corruption scandal, Lam took justice into his own hands and convinced Vander Zalm to step down. This was something that most Lieutenant Governors would feel reluctant to do. He also donated all of his salary from the lieutenant governor position, using the money to expand the Government House garden; he also invited and organized citizens and volunteers to get involved in the garden's construction and maintenance, thus breaking a barrier in social hierarchy. He worked together with the businessperson Milton Wong to establish the Canadian International Dragon Boat Festival, which then became a famous trademark of Vancouver. He also received a visit from the Queen during the Commonwealth Games; his humour and nobility left a great impression on the Queen and the Royal Family. Such actions significantly boosted the international visibility of Chinese Canadians. Due to his remarkable contributions during his years of service, he was awarded membership in the Order of Canada and Order of British Columbia after he left office. It could be said that the "historical gene pool" of Chinese people in Canada was modified to become more socially active and healthier due to the contributions made by David See-chai Lam.

The success of Dr. Lam also caused people in different fields to recognize and affirm Chinese Canadians as being eligible to assume important government positions in Canada, including the possibility of becoming head-of-state.

Governor General Adrienne Louise Clarkson

Adrienne Louise Clarkson's ex-husband Stephen Clarkson was a political science professor at the University of Toronto; they married in 1963 but divorced 12 years after their marriage. Adrienne Louise Clarkson still keeps her ex-husband's family name.

Her father, William Poy, was an Australian Chinese with UK citizenship; her mother was Hakka. William Poy was captured by the Japanese during the Second World War and was later released after a POW exchange between the UK and Japan. Their entire family went to Canada in 1942 as refugees from Hong Kong. Clarkson was only three years old at the time. Although Canada still maintained the barrier of the Chinese Exclusion Act, they were still allowed entrance as a "special case". Some people therefore claim that Clarkson's advancement from refugee to head-of-state highlights Canada's generosity.

With her excellent literary skills, Clarkson became a program host at the CBC and therefore became known to every family in Canada. Her position at the time was similar to that of Connie Chung of the United States, but Clarkson was much more talented and had fewer controversies. Also, Clarkson became the Agent General for Ontario in France in 1980 because of her fluency in both English and French, which she learned at the University of Toronto, and in Paris where she stayed as an international student. 11 years after Dr. Lam's appointment as the Lieutenant Governor of British Columbia, Adrienne Clarkson was sworn in as the 26th Governor General of Canada on October 7th, 1999, after Prime Minister Chrétien's recommendation to Queen Elizabeth II. She was the first visible minority and the second female Governor General of Canada.

She spoke up about her Chinese ancestry after she went into office. Although she went to her hometown Taishan to look for her roots, she doesn't speak Chinese, nor does she use her Chinese family name. These acts are very westernized. Her "lavish" lifestyles were also considered to be uncharacteristic of Chinese people. The expenditures of the Governor General's Residence doubled during her term, which caused a great deal of controversy.

However, as many non-Chinese groups still categorize people "by face", Clarkson's Chinese appearance brought an extraordinary boost to Chinese Canadian visibility, especially since Canada used to be a nation that aggressively discriminated against no other ethnics but Chinese; that period of history still goes under-recognized in the public education system. While Clarkson was in office as the Governor General, having a Chinese Canadian as the symbolic head-of-state and Commander-in-Chief of the Canadian military forces was a huge encouragement to Chinese Canadians, even though the head-tax was still not accounted for at the time.

In fact, the Poy family had another notable person in history—Adrienne's brother, Neville Poy. Neville Poy was the first doctor to receive the Order of Canada; his wife Vivienne Poy was appointed to the Senate of Canada in 1998 by Prime Minister Chrétien, one year before Adrienne Clarkson became the Governor General. Vivienne Poy was the first Chinese Canadian in the Senate. After Vivienne Poy, the next Chinese Canadian appointed to the Senate was in 2013, Victor Oh by Prime Minister Harper; the third was Yuen Pau Woo in 2016, by Justin Trudeau. Woo was also the first Chinese Canadian from British Columbia to be appointed to the Senate.

The saga of Adrienne Clarkson negated the conclusions of the two investigations by the Royal Commission on Chinese Immigration. Chinese Canadians do indeed integrate into Canadian society.

Lieutenant Governor Norman Lim Kwong

Having had Lam and Clarkson as notable Chinese Canadian leaders, Canadian society was no longer surprised to see another Chinese Canadian hold one of these positions. Alberta, a stronghold of the Conservatives, had its first Chinese Canadian lieutenant governor, Norman Lim Kwong.

In contrast to Dr. David Lam's status as a new immigrant, Norman Lim Kwong was the descendent of early 20th century immigrants; his parents came from Taishan, Guangdong. Kwong was born on October 24, 1929 in

Calgary; he received a Canadian education from start to finish.

There was another difference between Kwong and other Chinese Canadian children at the time: he became extremely active in football during his high school years, became a professional player and participated in the Canadian Football League when he was 19 as a player for the Calgary Stampeders. Luckily, the Chinese Exclusion Act had already been abolished by then, and Chinese Canadians faced far less discrimination. Kwong became the first Chinese Canadian player in the CFL. The Stampeders also happened to win the Grey Cup during the same season that Kwong joined, making him the youngest player of a Grey Cup champion team. Later on, he joined the Edmonton Eskimos, and contributed to a glorious moment in history by winning the Grey Cup for three years in a row from 1954 to 1956 together with his teammates. Nicknamed the "China Clipper", Kwong broke 30 records in his 12 years in the CFL, became the most valuable Chinese Canadian professional football player, and was inducted into the Canadian Football Hall of Fame and Canada's Sports Hall of Fame.

After retiring from football, Kwong went into the world of business where he achieved success on the stock market, investment and real estate; from 1980 to 1994 he became one of the owners of the NHL Calgary Flames, the team that won the Stanley Cup in 1989.

He was awarded the Order of Canada in 1988 due to his contributions in athletics and to society in general, and in January 2005 he became the first Chinese Canadian Lieutenant Governor of Alberta when he was appointed by Prime Minister Harper. In June of the same year, he personally welcomed Queen Elizabeth II to Alberta to celebrate Alberta's 100th anniversary. He held the position until May of 2010.

On September 3, 2016, Norman Lim Kwong passed away peacefully in his sleep at 86 years of age.

Kwong's success completely overturned the stereotypical image of Chinese Canadian professions in Canadian society, and again confirmed that Canada's "Chinese gene" continued to be transmitted in the postwar community of immigrants.

Lieutenant Governor Philip S. Lee

Philip S. Lee became Manitoba's first, and Canada's third Chinese Canadian lieutenant governor, when he was appointed to the position in August 2009 by Prime Minister Harper. Lee was born in Hong Kong in 1944, studied at Tak Sun School and Wah Yan College of Kowloon. He immigrated to Manitoba when he was 18 and studied chemistry at the University of Manitoba. He was one of our post-war international students. After graduation, Lee worked as a research chemist for the municipal government of Winnipeg, with responsibilities in water and waste treatment; he went on to become the city's top expert in water treatment and a locally famous professional. As a first generation immigrant, Lee speaks both Cantonese and Mandarin, which helped him greatly in his work in social services, especially in Chinese communities.

His contributions to Chinese communities are mainly in three areas: assisting in the expansion and development of Winnipeg's Chinatown, founding the Folklorama festival in Manitoba, and helping to construct the Winnipeg Chinese Cultural and Community Centre. Most would agree that Lee was the leader of Chinese Canadians in Manitoba due to his extraordinary contributions to the community; he was awarded the Commemorative Medal for the 125th Anniversary of Canadian Confederation in 1993, and the Order of Canada in 1999.

Lee's appointment as Lieutenant Governor was not only widely approved by the Chinese communities, but also affirmed by the provincial political parties in Manitoba. He was a well-respected individual in the province. During the 6 years of his service, Lee travelled to different places all around the country and the world to build economic, cultural and people-to-people bridges. He made tremendous contributions to Manitoba and brought great honour to Chinese Canadian communities.

Outlook for Chinese Canadians in Politics

Chinese Canadian participation and discussion in Canadian politics was a forced result of historical racial discrimination, and also a result of Canada's improved development of democratic policies. Looking into history, the starting point of Chinese Canadians taking part in politics was in British Columbia and other western provinces, where the worst cases of discrimination against Chinese people were also observed. This tradition also revealed a strong sense of continuity. In terms of federal politics, aside from the first two Chinese Canadian MP's (Douglas Jung and Art Lee) having been born in British Columbia, the first male Chinese Canadian (Raymond Chan) and the first female Chinese Canadian (Alice Wong) to be selected into Cabinet also started in B.C. It was not until the federal election in 2015 for Ontario (3 elected) to overtake British Columbia (2 elected) in the number of Chinese Canadian MPs elected as MPs. British Columbia had the highest number of Chinese Canadian MPs among all provinces and territories in all previous elections.

However, when viewed from the perspective of government policy making and power operations, Chinese Canadians have had very little power in politics and have had limited influence on Canada's national progress. In terms of voter turnout, Chinese Canadians are quite weak in political participation and influence, listing themselves near the bottom of all visible minorities. This situation is inconsistent with the status of the Chinese people who provided their share of Canada's "founding genes".

The bottom line is that Chinese Canadians have not recognized their identity as founders of Canada. They seem to be satisfied being "outsiders" who worry only about petty details; Chinese Canadians who do find a place in major political parties appear unable to go deep and dirty, which caused them to have little power in influencing the workings of political parties or in policymaking. In the history of Chinese Canadian politicians, only two have achieved leadership status in major federal political parties.

The first is Olivia Chow. She started as an NDP city councillor in Toronto, and with her outstanding experience, she eventually leaped into federal elections and became an MP. Due to her own political prowess and also due to her late husband Jack Layton (1950-2011) having been the most charismatic leader in the federal NDP's history (he led the party to become the official opposition party in 2011), Chow earned a great reputation in the party. After Layton's death from cancer, Chow was encouraged by the media to join the election for the party leader. However, Chow quit federal politics to put all her efforts into the Toronto mayoral election and lost much of her political influence after her loss in the election. The second is Michael David Chong; he was the first Chinese Canadian to launch a bid for Conservative Party leadership.

As for provincial politics, there still has not been an outstanding Chinese Canadian politician to hold the position of a major political party leader, which means there has never been a Chinese Canadian who could become the premier of a province. As for municipal politics, there are Chinese Canadians who have been elected mayor, but none who have created a pivotal influence on city development. For example, the former mayor of Victoria, the capital of British Columbia, was a Chinese Canadian, Alan Lowe. He was 38 years old in 1999 when he became Victoria's Mayor, and was the youngest mayor of a major Canadian city. He served three terms as mayor until 2008, and obviously was a great one. Unfortunately, he had little lasting impact as a Chinese Canadian mayor.

There are two obvious phenomena in the history of Chinese Canadians in politics. First, the politicians from the first generation immigrants had very little experience in political party operations and policymaking; however, they had the power to mobilize new immigrants to vote in large numbers to help them win elections. Yet they had very limited influence within their political parties and were typically the "token minority". Second, the politicians from second or later generations of immigrants, i.e. Canadian-born Chinese, have a much better foothold in political parties and a better understanding of the electoral districts. These are very important foundations for political participation. The problem is that they define themselves as a part of the "mainstream", rather than as representatives of Chinese communities. This made them extremely out of touch with their Chinese communities, having only a "Chinese" face but lacking a profound understanding of the challenges faced by more recent immigrants. These conditions have made them unable to speak for their Chinese communities and unable to win votes from those communities, leading mainstream political parties to not take them seriously.

These show that in order to have more Chinese Canadians participating meaningfully in politics, the first generation and Canadian-born Chinese must conquer their differences in values, interests, and cultures, work together to form an alliance with real strength and relevant political ideologies. This is the way for Chinese Canadians to have quality involvement in politics over the next 20 years, and the way for Chinese Canadian politicians to become better accepted by other ethnic groups in Canada.

Overall, for Chinese Canadians to play a larger part in Canadian politics, there is light at the end of the tunnel, but there still are many twists and turns ahead.

Chapter 6

A Multifaceted Community in Transformation

The 21st century has witnessed the robust momentum of Chinese Canadians becoming increasingly diversified and vibrant. This is partially due to continued flourishing of traditional Chinese communities that have put down deep roots in Canadian society, gradually growing and spreading its power and influence. Of equal importance is the fact that new generations of immigrants, from a variety of sources and through different classes of eligibility, continue to inject fresh blood into Chinese communities to keep them growing. Today, the social fabric of the community is seen as a multidimensional mixture and diversification, from residential patterns to economic activities, political participation, and community engagement, etc.

It is clear that a multifaceted portrait of Chinese Canadians is in the making. However, the diversity of Chinese Canadians used to be described as "a heap of loose sand". In fact, such a description only reflects one side of the story of Chinese Canadians not always agreeing on issues they care about and emphasizes inconsistencies on solutions to the problems they face. Despite the disagreement among the members of Chinese Canadian communities, the other side of the story shows that sometimes they are united and support each other for common goals. This kind of "agreeing to disagree" has been normal for a long time among Chinese Canadians and is perhaps just another part of the colorful features of Canada's multicultural society.

In this chapter, we will illustrate what multifaceted "Chineseness" looks like and discuss how such a diversity of Chinese is connected and linked through various organizations, and why Chinese Canadians need a strategy to seek common ground for everyone's benefit.

A Demographic Snapshot of Chinese Canadians

Chinese Canadians are a category of individuals who are Canadian, including Canadian-born and other residents of Canada, both permanent and temporary, who have full or partial Chinese heritage. Chinese Canadians constitute a group of overseas Chinese, and also a subgroup of East Asian Canadians which is itself a subgroup of Asian Canadians. Most importantly, Chinese Canadians are a part of the Canadian population. Many Chinese Canadians are immigrants and descendants of immigrants from mainland China, Hong Kong, Macao, Taiwan, as well as from other regions that include large numbers of the Chinese diaspora, especially Southeast Asia and some Western countries like United States, the United Kingdom, Australia, New Zealand, and Brazil.

The Canadian population of Chinese heritage has changed, is changing and will continue to change in many ways that will ultimately lead to its inclusion in and impact on many aspects of Canadian society. There is no longer a homogenous Chinese community in Canada due to a variety of demographic factors. From a statistical perspective, the Canadian census reports "Chinese Communities" in four categories, i.e., ethnic origin, visible minority, place of birth, and mother tongue, each of which sheds some light on the Chinese Canadians from a different angle.

It is somewhat misleading when people talk about the Chinese community in Canada. The Canadian census (2016) reported four numbers that reflect numbers of people who consist of the Chinese community, namely,

- 1,769,195 people claimed their ethnic origin to be Chinese ;

- 1,577,065 people who considered themselves as Chinese and one of the visible minority groups in Canada;

- 649,260 people reported their place of birth being mainland China, with an additional 208,935 claiming Hong Kong, 5,750 claiming Macao, and 63,770 claiming Taiwan; and

- 1,249,030 people reported one of the "Chinese languages" as their mother tongue.

Compared with the 2011 census, the Chinese population in all categories has grown significantly over the 5-year interval, as shown in Table 6-1 below.

Table 6-1: Counting the Chinese Community by Census Category, 2011-2016

Census Category	2016			2011		
	Total Chinese	Population in the Category	Share of Chinese	Total Chinese	Population in the Category	Share of Chinese
Ethnic Origin	1,769,195	34,460,065	5.1%	1,487,580	32,852,325	4.5%
Visible Minority	1,577,065	7,674,580	20.5%	1,324,745	6,264,750	21.1%
Place of Birth (outside of Canada)*	927,715	8,219,550	11.3%	817,420	7,217,295	11.3%
Mother Tongue (non-official language)	1,249,030	7,260,080	17.2%	1,066,950	6,551,515	16.3%

Note*: 2016 includes PRC, Hong Kong, Macao and Taiwan; 2011 includes PRC, Hong Kong and Taiwan.

Source: *Statistics Canada*, 2016 Census of Population; 2011 National Household Survey.

A close look at this census data (*Statistics Canada*, 2017) draws a few remarkable observations such as the following:

• Ethnic Chinese have become the 7th largest ethnic group and the largest group with an Asian ethnic heritage in Canada, representing 5.1 per cent of the total Canadian population. Canada has more people of Chinese ancestry per capita than any other country outside of Asia.

• Ethnic Chinese make up the single largest visible minority group in Canada, accounting for 20.5 per cent of the total visible minority population in Canada . Nearly 22.3 per cent of Canada's population are reported as one of the visible minority groups.

• First generation Chinese immigrants remain the largest immigrant group, representing 11.3 per cent of total immigrant population in Canada. The foreign born population accounts for 21.9 per cent of the total Canadian population, the highest among the

G7 countries.

• People who speak one of the Chinese languages as their mother tongue are the 2nd largest group of non-official language users in Canada.

• The difference between the four types of Chinese reported by the 2016 Canadian census further illustrates that not all ethnic Chinese consider themselves a visible minority; not all ethnic Chinese were born outside of Canada; and not all ethnic Chinese speak a Chinese language as their mother tongue. All of these will be included in the following discussion of major features of Chinese Canadians.

People of Chinese ethnic origin are highly concentrated in certain provinces and cities. Nearly 90 per cent of all ethnic Chinese live in three provinces in Canada, namely, Ontario, British Columbia and Alberta, compared to 63 per cent of entire Canadian population living in the same provinces. Ontario alone boasts the largest ethnic Chinese population reported at 849,345 individuals (or 48 per cent) of all ethnic Chinese in Canada, followed by British Columbia at 540,155 men and women (or 31 per cent) and Alberta at 188,280 men and women (or 11 per cent). Only 10 per cent of ethnic Chinese call the rest of Canada's provinces or territories their home (see Table 6-2 below).

Similarly, people of Chinese ethnic origin prefer to live in major cities, especially in 6 cities (CMA), Toronto, Vancouver, Montreal, Calgary, Edmonton and Ottawa, each of which has ethnic Chinese population close to 50,000 or more. All 6 cities together boast over 1.5 million (87 per cent) of ethnic Chinese in Canada, compared to only 47 per cent of entire Canadian population living in these same cities. Toronto (CMA) has the largest

Chinese population in Canada of 700,705 men and women (or 40 per cent) of ethnic Chinese in Canada, followed by Vancouver (CMA) of 499,175 (or 28 per cent).

Table 6-2: Distribution and Visibility of Ethnic Chinese in Canada by Regions in 2016

Provinces/Territories/Census Metropolitan Areas	Ethnic Chinese		All Ethnics in Canada		Share of Ethnic Chinese in the Region
	Population	%	Population	%	%
Canada	1,769,195	100.0	34,460,065	100.0	5.1
Ontario	849,345	48.0	13,242,160	38.4	6.4
British Columbia	540,155	30.5	4,560,240	13.2	11.8
Alberta	188,280	10.6	3,978,150	11.5	4.7
Quebec	121,445	6.9	7,965,450	23.1	1.5
Manitoba	30,150	1.7	1,240,700	3.6	2.4
Saskatchewan	19,080	1.1	1,070,560	3.1	1.8
Nova Scotia	9,695	0.5	908,340	2.6	1.1
New Brunswick	4,485	0.3	730,710	2.1	0.6
Prince Edward Island	2,735	0.2	139,685	0.4	2.0
Newfoundland and Labrador	2,700	0.2	512,250	1.5	0.5
Yukon Territories	625	0.0	35,110	0.1	1.8
Northwest Territories	380	0.0	41,135	0.1	0.9
Nunavut	115	0.0	35,580	0.1	0.3
Toronto	700,705	39.6	5,862,855	17.0	12.0
Vancouver	499,175	28.2	2,426,230	7.0	20.6
Montreal	108,780	6.1	4,009,790	11.6	2.7
Calgary	104,620	5.9	1,374,650	4.0	7.6
Edmonton	71,955	4.1	1,297,280	3.8	5.5
Ottawa	49,930	2.8	1,300,730	3.8	3.8
Rest of Canada	234,030	13.2	18,188,530	52.8	1.3

Source: *Statistics Canada*, 2016 Census of Population, Statistics Canada Catalogue no. 98-400-X2016187.

The regional over-concentration has led to an interesting and notable distribution pattern that the visibility of Chinese Canadians, measured as a share of ethnic Chinese in the local population, varies considerably from province to province and from city to city. In general, the national average odds of meeting a resident of Chinese ethnic origin in Canada is 1 in 20 (or 5.1 per cent of the visibility). However, there are dramatic differences from region to region. The ethnic Chinese are in fact most visible in the province of British Columbia (11.8 per cent), followed by Ontario (6.4 per cent), both of which are over the national average of 5.1 per cent. In other provinces or territories, the odds of seeing a Chinese resident differ from 4.7 per cent in Alberta to 0.3 per cent in Nunavut. At the city level, their visibility varies from as high as nearly one in five (20.6 per cent) in Vancouver (CMA) and over one in ten (12 per cent) in Toronto (CMA) to nearly zero in more remote Canadian towns or districts.

People of Chinese ethnic origin are not necessarily newcomers to Canada. Ethnic Chinese came to Canada as early as the periods of "Gold Rush" and building the Pacific Railway before Canadian confederation in 1867. Many of their descendants were born in Canada and their families may have lived in Canada for more than two generations. Canadian-born Chinese (CBC) has become a common phenomenon within the communities. The 2016 census reports 30 per cent of ethnic Chinese were born in Canada while the majority, or 70 per cent, were first generation or naturalized Canadians (see Chart below).

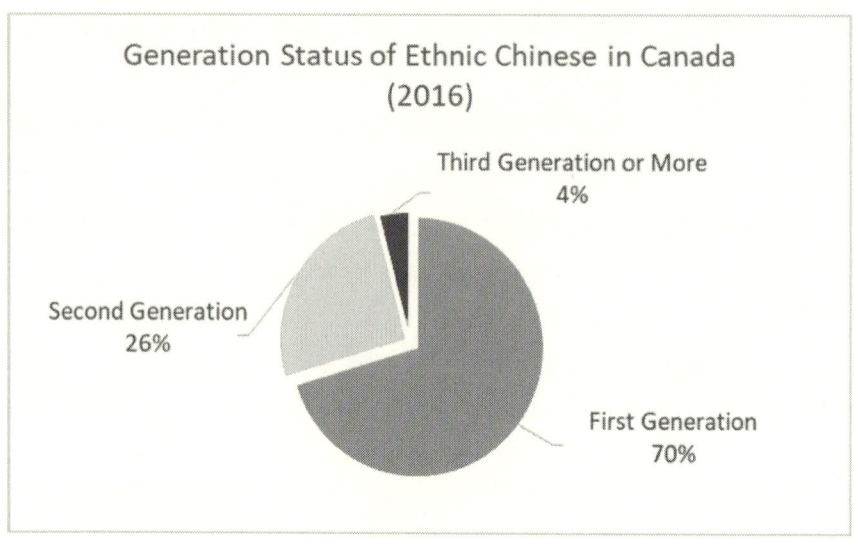

Generation Status of Ethnic Chinese in Canada (2016)

Third Generation or More 4%

Second Generation 26%

First Generation 70%

Source: *Statistics Canada*, 2016 Census of Population, Statistics Canada Catalogue no. 98-400-X2016187.

First generation Chinese immigrants who arrived in Canada at different periods from various source regions have completely different memories of their home towns at different historical moments when they left for Canada. Immigrants from mainland China are relatively newcomers to Canada, compared to their peers from Hong Kong, Macao and Taiwan. Shown in Table 6-3 blow, over 60 per cent of mainlanders came to Canada in the 21st century since China has been rising as a global economic powerhouse. The majority (70 percent) of immigrants born in Hong Kong arrived in the 1980s and 1990s, and Macao followed the same pattern. Over half of the immigrants born in Taiwan admitted to Canada in the 1990s for reasons discussed in Chapter 3.

Regardless of when they came to Canada or where they came from, ultimately there is a clear convergence of likelihood of being a Canadian in terms of the percentage of Chinese immigrants who have gained the Canadian citizenship. In general, the rate of having gained Canadian citizenship varies by place of birth. For example, men and women from Hong Kong and Macao have the highest rates of 94 per cent and 93 per cent of obtaining Canadian citizenship, followed by 86 per cent of those from Taiwan and 65 per cent of mainlanders. However, looking over a longer period of time, the rate of each cohort increases to a similar level as high as close to 95 per cent or higher 15 years after arrival in Canada.

Table 6-3: Chinese Immigrants in Canada by Year of Arrival and Place of Birth (2016)

Place of Birth	Total Immigrants	Before 1981	1981 to 1990	1991 to 2000	2001 to 2010	2011 to 2016
China	649,260	9%	8%	23%	41%	20%
Hong Kong	208,940	23%	27%	43%	5%	2%
Macao	5,750	26%	26%	39%	7%	3%
Taiwan	63,770	8%	11%	49%	26%	7%
Total	927,720	12%	12%	29%	31%	15%
	Percentage having gained Canadian citizenship	Before 1981	1981 to 1990	1991 to 2000	2001 to 2010	2011 to 2016
China	65%	98%	97%	94%	65%	6%
Hong Kong	94%	98%	97%	95%	88%	16%
Macao	93%	98%	97%	94%	91%	10%
Taiwan	86%	97%	96%	93%	84%	18%
Total	73%	98%	97%	94%	67%	6%

Source: *Statistics Canada*-2016 Census. Catalogue Number 98-400-X2016185.

People of Chinese ethnic origin have their roots in all five continents. Despite the fact that nearly 30 per cent of the ethnic Chinese population were born in Canada, Chinese immigrants who now call Canada home may have totally different memories of their country/region of birth. According to the 2011 census , as many as 95.7 per cent of them came directly from Asia, and the rest from the Americas (2.7 per cent), Europe (0.5 per cent), Africa (0.9 per cent), Oceania and other places (0.2 per cent). Among those from Asia, most were from mainland China (54 per cent), Hong Kong (20 per cent), Viet Nam (6 per cent), Taiwan (5 per cent) and the Philippines (4 per cent) (See table below). These statistical facts show that "Get out and go back to China!" which is the most frequent racist insult to ethnic Chinese (sometimes targeting the entire Asian community) is false, prejudiced, and ignorant.

Table 6-4: Origins of Ethnic Chinese in Canada (2011)

	Total	Percentage (%)
Population with Chinese Ethnic Origin	1,487,585	100.0
Non-immigrants (born in Canada)	434,345	29.2
Immigrants	1,004,485	67.5
Non-permanent residents	48,755	3.3
Chinese Immigrants Admitted to Canada by Place of Birth	1,004,485	100.0
China	538,885	53.6
Hong Kong Special Administrative Region	201,910	20.1
Viet Nam	59,335	5.9
Taiwan	48,230	4.8
Philippines	43,710	4.4
India	5,715	0.6
Japan	1,115	0.1
South Korea	490	0.05
Pakistan	470	0.05
Other places in Asia	61,085	6.1
Americas	27,585	2.7
Africa	8,695	0.9
Europe	4,915	0.5
Oceania and others	2,325	0.2

Source: *Statistics Canada*-2011 National Household Survey. Catalogue Number 99-010-X2011036.

Mandarin Speakers surpass Cantonese speakers. People of Chinese ethnic origin speak dozens of different Chinese dialects as their mother tongues, which is a direct reflection of changing sources of immigration to Canada. However, the Cantonese speaking group has always been the dominant group in terms of the population. On June 22, 2006, on behalf of all Canadians and the Government of Canada, Mr. Stephen Harper, then Prime Minister of Canada, offered a full apology to Chinese Canadians for the "head tax" and expressed the deepest sorrow for the subsequent exclusion of Chinese immigrants. When Mr. Harper spoke "Canada apologizes" in Cantonese, he received a 40-second round of applause by all MPs in Parliament. This also fully illustrates the importance of Cantonese in Chinese Canadian history—not only were most head tax victims originally from Cantonese speaking regions in China, but also native Cantonese speakers have been the largest group of Chinese speakers for a long time. It is no wonder that when the former Mayor of Vancouver, Sam Sullivan and the current Mayor Gregor Robertson, who both can speak Cantonese, preface their opening remarks to Chinese community rallies with a "Hello everyone!" in Cantonese, and often win warm applause from their audiences.

Nevertheless, there has been a gradual but notable change, in that Mandarin speakers (51 per cent) have surpassed Cantonese speakers (44 per cent) at the national level for the first time in Canadian history. There is even a slight difference between Canadian provinces: Mandarin speakers become the largest group among those whose mother tongue is one of the Chinese dialects, as reported in the 2016 census shown in the table below.

Table 6-5: Mother Tongue as Chinese Languages in Canada in 2016

Mother Tongue		Canada	BC	ON	QC	AB
Chinese-speaking population		913,365	297,675	441,615	76,490	120,375
Of which:	Mandarin	50.7%	49.2%	49.9%	57.1%	42.1%
	Cantonese	43.8%	46.0%	45.0%	31.9%	49.1%
	Min Nan (Chaochow; Teochow;					
	Fukien; Taiwanese)	1.5%	1.6%	1.3%	4.2%	2.5%
	Hakka	0.4%	0.2%	0.6%	0.6%	0.8%
	Wu (Shanghainese)	0.8%	0.9%	0.8%	1.4%	0.5%
	Min Dong	0.0%	0.0%	0.1%	0.0%	0.1%
	Other Chinese languages	2.6%	2.0%	2.2%	4.7%	4.8%

Source: *Statistics Canada*. 2017. Census Profile. 2016 Census. Statistics Canada Catalogue no. 98-316-X2016001. Ottawa. Released September 13, 2017.

People of Chinese ethnic origin prefer studying in business and sciences. Canada shows the highest level of tertiary education attainment among OECD countries. Nearly two-thirds of Canadians have received some postsecondary education as reported by the 2011 census. Ethnic Chinese attain similar level of schooling compared to the rest of the Canadian population (P>0.05), although Chinese families seem more likely to encourage their children to attend postsecondary education. It is also interesting to note that the majority of both ethnic Chinese and non-Chinese received their postsecondary in Canada (P>0.05). Still, it is noticeable that 42 per cent of ethnic Chinese attended schools outside of Canada for their postsecondary education, which presents a severe challenge for foreign credential recognition in Canada, as was discussed in Chapter 4.

In terms of major field of study, "business, management and public administration," "architecture, engineering, and related technologies," and "health and related fields" are the top three choices in postsecondary education for all Canadians, including ethnic Chinese. However, there are significant differences in the selection of field of study in postsecondary education between ethnic Chinese and the non-Chinese population (P<0.01). Ethnic Chinese prefer studying business and science related subjects and are less likely to study in programs that require more official language skills. Specifically, they are more visible in programs of "business, management and public administration," "mathematics, computer and information sciences," and "physical and life sciences and technologies". Compared to non-Chinese groups, ethnic Chinese are less likely to study in "health and related fields," "education," "personal, protective and transportation services," and "agriculture, natural resources and conservation" (see Table below).

Table 6-6: Education Attainment of Ethnic Chinese vs. Non-Ethnic Chinese in Canada in 2011

	Ethnic Chinese	Non-ethnic Chinese
Population aged 25 to 64 years by highest certificate, diploma or degree	853,795	17,530,125
Of which: No certificate, diploma or degree	11%	13%
High school diploma or equivalent	18%	23%
Postsecondary certificate, diploma or degree	70%	64%

P Value > 0.05

	Ethnic Chinese	Non-ethnic Chinese
Population aged 15 years and over with postsecondary education by location of study	718,765	14,086,425
Of which: Inside Canada	58%	85%
Outside Canada	42%	15%

P Value > 0.05

	Ethnic Chinese	Non-ethnic Chinese
Population aged 15 years and over with postsecondary education by major field of study	718,755	14,086,430
Of which: Business, management and public administration	26.9%	21.3%
Architecture, engineering, and related technologies	20.5%	21.6%
Health and related fields	10.9%	14.1%
Social and behavioural sciences and law	9.7%	10.1%
Mathematics, computer and information sciences	8.8%	3.8%
Physical and life sciences and technologies	6.7%	3.6%
Humanities	5.2%	5.6%
Education	3.9%	7.7%
Visual and performing arts, and communications technologies	3.6%	3.7%
Personal, protective and transportation services	2.7%	6.3%
Agriculture, natural resources and conservation	1.1%	2.3%
Other fields of study	0.0%	0.0%

P Value < 0.01

Source: *Statistics Canada*-2011 National Household Survey. Catalogue Number 99-010-X2011036.

People of Chinese ethnic origin have experienced upward occupational mobility. After working hard as labourers in gold and other mines and as CP railway builders, ethnic Chinese in Canada were working in three most popular and visible jobs that were often referred to by Chinese media as "Three Knives," i.e., kitchen knife (restaurants), tailor scissors (tailor stores), and razor blades (barbershops). Nowadays, new generations of ethnic Chinese and new Chinese immigrants have received a much better education and are more likely to work in professional fields that have been classified symbolically by Chinese media as "Six Masters," i.e., lawyer, engineer, medical doctor, accountant, technician and professor/teacher (China News, 2007).

Perhaps related to their training background and the nature of Canada's service-oriented economy, ethnic Chinese work in "sales and service" and "business, finance and administration" as the top two occupations in the labour market, similar to everyone else in the Canadian labour force. "Natural and applied sciences and related" becomes the third most important occupation for ethnic Chinese workers, while "trades, transport and equipment operators and related" becomes the third most important occupation for non-Chinese Canadian workers. Although it is statistically insignificant ($P>0.05$), in certain occupations, the difference between ethnic Chinese workers and average Canadian workers is notable by a big margin. Taking the percentage of Canadians working in a particular occupation as 1, ethnic Chinese workers are over-represented in "natural and applied sciences and related" occupations (difference=2.0), and under-represented in "trades, transport and equipment operators and related" (difference=0.4) and "natural resources, agriculture and related" (difference=0.2) occupations (see Table 6-7 below).

Ethnic Chinese workers are also more active in industries such as "finance and insurance" (difference=1.8), "professional, scientific and technical services" (difference=1.6) and "accommodation and food services" (difference=1.6), but less so in "agriculture, forestry, fishing and hunting" (difference=0.2), "construction" (difference=0.4), and "mining, quarrying, and oil and gas extraction" (difference=0.5).

Table 6-7: Occupations and Industries of Ethnic Chinese vs. All Canadians in 2011

	Ethnic Chinese	All Canadians	Difference (Canadian=1)
Labour force Population aged 15 years and over by occupation	773,195	17,990,080	
Sales and service	25.1	22.6	1.1
Business, finance and administration	18.9	16.1	1.2
Natural and applied sciences and related	13.5	6.9	2.0
Management	10.2	10.9	0.9
Education, law and social, community and gov. services	8.3	11.5	0.7
Trades, transport and equipment operators and related	6.0	14.1	0.4
Health	5.9	6.2	1.0
Manufacturing and utilities	5.5	4.5	1.2
Art, culture, recreation and sport	2.8	2.8	1.0
Natural resources, agriculture and related	0.5	2.2	0.2
Occupation - not applicable	3.2	2.2	1.4

P Value > 0.05

By industry

Professional, scientific and technical services	11.2	6.9	1.6
Retail trade	10.9	11.3	1.0
Accommodation and food services	10.2	6.3	1.6
Manufacturing	10.1	9.0	1.1
Health care and social assistance	8.7	10.8	0.8
Finance and insurance	7.8	4.3	1.8
Educational services	5.9	7.2	0.8
Wholesale trade	5.5	4.1	1.3
Public administration	4.5	7.0	0.6
Information and cultural industries	3.2	2.3	1.4
Transportation and warehousing	3.0	4.6	0.6
Administrative and support, waste management and remediation services	3.0	4.0	0.7
Construction	2.9	6.8	0.4
Real estate and rental and leasing	2.4	1.8	1.4
Arts, entertainment and recreation	1.6	2.0	0.8
Mining, quarrying, and oil and gas extraction	0.7	1.5	0.5
Utilities	0.6	0.8	0.8
Agriculture, forestry, fishing and hunting	0.5	2.4	0.2
Management of companies and enterprises	0.1	0.1	1.3
Other services (except public administration)	3.9	4.5	0.9
Industry - not applicable	3.2	2.2	1.4

P Value > 0.05

Source: *Statistics Canada-*2011 National Household Survey. Catalogue Number 99-010-X2011036.

People of Chinese ethnic origin are not necessarily millionaires. Ethnic Chinese often are stereotyped and exaggerated by some as rich people with boxes full of cash lining up to buy real estate properties, luxury goods, expensive services, etc. This might be true for a small group of high net worth individuals who immigrated to Canada with a big fortune that they accumulated through the fast economic growth in China in recent decades. It may also happen due to the short-term presence of Chinese tourists who have a shopping target built into their Canadian itinerary. However, this is only a small portion of Chinese Canadians. Ethnic Chinese in Canada have a median income that is below that of most visible minority groups (shown Table 6-7 below).

The 2016 census reports that there is significant income inequality in Canada between visible minorities and non-visible minorities, and between minority groups themselves. Non-visible minorities have the highest median income of $36,538 in 2016, while the total visible minority population earns 30 percent less with a median income of $25,514. Among all visible minority groups, the median income of ethnic Chinese was $22,973, which is only 63 per cent of what non-visible minority groups earned in 2016, and lower than that of most visible minority groups, except for Arabic, West Asian and Korean groups.

The same income inequality appears between these groups across the generations. There are some interesting observations to be made. Firstly, Pilipino Canadians have the highest median income among all visible minority groups. This is likely attributed to the outstanding performance of its first-generation immigrants who earn only 2 percent less than non-visible minority groups, the smallest gap between a visible minority group and non-visible minority group. Secondly, Japanese and Korean Canadians show the most significant catch-up progress over the generations. Their median income gaps with non-visible minority people narrows from first generation to third generation, especially the third generation Japanese Canadian have a median earning that is no less than 21 per cent higher than those of non-visible minority Canadians. Thirdly, second-generation Chinese have the smallest gap, but still earn nearly 20 percent less than non-visible minority Canadians.

Table 6-8: Median Income Comparison by Visible Minority Status and Generation: 2016

Visible Minority Status	Median Income ($)	Difference (Not a visible minority = 100)			
		Total Population	First generation	Second generation	Third generation or more
Not a visible minority	36,538	100	100	100	100
Total Visible Minority	25,514	70	76	55	74
Filipino	32,508	89	98	54	50
Japanese	32,200	88	71	92	121
Black	27,263	75	87	49	65
Latin American	26,843	73	82	48	55
South Asian	25,280	69	76	53	62
Southeast Asian	25,048	69	79	44	64
Chinese	**22,973**	**63**	**64**	**81**	**76**
Arab	20,803	57	62	44	68
West Asian	19,107	52	57	32	58
Korean	18,795	51	54	70	90

Source: *Statistics Canada*-2016 Census. Catalogue Number 98-400-X2016210.

People of Chinese ethnic origin are mainly Christian and Buddhist. In such a diverse country as Canada, where freedom of worship, equality of religions and mutual respect are well-regarded, Chinese Canadians have the full right to choose their own faith and can find an institution for their spiritual home. The 2011 census found Canada is primarily a Christian country in terms of population percentage. As shown in Table 6-9 below, overwhelmingly two-thirds of Canadians are Christians, followed by Muslim (3.2 percent) and Hindu (1.5 percent). Despite the fact that 59 percent of ethnic Chinese have no religious affiliation, the largest group of the Chinese population with a religious affiliation is the Christians, representing 28 percent of the total Chinese Canadian population, followed by 12 percent as Buddhists.

Table 6-9: Religions of Ethnic Chinese vs. Non-Ethnic Chinese in Canada in 2011

	Ethnic Chinese	Non-ethnic Chinese	Total Canadians
Population by selected religions	1,487,580	31,364,745	32,852,325
Of which: Christian	28.44%	69.12%	67.28%
Buddhist	11.66%	0.62%	1.12%
Muslim	0.19%	3.35%	3.21%
Jewish	0.05%	1.05%	1.00%
Hindu	0.05%	1.59%	1.52%
Sikh	0.02%	1.45%	1.38%
Traditional (Aboriginal) Spirituality	0.01%	0.21%	0.20%
Other religions	0.33%	0.40%	0.40%
No religious affiliation	59.25%	22.22%	23.90%

Source: *Statistics Canada*-2011 National Household Survey. Catalogue Number 99-010-X2011036.

This demographic snapshot has clearly shown that the portrait of Chinese in Canada today is vastly different than it was over much of the last two centuries when Chinese immigrants were stereotyped as railway coolies, laundrymen and waiters. Hollywood movies exaggerated the stereotype about opium dens, celestials in pig-tails with knives hidden up their silk sleeves, slant-eyed beauties with bound feet and ancient love potions (Lee, 1984). What the Chinese in Canada look like today is as diverse as Canada's multicultural society as a whole. General Victor Odlum (October 21, 1880-April 4, 1971) was a Canadian journalist, soldier, businessman, politician and diplomat. When he served as Canada's Ambassador (Envoy Extraordinary and Minister Plenipotentiary) to China (1942 to 1946), he once called for the day when Chinese Canadians would "not be distinguished from other Canadians." (Lee, 1984) That wish remains as relevant today as it was during General Odlum's lifetime.

Solidarity: Multiple Ties Hold Chinese Together

"A heap of loose sand" was often used by some to describe the differences and disunity among the Chinese. In fact, many overseas Chinese are well organized through various types of organizations, associations and groups as means to unify, connect and support each other. Professor Minghuan Li, one of the world-renowned scholars on the subject of overseas Chinese, described the emergence of organizations in Chinese communities in Europe and Southeast Asia as follows:

A saying in Chinese that "Blood is thicker than water" is a traditional concept that Chinese people always believe, especially for cross-border immigrants living in other countries. Immigrants with family connections or blood relatives often feel a natural intimacy between each other, and therefore it is easier to get together in groups, and then consciously or unconsciously use their blood ties to protect and fight for their legitimate rights and interests. In a modern society, this natural emotion and ties tend to develop or manifest themselves as a group for the common interests of the group. (Li M. , 2002)

Li further emphases in her book that many objectively existing, natural and special ties provide a basis for overseas Chinese to keep close connections, and the formation of associations is the practice of consciously or unconsciously trying to institutionalize these ties. Li's book illustrates 10 types of Chinese community organizations in Europe.

An online survey of Chinese organizations in Canada finds many similarities to those ties existing in this country. As of the end of 2016, we have identified over 1,000 Chinese community organizations across Canada that have a presence or records on the website. Among these organizations, over two thirds are religious groups or organizations, and nearly 90 per cent of them are located in Ontario, British Columbia and Alberta.

The other one third, non-religious organizations, include various types of groups, predominantly established in Toronto, Vancouver, Calgary, Montreal and Victoria. Some national organizations have branches in several cities. Chinese community organizations have existed in Canada for over a century. The earliest ones were established in the time of Canada's early development in the 19th century; however, the majority mushroomed in the post-1980 period, accounting for two thirds of all Chinese organizations. This emerging trend corresponds to the growing number of immigrants coming to Canada, starting from Hong Kong and followed by those from Taiwan and mainland China.

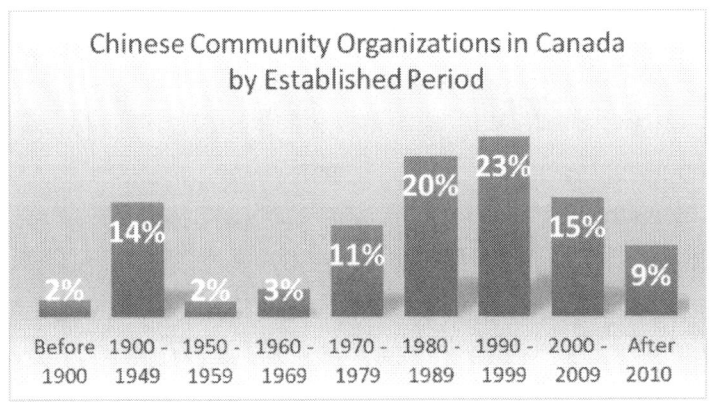

Chinese Community Organizations in Canada by Established Period

Before 1900: 2%
1900 - 1949: 14%
1950 - 1959: 2%
1960 - 1969: 3%
1970 - 1979: 11%
1980 - 1989: 20%
1990 - 1999: 23%
2000 - 2009: 15%
After 2010: 9%

Source: The authors' calculation based on an online survey as of December 2016, N=375.

Interestingly, Chinese communities in Canada are organized in complex ways connected through many different ties, such as family ties, alumni ties, business ties, etc. Our online survey classifies these ties into 14 categories and finds that hometown associations and alumni groups are the most popular types of organization among Chinese in Canada as shown in the chart below.

TYPES OF CHINESE ORGANIZATION IN CANADA

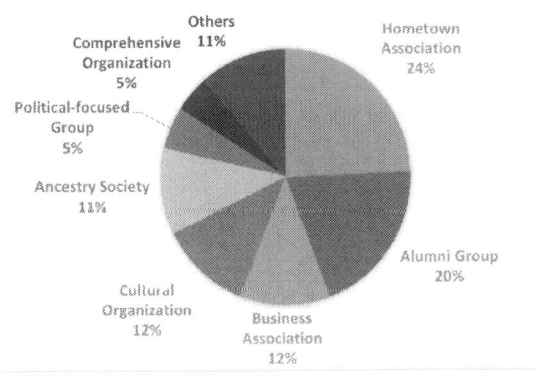

Others 11%
Comprehensive Organization 5%
Political-focused Group 5%
Ancestry Society 11%
Cultural Organization 12%
Business Association 12%
Alumni Group 20%
Hometown Association 24%

Source: The authors' calculation based on an online survey as of December 2016, N=375.

Hometown Associations—Geo-kinship Ties. In the study of international migration, "Chain Migration" is a very common phenomenon. After an immigrant has gained a foothold in a foreign country, he immediately tries to bring his relatives and friends over from the same hometown. As a result, the snowball effect gains greater and greater momentum in the chain migration process.

Chain migration has been a long tradition for most overseas Chinese assisting their families, relatives and friends from the hometown to migrate to another country. It also happened in early days when pioneer Chinese immigrants came to Canada for the "Gold Rush" and building the Pacific railway. These early arrivers found themselves lonely in a foreign land with foreign co-workers, and they were anxious to help their fellows from their hometown to come over and work together in Canada. On the other hand, those who were capable of bringing their family members and relatives from their impoverished home region to countries with better economic opportunities, were naturally regarded as heroes in their hometown and were widely respected by their loved ones. This kind of geo-kinship tie became a strong link to keep the chain migration pattern repeating from one family to another, from one village to another, and from one generation to another.

The snowball effect of Chinese chain migration objectively became an excuse for the emergence of anti-Chinese immigration sentiments when the "Gold Rush" was over and the Canadian Pacific Railway construction was finished, and they ultimately became the target of the "head tax" and the Chinese Exclusion Act. After World War II, Canada abolished the Chinese Exclusion Act and the immigration policy also gave a green light to relatives on humanitarian grounds, a move that coincided with the tradition of Chinese immigration. The number of Chinese immigrants started to grow again.

Under the influence of such a history and background of Chinese immigration, various hometown associations were among the earliest overseas Chinese organizations that have emerged and are still undergoing continuous development to this day. At present, hometown associations established across various parts of Canada are ubiquitous, cohesive and relatively active.

Nevertheless, the geo-kinship links to a hometown may have different implications. For many, a hometown is referred to as a village or town where the individual and family have roots. Others may consider the place their hometown where they have lived or worked for most of their life. In some cases, a hometown refers to the place of origin before they moved to Canada, including not only mainland China, Hong Kong and Taiwan, but also many other parts of the world, especially Southeast Asian countries as shown in Chapter 3. Therefore, a hometown association usually includes members who share one of the above three definitions, and the common geo-kinship tie becomes the unique group identity that all the members feel proud of. In early times, the hometown associations in Canada were those few from China's Guangdong province, but nowadays, the hometown associations consist of almost all major cities or provinces from the countries or regions they come from.

There is an interesting trend of closer inter-regional connection and more frequent interaction between associations from the same hometown in different locations in Canada and other countries. For example, with the support of 10 Teochew-related associations across this country, the Canada Teochew Business Association hosted the 18th Convention of Teochew International Federation at the Vancouver Convention Centre from August 19 to 21, 2015. The event attracted members from over 200 Teochew associations from over 100 countries or regions around the world, bringing over 3000 delegates to Vancouver for the three-day convention. The principle of the Convention of Teochew International Federation is to disseminate Teochew culture, unite people of Teochew descent around the world, and promote collaboration in areas of trade, culture and social welfare between communities and internationally. The 18th Convention of the Teochew International Federation was the first time the event was held in Canada and became a rare and excellent opportunity for Canadian business executives and entrepreneurs to network and work together to build relationships with their counterparts from around the world.

In fact, as Li (2002) pointed out, what we call geo-kinship is nothing more than a common dialect and culture, similar customs and practices, or shared identity and mutual trust that come with similar personal experiences in times of dramatic political and economic changes. Therefore, the ancient geo-kinship ties originating in China are constantly being transplanted, copied, innovated and institutionalized through established organizations and associations, thus becoming the collective social resources for overseas Chinese to unite and support each other.

Family Society—Ancestral Ties. A family society looks similar to the hometown association, but the former emphasises ancestral ties, i.e., blood and marital relationships. A nuclear family becomes the core of the ancestral tie which consists of someone's spouse and children. An extended family relationship often includes other family members and relatives such as parents and grandparents, children and grandchildren, brothers and sisters, mothers-in-law and fathers-in-law, brothers-in-law and sisters-in-law, daughters-in-law and sons-in-law, aunts, uncles, nephews, nieces and cousins, etc. Adopted, half, and step members are also included in such an extended family structure.

A significant identity of family relationship is the family's surname. Therefore, a family society is usually named after the family's surname. In other words, members of the family society normally belong to the same extended family. There is a large number of population in Canada who have family names related to big surname families and clans from major overseas Chinese hometowns, such as Guangdong and Fujian in mainland China and large families from Hong Kong, Macao and Taiwan. A survey of telephone directories across Canada finds that the top 20 common surnames include four Chinese family names, of which Li ranks the first, well above the second ranked Smith. The other Chinese names include Lam as the third, Lee as the eighth, and Chan as the nineteenth (Sieben, 2013).

In fact, Li and Lee may be a romanized spelling of such common Chinese surnames as " 李 ", " 黎 " or " 厉 " in Chinese characters, but it is more likely that " 李 " is the most common family name among them. In Canada, there is not only a large number of descendants of Li or Lee families, but also these individuals have made remarkable achievements. For example, Philip S. Lee was the first Chinese to serve as Lieutenant Governor of Manitoba. He received the Order of Canada in 1999 and The Queen's Golden Jubilee Medal in 2002. Independent film director Luo Li, T&T Supermarket founders Cindy Lee and Jack Lee, and business tycoon Victor Li are just some examples of outstanding individuals in the Li/Lee families.

After Canada opened its doors to Chinese for family reunification, all these family and clan relationships further expanded. The tradition of "blood is thicker than water" not only maintained a strong affinity and support among the members of the family societies or clan associations, but also interacted closely with their ancestral homeland. Returning to the ancestral home to pay homage to ancestors is an indispensable activity for many family societies. Every year, many families return to their hometowns to visit and honor their ancestors. In the same vein, from time to time senior family members, official or non-official organizations from their ancestral homeland come to visit their relatives in Canada.

Alumni Groups—Campus Ties. Alumni groups are associations or organizations whose members are linked by alma mater ties. This relationship emerges as Chinese immigrants become more highly educated. In contrast to old generations of immigrants dominated by low skilled laborers and family reunification, Chinese immigrants have been much more highly educated in recent decades. One of the basic requirements of immigration to Canada is to have a college degree or higher, especially after the independent skilled immigrant and other economic categories of immigrants are open to Chinese applicants. At the same time, the number of Chinese students studying in Canada has also increased considerably.

As a result, Chinese alumni organizations in Canada have mushroomed in the past two decades and become the second most popular type of Chinese organization in Canada, after the hometown associations. Generally, there are three types of alumni groups according to the location of the alma mater. The first group is organized by graduates of Chinese universities or schools. Nearly all large or small Chinese universities have their alumni organizations or their branches in Canada, and even some popular high schools and elementary schools have formed alumni groups thanks to the power of social media tools such as WeChat. The second type is formed by graduates of universities or schools in Canada, and the third is established by those graduated from universities or schools in U.S.A. or other international destinations. Unlike a unique membership identity of hometown or family associations, membership in alumni groups could be multiple depending on the number of schools an individual has attended.

The members of an alumni group share similar background and interest. The common experience and memories from the same school become an extremely important form of social capital that Chinese immigrants can trust and rely on after moving to a new homeland. It is much easier to keep members united and connected for purposes of social, cultural, business and community activities.

Chambers of Commerce—Business Ties. Chambers of commerce or industrial associations are business groups formed as a result of common or complementary commercial interests of their members. They are often organized by industry sector or business type. Many of them like to use names that include Canada and China. Some prefer to add a name of province or city in Canada to identify their regional location. It is also common to include a name of the hometown back in China that most of the members come from. The early industrial associations in Canada sought to promote commercial benefits for retail and sales in local regional markets. Gradually they became active in promoting cross-border trade and investment, especially between Canada and China, when China emerged as a world powerhouse of manufacturing and trade.

There is an impressive number of ethnic Chinese business groups in Canada, covering a wide range of industries and regions. They maintain very close business and commercial ties with their counterparts in their places of origin or major markets in the world often described as the "Bamboo Network" which plays significant roles as an effective platform to link and promote business transactions in different markets. Various types of Chinese chambers of commerce have made remarkable achievements in actively promoting trade and investments between Canada and China and other markets where ethnic Chinese populations are concentrated. It is easy to see that countless Chinese-Canadian individuals and associations in Canada have played and are playing significant roles in promoting Canada's commercial interests on the global stage through the "Bamboo Network" effect. A good example is perhaps the 4th World Chinese Entrepreneurs Convention which took place in Vancouver in 1997.

Initiated in 1991 in Singapore, the World Chinese Entrepreneurs Convention (WCEC) aims to draw together Chinese entrepreneurs and other interested parties from all over the world to network with each other. WCEC has become the largest event for the global Chinese business community, held once every two years, rotating to selected cities. The second WCEC was held in 1993 in Hong Kong, followed by the third one in 1995 in Bangkok. Hosted by Chinese Entrepreneurs Society of Canada (CESC), the 4th WCEC was held from 25 to 28 August 1997 in Vancouver. Under the theme "Telecommunications & Information Technology—Its Impact on the Global Marketplace", the Convention brought together nearly 1,400 Chinese entrepreneurs from 30 countries or regions.

Since its launch in 1991, the WCEC has held 14 conventions rotating in different cities in the Asia Pacific region. It is remarkable that Vancouver has been the only city in North America to host the WCEC. It would have been impossible to bring it to Vancouver without the extraordinary efforts and contributions by the CESE and its members. For the purpose of receiving the bid in Vancouver for the 1997 WCEC, Mr. Richard Wong, founding president of the CESC, organized and successfully led the bid team in May 1995 to win the right to host the 4th WCEC. During the process, Mr. Wong and the bid team were strongly backed by both Chinese and mainstream business associations, the community service associations, and many business leaders, those from three levels of Canadian government to business corporates and communities, including former lieutenant governor of B.C., Dr. David Lam and a businessman, financier, and philanthropist, Dr. Milton Wong.

When the 4th WCEC opened in Vancouver in 1997, Mr. Raymond Chan, then Canada's Secretary of State for Asia-Pacific and Convention Honorary Chairman gave a welcoming address. Mr. Jean Chretien, then Prime Minister of Canada delivered a keynote speech on the topic of "Canada and Chinese Entrepreneurs" to fully affirm the outstanding contributions made by the majority of Chinese businesspersons to the Canadian economy. Dr. David Lam, former lieutenant governor of B.C. and Convention Hon. Chairman gave a talk on the topic of "The Overseas Chinese Way: Adopting, Adapting, and Improving," which still inspires and encourages many recent Chinese immigrants to participate in and contribute to Canadian society.

The 4th WCEC was widely regarded as such a successful event that it not only attracted a large number of overseas Chinese entrepreneurs to Vancouver with benefits for tourism, investments, development of small- to mid-sized businesses, expansion of overseas markets and opportunities, increase in job opportunities and increase in the status of Chinese entrepreneurs, it also developed synergies between Chinese entrepreneurs and local businesspeople as they worked together on this event. It further united Vancouver and the entire body of Canada's Chinese entrepreneurs, business and community associations to become a powerful force. This force can help contribute to Canada's Chinese business people and those of other nationalities around the world.

Professional Organizations—Career Ties. Canada's skilled immigrant category has attracted a large number of highly educated and highly-skilled Chinese professionals from China, Hong Kong, Taiwan and other regions. At the same time, there is a growing group of Canadian-trained Chinese professionals thanks to the increasing number of Chinese students in Canada and Chinese families always encouraging their children to study subjects leading to a professional career, such as doctor, engineer, accountant, lawyer, professor, etc. As discussed in Chapter 3 of this book, Chinese professionals have faced many problems in employment and career development. Therefore, professional organizations have emerged as a separate group adding new faces and voices to traditional Chinese communities.

These professional associations are organized according to specific practitioners, such as acupuncturists, IT professionals, Chinese writers, etc. Some associations are structured for general professional purposes. A common objective of professional organizations is to help their members to address common problems in their career development.

The Chinese Professionals Association of Canada (CPAC) is one such example. According to its website, it was founded in 1992 as a registered not-for-profit organization, headquartered in Toronto. Its mandate is to assist internationally trained professionals in gaining recognition, cultural integration, career advancement, civic engagement in Canada and expanded international opportunity through quality service and advocacy. As a service provider, CAPC has over 30,000 members with multicultural backgrounds. It has advocated for and served the internationally trained professional community for over two decades, especially helping them obtain licences, find employment, advance careers, integrate into society and develop leadership skills.

In line with its mandate, the CAPC provides services in areas of career development, member's benefits, and international cooperation. CAPC also includes the CPAC Foundation which was founded in 1999 as a registered Canadian charity that raises funds in support of CPAC's mission within the immigrant community as well as the Foundation's own education related initiatives including activities that provide educational information to parents and students. It also provides scholarships and bursaries to secondary and post-secondary students who have demonstrated social responsibility as well as determination to pursue academic excellence. Since 2000, the CPAC Foundation has given out 216 scholarships and bursaries worth a total value of 264,000 dollars. It has also built two schools in poverty and disaster stricken areas in China.

Political Organizations—Political Ties. A political organization is obviously created in pursuit of certain political interests and goals that are shared by its members. This type of organization has a long history among Chinese in Canada.

For a long time, these Chinese Canadian political organizations have often been tied to the politics of their ancestral home. As early as the beginning of the 20th century, the clash between "royalists" and "revolutionists" was the main theme of the political struggle among Chinese in Canada, taking place mainly in Chinatowns. At that time, the main battlefield of the Chinese Revolution of 1911 was in China. However, Chinese in Canada were deeply divided with one group supporting the royalist party and the other supporting the revolutionary party. The two sides had totally different ideologies and fought each other fiercely. Before the Chinese Revolution of 1911, both the headquarters of the Chinese Reform Association representing the royalists, and the Chinese Freemasons in Canada supporting revolutionists led by Dr. Sun Yat-sen, were located on the same block in Vancouver's Chinatown. The confrontation between "royalists" and "revolutionists" also appeared in the Chinatowns of Toronto and other cities. Because the patriotic overseas Chinese supported the Revolution of 1911 led by Dr. Sun Yat-sen in various ways, Dr. Sun once gave high praise for the "overseas Chinese as the mother of the revolution". Chinese communities in Canada not only were among the most active overseas Chinese groups to support the Revolution of 1911, they also supported China without hesitation in the War of Resistance against the Japanese invasion.

After the founding of the People's Republic of China in 1949, political tensions continued within Chinese communities as the Beijing based Communist Party and Taiwan's Kuomintang (Nationalist Party) opposed each other in overseas Chinese communities and sought sympathy and support of local overseas Chinese communities. Naturally, there were also "pro-Beijing" and "pro-Taiwan" campaigns among different Chinese organizations.

This confrontation was not eased until 1970 when Canada established formal diplomatic relations with the PRC, and the Canadian government recognized the Beijing government as the sole legitimate government of China. After that, the anti-Beijing pro-Taiwan groups were unable to organize large-scale public political activities in local overseas Chinese communities because their political positions were contrary to Canadian foreign policy. Eventually, their political activities were gradually weakened and replaced by a wide range of cultural and economic activities.

Nevertheless, the anti-Beijing sentiment has never gone away, and political clashes have been a normal occurrence in Chinese communities. After the June 4th incident in Beijing in 1989, some pro-democracy groups or branches of those organizations based in Hong Kong, Taiwan, or U.S.A. emerged in Chinese Canadian communities with the stated aim of "supporting the Chinese democratic movement." Often, a number of demonstrations, protests, speeches, parades and other activities have been organized every year commemorating June 4th. Entering the 21st century, some political-purposed groups emerged to support "Falungong," "Taiwan Independence," "Tibetan Independence," and "Xinjiang Independence". However, the "anti-independence and pro-unity" groups are often overwhelmed with the support of other non-political Chinese community organizations. There are also organizations established to support China's stance at times when tensions escalate between mainland China and other countries, such as the South China Sea territorial disputes, and the dispute over the island called Diaoyutai by China and the Senkaku by Japan. It should be no surprise to see Chinese Canadian protests and counter-protests between the two sides emerge from time to time on Parliament Hill or near city halls of various places where Chinese communities are concentrated.

Despite such organizations tied to the politics of their ancestral home, there are a growing number of Chinese Canadian political organizations that are focused on domestic politics and public policy issues in Canada. For example, the Chinese Canadian National Council (CCNC) , known in the Chinese-Canadian community as the Equal Rights Council, is one of the Chinese Canadian organizations that pressured the Government of Canada to apologize and redress the head tax that Chinese had to pay from 1885 to 1923. The Chinese Canadian Military Museum Society collects, preserves, documents, and commemorates the role of Chinese Canadian veterans in the service of Canada's military and its impact on Chinese Canadian history and civil rights.

Many Chinese Canadians are no longer satisfied being treated as a "model minority." They are no longer happy being respected economically and marginalized socially and politically in society. They even become angry whenever government policies contradict the fundamental values of Chinese culture and Chinese families. More and more Chinese Canadians have begun to realize that there is no other way to have their voice heard in Canada than by mastering and participating in the Canadian democratic political system. From demonstrations, protests and speeches to parades, they are "learning by doing" to protect the civil rights that many recent Chinese immigrants were not accustomed to back in their home country. Encouraging Chinese Canadian political participation and promoting full inclusion for Chinese Canadians in all aspects of Canadian society have become top priorities for many political organizations within communities. The newly established Chinese Canadian Society for Political Engagement and Action Chinese Canadians Together Foundation (ACCT Foundation) are typical examples of responses to the emerging desires of the community.

Cultural Organizations—Social Hobby Ties. Such organizations often consist of amateurs who share a common hobby, of which the most active are related to all types of sports, culture and entertainment. Canadians love nature and generally advocate outdoor sports activities. In summer people are keen on mountain hiking and biking, while in winter everyone is involved in various types of ice and snow activities. Chinese also retain their own favorite traditional sports, such as martial arts, table tennis, badminton, cycling and so on. As a result, many Chinese associations distinguish themselves through organizations like a "martial arts club," "dragon boat club," "table tennis hall," "karate association," "fishing club," "outdoor activities camp," "ski club" and so forth.

In terms of cultural and entertainment activities, all kinds of associations are organized for a variety of hobbies, such as "stamp and coin collection association," "photography club," "choir," "arts and culture association or foundation," "music club" and so on.

The cultural organizations are very popular among Chinese Canadians because they are connected purely by personal amateur interest. Members can participate voluntarily and enjoy the sports or cultural activities with the spirit of free will. While Chinese new immigrants admire Canada's beautiful natural scenery and clean environment, some also feel lonely being far away from other family members, relatives and friends and being unable to continue enjoying the social and cultural hobbies back in their home country. The rise of such cultural and amateur organizations undoubtedly infuses positive energy and new impetus into Chinese communities. It is not only conducive to personal, physical and mental health, but is also helpful in furthering interaction and solidarity among Chinese people.

New Immigration Service Organizations—Community Service Ties. In the late 20th century, many community service organizations were established in response to the growing number of Chinese new immigrants and the complexity of their source country or region and its composition. Community service organizations provide settlement services for new immigrants when they first arrive in Canada, as well as other ongoing assistance in establishing of their new lives in Canada.

S.U.C.C.E.S.S., for example, is recognized as one of British Columbia's largest social service providers . According to its official website, S.U.C.C.E.S.S. was founded in 1973 and incorporated in 1974 as a non-partisan and non-profit charitable organization. It was initially founded to assist new Canadians of Chinese descent to overcome language and cultural barriers. Today S.U.C.C.E.S.S. has evolved into a multicultural, multi-service agency assisting people with different heritage backgrounds at all stages of their Canadian experience. With over 20 locations, S.U.C.C.E.S.S. provides services to local communities in B.C. and via overseas offices in Beijing, Taipei and Seoul. The organization has over 400 professional staff and 2,000 volunteers who deliver a multitude of services in the areas of settlement, employment, health and housing as well as business, auto insurance, economic, community and social development skills. Its major funding comes from Canadian federal and provincial governments. The S.U.C.C.E.S.S. Foundation was incorporated in 2001 to raise funds essential for under-funded and non-funded programs. Annual major fundraising events include a Gala Dinner, Charity Golf Tournament and the "Walk with the Dragon," one of Vancouver's largest community-based fundraisers which draws over 12,000 individual and corporate participants.

Women, Senior and Youth Organizations—Demographic Ties. Despite many common issues faced by all Chinese Canadians, there are some special challenges for particular demographic groups, such as women, seniors and youths. Therefore, many organizations have been created to address the needs of these groups. Others are organized to provide caring assistance to people with special needs, such as cancer patients, people with mental illness and people with disabilities.

These organizations are either established as standalone societies to serve targeted members or are created as a sub-group or committee within a larger umbrella organization to serve members with particular needs. These organizations are aware of the need to respect Chinese culture and provide language assistance while protecting women's rights, senior care, and service for youth, etc. Their practices have proven the importance of addressing the double jeopardies of these demographic groups within Chinese Canadian communities in areas that existing non-Chinese structures may have overlooked.

Charitable Organizations—Empathetic Ties. Many Chinese community organizations have been created in the form of charitable institutions. They are regulated by Canadian law and government regulations and provide a wide range of services and support to their communities. Canadians are well-known for being open and warm-hearted, and so are Chinese Canadians. Every year, Canadians contribute both money and time to improve the well-being of their communities. In 2013, for example, over 24 million (or 82 percent) of Canadians, aged 15 years or older, made financial donations to a charitable or non-profit organization, with a total amount of 12.8 billion dollars donated, the average annual amount per donor being 531 dollars. Their financial donations help a variety of causes, such as ensuring that shelters, social service organizations and food banks are able to deliver their services, universities and hospitals are able to advance medical research, and ensuring that political, religious and environmental groups can have their voices heard. Volunteering also has a direct impact on the lives of Canadians, whether it is through teaching and supporting children, providing health care, or supporting by providing companionship. In 2013, 12.7 million Canadians (or 44 percent of the population) aged 15 and older, participated in some form of volunteer activity, contributing a total of 2 billion volunteer hours with an average of 154 hours per volunteer (Turcotte, 2015).

There are no statistics that can be broken down by ethnic background of donors or volunteers. However, Chinese people have been active and proud of donating to and volunteering for a variety of charitable champions organized by major Canadian charitable organizations, such as the Canadian

Red Cross B.C. Fires Emergency in 2017, the Alberta Fires Appeal in 2016, the Sichuan Earthquake relief in 2008, etc. It is also getting more common to see the names of Chinese companies, organizations or individuals on the list of contributors of Canadian community cultural and hospital fundraising events, such as the Vancouver Art Gallery's Claude Monet's Secret Garden exhibition, fundraising galas for the Vancouver General Hospital and UBC Hospital Foundation, the Richmond Hospital Foundation, etc.

A growing number of charitable organizations have been established by Chinese Canadians. For example, the Buddhist Compassion Relief Tzu Chi Foundation, Canada (also known "Tzu Chi Canada" for short) was founded in 1992, inspired by Dharma Master Cheng Yen to inaugurate Tzu Chi's charitable work in Canada. From the national head office in Vancouver, B.C., the Tzu Chi Foundation Canada's regular donors and volunteers have expanded their unconditional love and charitable contributions across the country through their missions of charity, medicine, education, culture, international relief, and environmental care. Currently, Tzu Chi Canada has over 40,000 regular donors and over 2,200 volunteers with 9 offices coast to coast including Vancouver, Richmond, Surrey, Calgary, Toronto, Mississauga, Richmond Hill, Montreal, and Ottawa .

Chinese in Canada—specifically, newer immigrants mostly from PRC— have in recent years also stepped up charity work with a number of Canadian causes, often led by business and community groups. In Vancouver, for example, within a two week period in 2016, two major fundraisers (the corporate-led CA Chinese Night on July 30, and a ceremony by the Canadian Alliance of Chinese Associations on Aug. 3) brought together several hundred people to raise 160,000 dollars for the Canadian Cancer Society, and to support Fort McMurray wildfire victims through the

Canadian Red Cross. On June 20, 2014, a newly established Foundation of Charitable Chinese Immigrants held its first fundraising gala which raised a total of 250,000 dollars. Most of the funds would be used to build a monument to honor historical contributions made by Chinese Canadians. Funds were also donated to the B.C. Women's Hospital, B.C. Children's Hospital, The Sam Sullivan Disability Foundation and the Canadian Cancer Society of B.C.

Religious Organizations—Faith Ties. According to Statistics Canada, religious organizations are groups promoting religious beliefs and administering religious services and rituals (such as churches, mosques, synagogues, temples, shrines, seminaries, monasteries and similar religious institutions) and related organizations and their auxiliaries. Canada has almost 31,000 Religious organizations, which account for 19% of the nation's 161,000 non-profit and voluntary organizations. Religious organizations are the second most common type of non-profit and voluntary organization in the country (*Statistics Canada*, 2005).

Chinese immigrant religious groups have flourished in Canada. Our online survey found that over 750 religious organizations of all sizes exist in Canada as of the end of 2016, which accounts for two thirds of all types of Chinese organizations in Canada. As observed by a practitioner, "In the past, Chinese restaurants opened wherever Chinese immigrants went. Nowadays, Chinese churches open wherever Chinese immigrants go."

The Chinese community religious organizations are predominantly Christian and Buddhist groups scattered throughout the urban and rural communities where Chinese Canadian population is concentrated. This trend has an obvious correlation to the share of Christians and Buddhists in the population as Table 6-9 reported.

All-inclusive Organization—Cooperation Ties. There is a separate group of Chinese organizations that are not based on one of the aforementioned single ties, but rather emphasize that they try to be all-inclusive for all targeted ethnic Chinese in a certain geographic region. They emphasize that Chinese Canadians from different places of origin, speaking different dialects, having different faiths or political views, should be united and enjoy equal treatment. In the constitution and activities of such associations, all Chinese Canadian organizations are regarded as their service targets, emphasizing mutual cooperation and support.

There are many good examples of such all-inclusive organizations. The Chinese Benevolent Association of Canada (CBAOC) was founded in 1889 and registered with the provincial government of British Columbia in 1916 under the Benevolent Society Act as a society and acted as the sole leader and representative of the Chinese communities across Canada. It is the first registered organization in Canada to provide free services and assistance to the Chinese Community. CBAOC assists new immigrants to settle and integrate, to improve their standard of living, to promote Chinese culture while exchanging and communicating with the mainstream and other ethnic groups .

The Chinese Benevolent Association of Vancouver is another Chinese Canadian organization headquartered in Vancouver. As of 2006 it has 2,000 members and serves as a federation of various Vancouver-based Chinese organizations. It was reported by the local media that the CBA was the most important organization operating in the Vancouver Chinatown in the first half of the 20th century, and "They were, for all intents and purposes, the government of Chinatown."

More recently, the Canadian Alliance of Chinese Associations (CACA), established in May 2008, is an amalgamation of over 100 B.C.-based Chinese organizations consisting mostly of mainland Chinese immigrants with a shared mission, which is to strengthen cooperation between China and Canada in economic development, trade, education, scientific research and technological development.

Cross-ethnic Alliances—Friendship Ties. In Canada, there are also cases where non-Chinese organizations accept Chinese for membership and vice versa. From time to time, Chinese and other ethnic groups have formed joint alliances based on shared interests and goals.

According to "Chinese Canadian Stories," as early as 1916, Chinese labourers in the lumber industry organized themselves into a union known as the Chinese Labour Association and used strikes as a means to bargain for treatment similar to that of white workers. White labourers, who once led the anti-Chinese movement, began to recognize the power of Chinese unions. Some white worker unions discussed Chinese membership and saw advantages to forming an alliance with Chinese labourers. In the 1920s, the Chinese Workers' Protective Association, a left-wing organization, had some fraternal affiliations with the Communist Party of Canada. In March 1935, the Chinese Workers' Protective Association and the Unemployed Workers Association held a joint meeting and called for equal treatment in the employment and welfare of Chinese workers.

On the business side, the Canada China Business Council (CCBC), is a bilateral non-profit organization with six offices in Canada and China. Founded in 1978, the CCBC has been the leading voice for Canadian businesses in China for 40 years and provides knowledge and connections needed to succeed in China and Canada. In addition to its thematic focus and practical services, the CCBC is the voice of the Canadian business community on issues affecting Canada-China business, trade, and investment. CCBC members include some of the largest and best-known Canadian and Chinese firms, as well as small to medium-sized enterprises (SMEs), entrepreneurs, and non-profit organizations. Members represent a wide range of sectors, including financial services, professional services, manufacturing, construction, transportation, oil and gas, natural resources, ICT, public sector, and education.

Social Media Platform—Internet Ties. The internet, cloud computing, and mobile communications have transformed the ways we work and play. People use the internet every day to receive information, send messages and communicate with relatives and friends in a virtual world.

For many immigrants to Canada, online tools have become a very useful and open source of assistance for settlement and establishing themselves in Canada. As for Chinese communities, various social media platforms have played an incomparable role in traditional community organizations in the past, in ways that are efficient, instant, low-cost, wide-spread, and used for networking. Facebook, YouTube, Twitter, Pinterest, Google, Instagram, Linkedin, Snapchat, Tumblr and Reddit are the top 10 most popular social media platforms used by most Canadians. However, WeChat, WhatsApp and Line are more common among Chinese users, due to their extensive user numbers and other powerful functions. According to Wikipedia, WeChat is so powerful because it is a Chinese multi-purpose social media mobile application software developed by Tencent. It was first released in 2011, and by 2017 it was one of the largest standalone messaging apps used monthly by active users, with over 980 million monthly active users (902 million daily active users). It has been called China's "App for Everything" because of its many functions and platforms and is lauded as one of the world's most powerful apps. In addition to China, it is also a popular messaging app used in over 200 nations or regions, supporting 23 major languages around the world.

Among many of these convenient functions, a Group Chat can be easily created for any purpose at any location and any time as a virtual communication network. Membership in any Group Chat can grow to whatever limit that the system allows. Even Prime Minister Justin Trudeau, former B.C. Primer Christy Clark, and Mayor of Vancouver Gregor Robertson all opened official accounts on WeChat.

Seeking Common Ground

So many Chinese associations and organizations have existed for such a long time and grow continuously in Canada, and there are many reasons for this. The most fundamental reason is perhaps that members share something in common whether it be reflected in kinship ties, identity ties or social ties, etc. Based on these common interests and goals, the organizations tend to unite, cooperate and support each other, and sometimes even "agree to disagree".

Nevertheless, why is it that Chinese are still seen by many as "a heap of loose sand," even though they have so many organizations and share so many common grounds? Three reasons may be found for this. First, the high-level of homogeneity within a group normally leads to greater trust, support and collaboration among its members who share the same identity or have common interests. However, when internal disagreement arises, which happens often, the group may ultimately be divided into two or several subgroups. Once divided, the level of trust, support and collaboration between groups diminishes.

Secondly, even though Chinese communities have been transforming for over 150 years in Canada, the original types of opposition and struggle rooted in historical Chinatown's tit for tat between the "royalists" and "revolutionists" have never gone away. The difference in political stance, business interests and associations with the original home places, etc. keeps dividing Chinese communities. It is naive to believe that interacting with only one group or two will be enough to get to know and understand the Chinese in Canada.

Finally, what is truly challenging is how multifaceted Chinese communities react collectively when being targeted with suspicion, blame, discrimination, or political attack whenever there is a general public outcry on certain issues that may or may not be related to Canada's Chinese. For example, "go back to China" is often used as an insult to all Chinese Canadians. Chinese home-buyers, regardless of their immigration status in Canada, are always blamed for being "foreign buyers" who caused housing price hikes and unaffordability in some Canadian cities, just to name a few.

Gradually, Chinese in Canada, including individuals and groups, have come to realize the importance and mutual benefit of solidarity and support for each other within their communities regardless whether they are old or newcomers to Canada, home place origins, spoken dialects, political preferences and religious beliefs, etc.

Acting collectively through mutual cooperation and support is becoming a general trend with the transforming multifaceted community, which raises a new challenge for Chinese to develop community strategies based on which individuals and groups can really agree to disagree. In a foreseeable future, a new type of organization may emerge—a think tank that functions in the best interest of all Chinese in Canada.

References

Asia Pacific Foundation of Canada. (2017). Investment Monitor 2017-Report on Foreign Direct Investment from the Asia Pacific into Canada. Vancouver: Asia Pacific Foundation of Canada.

Canada's 100 Best Restaurants. (2016). Retrieved from http://canadas100best.com/canadas-100-best-restaurants-2016/#1466432694478-4a0f1050-4cf8

CBC News. (2013, April 9). B.C. mine's temporary foreign workers case in Federal Court. Retrieved from http://www.cbc.ca/news/canada/british-columbia/b-c-mine-s-temporary-foreign-workers-case-in-federal-court-1.1374502

CBCNews. (2016, 5 4). Deal of the century: Expo 86 land purchase changed Vancouver. Retrieved from http://www.cbc.ca/news/canada/british-columbia/expo-86-china-business-vancouver-1.3560255

China News. (2007, 12 5). 从 " 三把刀 " 到 " 六个师 " 澳华人主流意识增强 (From the "three knives" to "six masters," the Australia Chinese mainstream awareness increased). Retrieved from http://www.chinanews.com/hr/dyzhrxw/news/2007/12-05/1095678.shtml

Chinese Canadian National Council. (2012, June 12). Our Stories-Paper Sons and Daughters. Retrieved from https://ccncourstories.wordpress.com/videos/paper-sons-video/

CIC. (2011). Facts and Figures.

Economist (2011, Nov 19). The Magic of Diasporas. Retrieved from http://www.economist.com/node/17797134

Fairchild TV. (2017). Mandarin Profile Awards Presentation. Retrieved from http://www.fairchildtv.com/shows/mpa/index.php

Globe and Mail. (2006, 7 15). PM brands Canada an "energy superpower". Retrieved from https://beta.theglobeandmail.com/news/world/pm-brands-canada-an-energy-superpower/article1105875/?ref=http://www.theglobeandmail.com &

Globe and Mail. (2015, 12 31). China Investment Corp. closes Toronto office in wake of commodity rout. Retrieved from https://www.theglobeandmail.com/report-on-business/industry-news/energy-and-resources/commodity-rout-forces-china-investment-corp-to-shutter-canadian-office/article27972618/?arc404=true

Gluszynski, T., & Peters, V. (2005). Survey of Earned Doctorates: A Profile of Doctoral Degrees.

Goverment of Canada. (2017, July 18). Immigrate as a skilled worker through Express Entry. Retrieved from http://www.cic.gc.ca/english/immigrate/skilled/index.asp

Government of Canada. (2001). Justice Laws Website. Retrieved from Immigration and Refugee Protection Act (S.C. 2001, c. 27): http://laws-lois.justice.gc.ca/eng/acts/I-2.5/FullText.html

Government of Canada. (2012). Canadian Multiculturalism: An Inclusive Citizenship. Retrieved from http://www.cic.gc.ca/english/multiculturalism/citizenship.asp

Government of Canada. (2017, 6 20). Statistics and Open Data. Retrieved from http://www.cic.gc.ca/english/resources/statistics/index.asp

Guo, S., & DeVoretz, D. (2007, August). The Changing Face of Chinese Immigrants in Canada. Retrieved from IZA Discussion Paper No. 3018 : http://ftp.iza.org/dp3018.pdf

Husky Energy. (2017). History. Retrieved from http://www.huskyenergy.ca/about/history.asp

Institutional Investor. (2012, 1 30). The CIC and Felix Chee. Retrieved from http://www.institutionalinvestor.com/blogarticle/2970178/blog/the-cic-and-felix-chee.html#.WbiieMiGMyU

IRCC. (2015). Facts and Figures 2015. Retrieved from Immigration Overview-Temporary Residents—Annual IRCC Updates: http://open.canada.ca/data/en/dataset/052642bb-3fd9-4828-b608-c81dff7e539c?_ga=2.140835762.1854832651.1502753991-1488428533.1429565837

KPMG. (2016). China Outlook 2016. Retrieved from https://assets.kpmg.com/content/dam/kpmg/pdf/2016/03/china-outlook-2016.pdf

Lee, W.-m. (1984). Portraits of a Challenge: An Illustrated History of the Chinese Canadian. Toronto: The Council of Chinese Canadians in Ontario.

Ley, D. (2011). Millionaire Migrants: Lessons for Immigration Policy Today. Vancouver: Presentation at 2011 Metropolis Conference.

Li Kai Shing Foundation. (2017). Canada. Retrieved from https://www.lksf.org/locations/canada/

Li, M. (2002). 欧洲华人华侨史 (History of Overseas Chinese in Europe).

Li, P. S. (1998). Chinese in Canada second Edition. Oxford University Press.

Li, P. S. (2011). Immigrants from China to Canada: Issues of Supply and Demand in Human Capital. In P. B. Adams, Issues in Canada-China Relations. Canadian

International Council.

Lin, X., Guan, J., & Nicholson, M. (2008, Dec). Transnational Entrepreneurs as Agents of International Innovation Linkages. Retrieved from Asia Pacific Foundation of Canada: Research Report: http://www.asiapacific.ca/sites/default/files/filefield/ImmigEntrepreneurs.pdf

Ministry of Commerce of the PRC. (2016). REPORT ON DEVELOPMENT OF CHINA'S OUTWARD INVESTMENT AND ECONOMIC COOPERATION. Beijing: MINISTRY OF COMMERCE OF THE PEOPLE'S REPUBLIC OF CHINA.

Olds, K. (2001). Globalization and Urban Change: Capital, Culture, and Pacific Rim Mega-Projects. Oxford: Oxford University Press.

Poy, V. (2013). In V. Poy, Passage to Promise Land. McGill-Queen's University Press.

Qiang, Z. (2013). CANADA'S "THOUSAND TALENT PROGRAM" HOW CANADA RESEARCH CHAIR PROGRAM ATTRACTS CHINESE ACADEMICS. Retrieved from https://www.asiapacific.ca/sites/default/files/filefield/researchreport_qiang_zha_0.pdf

Sieben, D. (2013). Canada's Top 20 Surnames Dissected. Retrieved from http://www.darby.ca/white-pages/236/canadas-most-common-surnames-dissected/

Statistics Canada. (2005). Cornerstones of Community: Highlights of the National Survey of Nonprofit and Voluntary Organizations. Retrieved from Catalogue no. 61-533-XPE: http://www.imaginecanada.ca/sites/default/files/www/en/library/nsnvo/nsnvo_report_english.pdf

Statistics Canada. (2013, Sept 11). NHS Profile. . Retrieved from Catalogue no. 99-004-XWE: http://www12.statcan.gc.ca/nhs-enm/2011/dp-pd/prof/index.cfm?Lang=E (accessed September 29, 2017).

Statistics Canada. (2017, Oct 25). Immigration and Ethnocultural Diversity Highlight Table, 2016 Census. Retrieved from Catalogue no. 98-402-X2016007: http://www12.statcan.gc.ca/census-recensement/2016/dp-pd/hlt-fst/imm/index-eng.cfm (accessed November 03, 2017)

Statistics Canada. (accessed: 2017, 9 10). Table 376-0051. Retrieved from International investment position, Canadian direct investment abroad and foreign direct investment in Canada, by country, annual (dollars), CANSIM (database).: http://www5.statcan.gc.ca/cansim/a26?lang=eng&id=3760051

The Metro Toronto Chinese & Southeast Asian Legal Clinic (MTCSALC). (2011). Road to Justice-The legal struggle for equal rights of Chinese Canadians. Retrieved from http://www.roadtojustice.ca

Torgan Group. (2017). About Us. Retrieved from http://www.torgan.com/About-Us.8.0.html

Toronto Star. (2009, 6 19). A huge gamble on Markham Asian mall. Retrieved from https://www.thestar.com/business/2009/06/19/a_huge_gamble_on_markham_asian_mall.html

Turcotte, M. (2015, 1 30). Volunteering and charitable Giving in Canada. Retrieved from Statistics Canada: Catalogue no. 89-652-X2015001: http://www.statcan.gc.ca/pub/89-652-x/89-652-x2015001-eng.pdf

Zhang, K. Q. (2013). Chinatowns. In I. N. (Ed), The Encyclopedia of Global Human Migration. Blackwell Publishing Ltd.

Zhang, K., & Chen, V. (2011). Growing and Diversifying Chinese Investment in Canada: 2000-2010. Asia Pacific And Globalization Review, 1(1), 37-54. Retrieved from https://journals.macewan.ca/apgr/article/view/33/42

Zhang, K., & DeGolyer, M. E. (2011). Hong Kong: Canada's Largest City in Asia-Survey of Canadian Citizens in Hong Kong. Retrieved from Asia Pacific Foundation of Canada: https://www.asiapacific.ca/sites/default/files/filefield/hk_survey_feb2011_v8.pdf

Chapter 7

Listen: Voices of Media in the Chinese Language

An old saying goes: where there are people, there are Chinese; where there are Chinese, there are Chinese restaurants; where there are Chinese restaurants, there are Chinatowns. This was said about the history of early Chinese immigrants. Today over 60 million Chinese are spread around the globe, and Chinese restaurants have become a core part of the world's dining cultures. Chinatowns have also become much more diverse in their appearances. No longer are they confined to one specific area called "Chinatown"; these "New Chinatowns" are blossoming all over town. The early, traditional Chinatowns have mostly become precious historic and cultural relics that are protected by local governments or tourism bureaus in their respective countries. However, at the same time they are undergoing a process of debate, survival and revitalisation between traditions and modernity.

Newspapers and magazines in Chinese have played an important role in the past hundred years along with the struggles of Chinese people in Canada. As time passes, many of these Chinese media have become a part of history themselves after having created rich and colorful pages over time.

Early Chinese Media—Born from Political Parties

The Chinese who came with European explorers to Canada were few in number, thus the thousands of Chinese labourers were the first people to build the social foundations for welcoming future Chinese to Canada; yet most of them were illiterate peasants. That was the reason there were no Chinese newspapers or magazines to record contemporary conditions and events in the late 19th century, i.e. the era of Gold Rush and railway construction. For the few educated Chinese who needed information on business and politics, Chinese media from San Francisco in the US was the typical choice, such as the China Ocean Daily.

It is interesting to note that after the failure of the Reformation Movement in the late Qing Dynasty, its supporters went abroad and slowly turned into loyalists supporting imperial power. As Chinese communities grew stronger in Canada, Kang Youwei and Liang Qichao established the Chinese Empire Reform Association in Canada and quickly spread across Chinese communities around the world and wrote newspapers to promote and publicize ideas for protecting imperial power, as well as gaining approval from overseas Chinese. The earliest Chinese newspaper published in Canada was the China Reform Gazette in August 1903. Although Canada was the origin point of the Chinese Empire Reform Association, the size of associations and the scale of newspapers in San Francisco and Southeast Asia were much greater than those of Canada, as Canada at the time had a limited Chinese population. For example, there were almost ten thousand members in the Association in San Francisco. In 1899, the Mon Hing Po was changed into a Loyalist newspaper, first published in 1892 by Hui Kan, and the Golden Harbor Daily were distributing far more issues than their Canadian counterparts. There were over 30 publishers of Loyalist Chinese newspapers in the Americas and Southeast Asia.

Of course, the Loyalists had an adversary—the Revolutionaries. The growth of the Loyalists was immediately met with counteraction from Revolutionaries such as Dr. Sun Yat-sen; as a method of breaking the monopoly of overseas propaganda by the Loyalists, Revolutionist newspapers soon became popular. Chinese Revolutionist newspapers from the Americas led by the Hawaiian Chinese News began their public opinion battle against the Loyalists. In 1904, the Datong Daily from San Francisco took the lead in switching sides, and announced: "Expel the Manchu invaders, restore China's glory, establish a republic, and equalize land ownership" as its new tribunal hall policies. Revolutionist newspapers bloomed in Canada and the US thereafter. Chinese newspapers sprouted in Canada, including the Chinese-English Daily News from Vancouver Chinatown in 1906 (discontinued in 1908), the Chinese Daily News in 1907 (crowdfunded by the Wo Hing Temple), and the KMT's official newspaper, the New Republic. Its corresponding newspaper, the Shing Hua Daily, was first published in Toronto (formerly the Shing Wah Weekly) in 1916. As the Revolutionist newspapers stood on the winning side of history after years of see-sawing with the Loyalists, they eventually made immense contributions to the revolution by leading public opinion, uniting overseas Chinese, and acquiring funds to support the revolution.

The great newspaper debate between the Loyalists and Revolutionaries formed the political contents of early Chinese newspapers in Canada. Their secondary functions were to provide information on situations back home in China, allow overseas Chinese to give vent to their homesickness, and connect with their countrymen. The early battle between Loyalist and Revolutionist Chinese newspapers in Canada forged the "traditional gene" of political rivalries between Leftists and Rightists, which have continued to this day.

Chinese Newspapers and Movements Against Discrimination

The fighting over political orientation continued for a long time in Canadian Chinese newspapers; the primary content of the papers did not change until the wave of anti-Chinese sentiment in Canada and the War of Resistance against Japanese Occupation in China.

The success of the 1911 Revolution in China turned the Revolutionist newspapers into the mainstream, and the Loyalist newspapers became miniscule. Speaking in terms of longevity, the newspapers run by the KMT and the Hongmen survived the longest because they had the most stable sources of income and the greatest political strength abroad. As previously described, the New Republic, published by members of the Tongmenghui Vancouver Chapter, continued for almost 70 years, ending its publication in 1984. The Shing Wah Daily News from Toronto played an important role in the development of Chinese communities in Toronto by promoting nationalism according to KMT ideology. Its masthead was penned by Chiang Kai-Shek himself to show the paper's official status as the voice of the KMT. The paper was discontinued in 1990. The opposing newspaper of Toronto's the Shing Wah Daily News was the Hong Chung Pao, first published in 1928 by Hongmen (Chinese Freemasons) but shut down in 1957 due to lack of funding. There were discussions of resuming publication in 1970 but the attempt was unsuccessful.

Among the major Chinese newspapers in Canada up to the 1980s, the Chinese Times was by far the most deserving to be called the core media. As mentioned, the Chinese Daily News was first published in 1907 by a major member of the Tongmenghui, Feng Ziyou. In 1915 the Chinese Daily News was renamed the Chinese Times and began its dominance of Chinese media in Canada for decades to come. It provided first hand media reporting and historical information for political parties and ideologies competing for public opinion and organizing events among overseas Chinese. It also left a treasure house of information on the Chinese people's struggles in Canada, as they were unable to enter the mainstream English and French societies of Canada. The paper is an irreplaceable primary media source for researching the history of early Chinese communities in Canada. The Chinese Times and other early Chinese newspapers are the greatest witnesses to history for Chinese Canadians that severely lack other written sources.

The Chinese Times and other major Chinese newspapers showed an immense influence on public opinion in the following three aspects: First was the full-scale reporting and the crucial influence it had in leading Chinese resistance to discrimination from the start of head-tax implementation to the Chinese Exclusion Act in Canada. Second was the comprehensive reporting on the Japanese invasion of China and the

War of Resistance against the Japanese Invasion, as well as calling out to overseas Chinese to join the resistance. These reports made records of the longest ongoing reporting of a single event in overseas Chinese media. They also had unprecedented effects in leading people to donate to China or to go back to China and directly join the battle of resistance. Third was their focused reporting on Chinese Canadians fighting against fascists, pressing for the abolishment of the Chinese Exclusion Act, and restoring citizenship to Canadian Chinese. These reports were extremely effective in helping achieve equal rights by pressuring the government through public opinion. It may be said that during this time of anti-discrimination, interactions between the Ottawa government and groups such as the Chinese Consolidated Benevolent Association were all reported in detail in the Chinese Times. Public resistance movements were also organized by these news agencies.

A longitudinal view of the Chinese Times and other Chinese newspapers showed that they were very professional in their range of reporting, comprehensiveness of information, and timely reporting on the opinions of their readership, to the point that they were just as good as the professional newspapers that came later. It is important to note that after the end of the War of Resistance against Japanese Invasion, newspapers from Hong Kong began flooding into Canada and the US, including: Kung Sheung Daily News, Sing Tao Daily, Overseas Chinese Daily News, Sing Pao Daily News, and the Wah Sheung Po. After the abolishment of the Chinese Exclusion Act (1947), Hong Kong became the largest base of interaction for Chinese people to immigrate to Canada in the 1950s and 1960s. In the 1980s and 1990s the Sing Tao Daily and Ming Pao Daily News were published in both eastern and western Canada;

the World Journal from Taiwan also entered Canada from the US. These three newspapers became dominators of the market, and competed head to head through weekly newspapers and minor papers in a period of "trade wars for newspapers". The traditional papers such as the Chinese Times, the Shing Wah Daily News, and the New Republic were no match for the newcomers and continued to lose readers and funds until they had to close, one by one. The loyal readership of the traditional Chinese newspapers was mostly acquired by the Sing Tao Daily.

Chinese Newspapers and Canada's Immigration Policy

For Chinese newspapers in Canada, the most important content in reports on Canadian policies was none other than immigration. The reason being these immigration policies have the strongest influence on Chinese Canadians, far exceeding the influence of changes to the party in power or the Prime Minister. Over the past one hundred and some years, with Canadian immigration policies changing, Chinese Canadians either faced discrimination, or rose up in resistance, or cheered with joy. It can be said that the evolution of Canadian immigration policies has shaped the features of Canada's Chinese population to a certain degree and influenced the progress of Chinese Canadians in terms of politics, economy, participation in community events, daily living, and ways of thinking.

Therefore, a discussion on the reactions of Chinese media to immigration policies, or in other words, their interaction with the makers of immigration policies, would show the general process of evolution of Chinese media, the development of Chinese communities, and the inadequacies and weaknesses of Chinese communities, especially regarding their integration into the mainstream of Canadian society.

Before the War to the 1950s

Chinese media have played vital roles in the evolution of Canada's immigration policy. Canadian immigration policies were highly discriminatory towards East Asians, especially towards Chinese immigrants during the anti-Chinese period before the Second World War. Chinese media joined forces against the common adversary during this period. On the one hand they protested against the anti-Chinese policies and requested equal treatment with East Asian immigrants. They asked the government to provide the Chinese immigrants the same basic rights as every other citizen as per the spirit of the Canadian constitution and stop the injustices in a timely fashion. On the other hand, they encouraged Chinese Canadians to never give up and to work together to support each other in the continuous struggle for equality in immigration policies.

There were few Chinese media during that period, and even fewer at a scale similar to the Chinese Times. However, in spite of the small Chinese Canadian population at the time, the limited number of Chinese media were able to speak from the same page. The discrimination and oppression that Chinese communities faced in society forced them to unite closely in order to struggle against the oppressors, and there was little divergence in public opinion regarding immigration policies. The problems internal to the Chinese communities however, such as opposing political parties (Hongmen versus the KMT, and Loyalists versus the KMT) had a much greater divergence, and heated struggles for public opinion were commonplace.

During the period of Chinese exclusion, the Chinese had no right to vote. Compounded by the fact that the majority of the Chinese Canadian population were either labourers or small business owners (with the exception of a few large business owners and community leaders), most of them had no power to fight against the government, and even fewer had the mindset of political resistance. As for the second generation Chinese Canadians, although many of them fought hard to become a part of the mainstream and enjoyed much greater achievements in their careers compared with their parents and grandparents, they were still most concerned with gaining equal status with other citizens, and less with immigration policies that only affect first generation immigrants. They were also limited in their Chinese reading and writing abilities, which kept them from venting their displeasure through the Chinese media.

In the Chinese exclusion period, the comments on the federal government's immigration policies from Chinese communities were mostly expressed through the Chinese Consolidated Benevolent Association. For a long time, the Chinese Consolidated Benevolent Association was definitely the leader among all of the clan associations and other associations in Chinese communities and in Chinatowns. This situation meant that the Association bore the responsibility to lead in communications as well as protests against the government. Whenever a new immigration policy came into effect, the Chinese Consolidated Benevolent Association was sure to react, while the Chinese media would also abide with the understandings and comments from the Chinese Consolidated Benevolent Association in their reports on immigration policies. It could be said that aside from some disputes within the Chinese Consolidated Benevolent Association itself, the Association's comments on federal immigration policies represented the voice of Chinese Canadian communities; the Association's understanding of Canadian immigration policies also represented the consensus among Chinese Canadian communities.

The media leadership status of the Chinese Consolidated Benevolent Association on Canadian immigration policies continued after the War and into the 1950s. In other words, the "channel" of which Chinese Canadians had to express their opinions on the government's immigration policies was limited, but it also simplified the communication process between the government and Chinese communities. The government's immigration policies would be disseminated through the Chinese media as long as it had communicated with the Chinese Consolidated Benevolent Association. The Chinese media and the Chinese Consolidated Benevolent Association could be regarded as so much "on the same page" that there was little divergence and ambiguity in their opinions on immigration policies that could offer different angles for analyzing the Chinese communities.

However, as Chinese Canadians were not highly active in political participation, it took until the end of the 1950s for the first Chinese Canadian Member of Parliament to appear. Voices of the Chinese media and communities were not transformed into pressure applied to political parties, nor were they effective in influencing votes, and therefore Chinese media had almost no special influence on changing immigration policies.

Changes after the 1960s

A second wave of Chinese immigration into Canada (first wave having started with the Gold Rush and railway construction period until the implementation of the Chinese Exclusion Act) occurred from the 1950s to 1967, when the Chinese Exclusion Act was abolished. Aside from a number of skilled immigrants who migrated to Canada independently at the end of this period, most of the Chinese during this period still had strong ties with their pre-war families and communities, such as those who went back to China before the war then returned to Canada, or family-class immigrants. These immigration characteristics determined that Chinese communities' understanding and comments on Canadian immigration policies were still to follow the same pattern of reaction as they had followed before the Chinese Exclusion Act was abolished. The Chinese Consolidated Benevolent Association still played its leadership role and acted as the middleman between Chinese communities and the federal government on immigration policy matters.

A third wave of Chinese immigration happened before Canadian immigration policies became truly "universal". This new wave of immigration was quite different from previous ones, because the immigrants came from a variety of locations and social backgrounds. Indeed, this had an apparent effect on Chinese communities' comments on the federal government's immigration policies, and the Chinese media also showed this divergence. This is a subject that requires attention.

As Chinese Canadians had a low level of political participation, they had miniscule influence on the agendas of the dominant political parties and were outside of the "closed doors" when it came to policymaking by the party in power. Therefore, the understanding and reactions of Chinese communities were mostly voiced through Chinese media with very few exceptions. A comprehensive analysis of these will become great reference material for learning about the political trends in Chinese communities, the roles of Chinese media, the interactions between Chinese communities and mainstream society, and the relative importance of Chinese communities in the eyes of the party in power.

Roles of Television and Radio

As more Chinese immigrated to Canada after the 1970s, Chinese media also became more and more diverse. Besides the traditional print-based media, Chinese radio stations, and later on the much more pivotal Chinese TV media also appeared in both eastern and western Canada. The birth of these digital media completely changed the dominance of print media. The appearance of radio stations gave Chinese Canadians in the lowest social groups a chance to learn about Canadian politics and news in their Chinese communities; TV media had immense coverage and influence which sped up the reaction time of Chinese communities towards important events in mainstream society, and thus accelerated the integration process of Chinese Canadians into mainstream Canadian society.

In the 1990s, Cathay International TV's newly founded Fairchild Group essentially monopolized Chinese TV media and all of the TV programs that Chinese communities watched. It wasn't until the appearance of OMNI TV under Rogers, and Channel M in Vancouver in 2003 that competition for Chinese TV dominance began. In 2008 Rogers

Media acquired Channel M, creating a head-to-head competition between the two big companies.

In terms of radio, Fairchild's Mandarin and Cantonese radio stations were also put into competition with Vancouver's Mainstream Broadcasting Corporation. The 21st century broke the tug-of-war. TV media from Mainland China and new media came into play, and Chinese media entered a period of battle royal. Such a situation wasn't necessarily positive for Chinese media. As the Chinese Canadian market is quite limited, the increase in the number of media expedited competition for advertising, which led to a shortage of funds in all media groups, and this severely damaged the quality of reporting. The situation was coincidentally contrary to that of mainstream English media, which entered a period of merger and monopoly, while Chinese media became fragmented and unconnected.

Chinese Media's Patterns of Reaction towards Immigration Policies

After sketchy research into the main historical Chinese media in Canada, we have discovered a few set patterns of reaction that Chinese media had on the government's immigration policies.

First was translation and introduction of the immigration policies, as well as some details of other policies. Chinese media were headstrong in their role as the "bridge" and tried to satisfy Chinese readers of this. There were two reasons for Chinese media to have taken such action. One was that they believed a large portion of people in the Chinese communities had enough difficulty in English reading and comprehension that it was necessary to use Chinese to satisfy their in-depth information needs; the second was that Chinese people were not interested in politics or government policies, and would not spend the required time and effort to learn more about the details of the policies even when they had access to tools to help them read English. This was the hundred-year-old principle of Chinese media—to always use Chinese to deliver government policies to first generation immigrants.

Chinese newspapers in the 60s and 70s of the 20th century were not yet "advertisement-centred"; they would use up as much space as necessary to report on important changes in immigration policies. For example, take the white-paper on changes to immigration policy published in 1966 by Jean Marchand which became the source for the complete change in immigration policy in 1967. The two main Chinese media at the time, the Chinese Times and the Shing Wah Daily News spent several months to fully translate and cover the changes in a series of reports. This type of large-scale series coverage was the only one in the history of the Chinese Canadian newspaper industry. The root cause clearly was that the policy changes were vital to Chinese Canadians, and thus it was necessary for the Chinese reader to understand the details.

The second was to show their effectiveness in speaking up to the government as representing the Chinese communities, and they grabbed every chance they could to do so. They wanted to let the Chinese communities believe that their voices could be heard by the government and could be taken into account during the policymaking process. This became a common pattern of reaction used jointly by the media and groups such as the Chinese Consolidated Benevolent Association. Yet the reality was often very different from their expectation, and only seldom did their words make a meaningful difference.

Based on the logic of history, the changes to immigration laws in 1967 were the work of all Canadians, including Chinese Canadians. However, it would be a bit far-fetched to say that Chinese communities were key players in making the changes, since Chinese Canadians held very little political power. Based on the report from the Shing Wah Daily News, at the end of September 1966, Minister of Immigration Marchand mentioned about changes to the immigration policies during his interview in Vancouver on the return trip from his visit to Tokyo. He claimed that the principles of Canada's immigration policies were to select and not to discriminate, but abolishing discrimination would not mean a large increase in immigrants from Hong Kong. He even pointed out that the people in Hong Kong may not meet the immigration requirements for Canada because Hong Kong provided a poor level of education. He further claimed that the Department of Citizenship and Immigration had already set up office in Tokyo, ready to take in skilled immigrants from Japan whose travelling expenses would be partly covered by the government.

This shows that even if the claim were true that Asian immigrants were pivotal in the massive changes to immigration policies, credit should go to the Japanese immigrants and the Tokyo government who stood behind them. New immigrants from Japan were the strongest agents of change and the greatest beneficiaries from the policy changes, not the Chinese, especially those from Hong Kong. These objective factors show that since Japan formed an alliance with Canada after the war, communication between their governments would be smooth, and diplomatic contacts would be much more effective. At the time Mainland China still had not established formal diplomatic relations with Canada. Without a strong backup through a powerful home country, Chinese Canadians were not as able to form synergies as Japanese Canadians did to influence Canada's immigration policies through effective, bilateral diplomatic means.

Chinese communities had neither opportunities nor the capability to conduct truly in-depth analysis of the logic behind the new policies; what they did was to create a scenario in which the media and community leaders would represent their communities to make a difference in changing Canada's immigration policies, gain support and unified power from the communities. Before Chinese in Canada had any power to influence the government's decisions, even a few scattered or completely decorative acts of suggestion to the government by community leaders were still quite effective in maintaining the image of Chinese Canadians. Chinese media of course would seize these opportunities to not only interact with their communities, but also increase their readership.

In 1975, the Department of Manpower and Immigration in Canada published a Green Paper on immigration policies. The Chinese Consolidated Benevolent Association in Toronto and Vancouver sent in a list of suggestions to the government after gathering opinions from immigrants in all regions. The list suggested that the Canadian government ease up on immigration requirements, simplify the examination procedures for immigrants, and shorten the waiting time for application processing, all based on family-class immigration policies. Chinese media posted reports on the Special Immigration Council of Canada's reply to Fong Lam, the president of Chinese Consolidated Benevolent Association at the time. The media used a headline that said the Council will "carefully consider" the suggestions made on immigration policies, which showed a direct attempt by the media to assure audiences that the Chinese Consolidated Benevolent Association had a level of influence on Canadian immigration policies.

The third pattern was to get Chinese Canadian politicians or candidates in elections to make suggestions on certain policies through Chinese media, which was a way to make audiences believe that their suggestions would be able to influence the government's decision-making process.

It is undeniable that Chinese politicians and candidates made quite a number of suggestions during elections, however, these suggestions can be put into two categories. One category came directly from their political party's agenda, with some added views that interested Chinese Canadians; the other category was so-called suggestions that entirely catered to the opinions of Chinese communities. Looking at the situation afterwards, those who weren't elected were obviously incapable of making a difference, but those who were elected and worked with the party in power never put forward any bills, and only followed their party's decisions and policies. The problem was that Chinese media never explained the general background of the situation when they published these types of information, nor did they address the responsibility to represent their audiences by requesting politicians to account for their commitments after elections.

In fact, even the Chinese Canadian MPs had a minimal level of influence and power to change immigration policies, let alone the Chinese Canadian candidates. The reason they talked at length about changes in immigration policies in the communities was essentially to gain votes for the political party they represented, and thus raise their own position in the party through the voices of the Chinese Canadian public. However, the Chinese media had not made any extensive reports or queries about their actions, but rather chose to continue acting as mouthpieces for Chinese Canadian politicians and gain publicity for them among the communities. Consider the example of Art Lee, the only Chinese Canadian MP at the time: he made a speech on Chinese media concerning the Green Paper on immigration in November 1974, in which he said that Canada had entered a period of "universal immigration policy", but the complete eradication of racism was going to be difficult because of human behavior. He therefore suggested that it was necessary for the immigration officers to learn more about Chinese culture and traditions and set up overseas immigration offices and officers. Lee also spoke against the suggestion to cancel nominated immigrants in the Green Paper because it was in conflict with the Chinese concept of "extended family". An overview of the Chinese media reports showed that no reporter asked about whether what he said was entirely his personal opinion or was a proposal that would be entered into the political party's decision-making process. For a long time, the Chinese media only wrote down the transcript of their interviews with Chinese Canadian politicians in their reports, and never explained to readers whether these suggestions that would benefit the Chinese had any chance of becoming policies. The fuzzy interview method made the Chinese audiences falsely believe that these Chinese Canadian politicians had a real voice in the policymaking process in their parties and continued to support these politicians with their votes. The truth was that the personal opinions of these politicians were rarely ever depicted in the policies of their parties.

Interactions between Chinese and English Media

The early Chinese immigrants to Canada were mostly illiterate to the point that they needed help with writing letters to their families back home in China, let alone reading English. As the communities developed and the second and third generations of Chinese Canadians appeared, the need for exchanging English information also increased. Interestingly, the worsening relationship between China and Japan and the War of Resistance Against Japan became an opportunity for publishing English newspapers catering to Chinese Canadian readers. Through publishing in English, Chinese Canadians could reveal the facts of Japan's invasion of China to Western society and called for Canada to stand up for justice and aid for the Chinese victims of the war, and to stop exporting resources to Japan for use by their military.

The English version of the *Chung Wah Chow Po*, the *China News Weekly*, was published in Chinatowns in 1936 for an audience of Westerners and second or third generation Chinese Canadians who could no longer read Chinese. In terms of content, these magazines were an extension of Chinese media that mostly introduced life in Chinatowns and trends among Canadian Chinese people. These contents were helpful in reducing racial discrimination and racial conflicts caused by stereotypes and misunderstandings. The Chinese media started to increasingly use English to disseminate information after the war. A notable example was the Chinese News, a semi-monthly magazine started by Roy Mah, a retired Chinese Canadian veteran in 1953. The magazine operated for a long period and became a major source of information on Chinatowns for mainstream society and later-generations of Chinese Canadians.

Irregular publications with both Chinese and English appeared since the 1950s, such as the Chinese Guide by Orient Publishing Co., and in anniversary publications by various clan associations.

Active interactions between Chinese media and mainstream English media started to take trend as the Chinese communities grew and relationships improved between Canada and Asia, especially China. After the Opening-up and Economic Reforms in China, trade between China and Canada skyrocketed, and China leaped to become the second largest trading partner of Canada from its original position at the bottom of the list. This also greatly increased the visibility of Chinese communities within mainstream society, and the inclusion of more Chinese elements in English media. Interaction between English and Chinese media has become increasingly frequent since the 90s. However there remains one problem: Chinese Canadians often complain that the mainstream English media only report news on Mainland China, Hong Kong, Taiwan, and local Chinese communities through negatively coloured lenses.

During the mid 1990s around the time of Hong Kong's return to China, the *Ming Pao Daily News* (Western Canada Edition) and the *Vancouver Sun* (the largest local English newspaper) showed unprecedented cooperation in British Columbia, the origin of Canada's Chinese media. The Chinese-English bilingual forum edited by the Ming Pao sent three short opinion pieces in English to the *Vancouver Sun* each week to be published on the Sun's forum pages. The special forum page even included the Chinese characters for "forum" (lun tan) and received widespread attention from both Chinese readers and mainstream society. This forum continued for dozens of issues.[1]

The *Vancouver Sun* put forth a Chinese version of its website in 2011 to appeal to a growing Chinese reader base. As the new media emerged, however, the Chinese site lacked the strength to compete and closed after a few years. Another noteworthy fact was that at the turn of the century, Canada's largest English language newspaper, the Toronto Star acquired stocks in the Eastern Canada Edition of the Sing Tao Daily, which became a model for in-depth interaction and cooperation between Chinese and English media, as opposed to simply sharing information in the earlier days.

Appearance of New Media and Social media

Following the appearance of traditional media such as newspapers, TV and radio, Chinese media in Canada have recently accelerated their entry into the age of innovative new media. Along with the age of digitization came an increase in the pace of life and work, as well as the popularization of computers and cellphones. This brought "online media" and "mobile media" to the world.

One by one, all major news media have now built their own websites and have taken the internet as a carrier to disseminate information via various channels. For example, the Sing Tao Canada's website has three sections: Toronto, Vancouver and Calgary. Their site provides information on headline news, business, society, sports, entertainment and fashion. The

---

1   Guo Ding, author and former senior editor responsible for the bilingual forum column of the Ming Pao Daily News.

Ming Pao Daily News, the Canadian City Post, and the Global Chinese Press all have set up their own respective websites. These websites currently provide news and information as electronic versions of their print media but also with many interactive and sharing functions. Similarly, TV and radio stations have set up their own websites, for instance: Fairchild TV and Radio.

Besides the corresponding internet pathways of traditional media, many other information platforms have sprouted up and became an important tool for communication and resource sharing between Chinese immigrants. Based on information provided by Amazon's Alexa51.ca[2], a website established in 2001 that provided news and information on immigration, international studies, employment, daily living and other forums, had the highest traffic in Toronto. It built a platform for Chinese international students and immigrants to access information and communicate among themselves. The website with the second highest traffic in Toronto was yorkbbs.ca.

Following its establishment in 2002, yorkbbs.ca boasted 100 thousand registered accounts in one year; its total number of members reached 465,000 in 2011, and 800,000 in 2016. Other websites including rolia.net, superlife.ca and am1470.com were all among the websites with the highest traffic in Toronto. As for Canada West and Vancouver, the sites with high CTR include westca.com, bcbay.com, vanpeople.com, vansky.ca, and lahoo.ca. These websites also function as methods to exchange information between Chinese Canadians.

The rapid development of online media and social media have helped audiences in exchanging and disseminating information, but also have

---

2   Traffic rankings of Chinese websites in Canada. http://www.cnweb. ca/#pos1

made a strong and direct impact on the traditional print media. For example: Facebook, Twitter, Weibo and WeChat have all filled up the fragmented time created by changes in peoples' lifestyle and reading methods. WeChat has become an especially sought after high ground for Chinese media in Canada. The major Chinese newspapers and websites have all started their own WeChat public accounts and platforms, such as Canada News Today, Canadanews, and Dushi.ca. Chinese speakers still prefer to use their mother tongue, their most familiar language to express their thoughts and feelings no matter how many years they have spent abroad. The unique features of social media, such as "user-generated contents that spread both ways", have created more interactive modes of expression and exchange on an equal footing, and have also boosted the speed of receiving and spreading information. These social media have become the centres for discussion of hot topics. Low-cost, personalized social media have toppled the dominant influence of traditional media and have helped more people to express their truest thoughts and feelings.

Having begun as the current fad in China, online live video broadcasting is now a growing trend among international students from China, the phenomenon still has not caught on among Chinese media in Canada. It is expected that there will be more high-quality live video programs in future.

The decentralization effect of new media on information dissemination has achieved equality and freedom in that regard and has also allowed the public to receive information at lower cost and higher efficiency. That being said, new media still has many shortcomings compared with traditional media. False information and rumours online have made the authenticity of such information come under question. The quality of user-supplied online information also remains to be improved. The information is highly homogenous and lacking in professionalism. Therefore, quality control and professionally presented information still relies on the authority of traditional media.

Overall, digital, internet and mobile technologies have brought innovation to the Chinese media; they are moving from traditional print to digitized new media. A combination of the advantages of traditional and new media is the expected trend, becoming a new source of revitalization for Chinese media.

Future Prospects of Chinese Media

Reviewing a whole century of Chinese media in Canada, we see that it took on soft roles in the early days as a method of maintaining cultural traditions, expressing sojourners' thoughts of home, and passing on information from the homeland. In the Chinese Exclusion era, it became a rallying tool (and a tool for political parties to gain favour) to unite and address the public. In the post-war period, they took on the above roles, but also became a bridge for communication between government and Chinese community organizations.

However, we must clearly recognize that Chinese media were not the same as English media; they did not position and expect themselves to be the watchdog of the government and other powers that affect political decisions. Under the limitations of their language and socio-political status, Chinese media had difficulty exercising "supervision by public opinion" and being a "watchdog of the government" like their English or French counterparts. They had the capability to complain or give suggestions about the government on immigration policies, but they were not able to influence policies before they were implemented or during the process of debate and research; neither were they able to help correct the mistakes of government policies in a timely manner. The quality and importance of Chinese media should not be blamed entirely as the cause of this circumstance. More likely, it was the weak level of political and social involvement of Chinese Canadians themselves that was the main cause of such a situation.

However, we must acknowledge that the growth of Chinese communities and Chinese immigrants after the war did bring a greater sense of confidence and strength to the Chinese media. They worked as bridges and clarions when they translated government policies and passed on the opinions of their Chinese communities. At the same time, Chinese media functioned as enlighteners, gatherers and leaders for Chinese Canadian involvement in politics and mainstream society. Such feats would have been impossible through English or French media. The trend has continued into the 21st century and brought along a substantial boost to the status of Chinese media in mainstream politics. This boost was not caused by Chinese media exceeding the quality of mainstream English and French media, but by the growth in political involvement and voter turnout on the part of Chinese Canadians. This brought attention to Chinese media from mainstream society and political circles. In fact, from the federal level to the provinces and cities with large Chinese populations, governments have designated offices or personnel to learn about the positions and focus of the Chinese media. All levels of government and media offices have employees who understand Chinese. Roundtable discussions about government policies are held periodically with Chinese media from the Prime Minister all the way down to local leaders and opposition parties in provinces and metropolitan areas. They hope to make advances with Chinese Canadian voters through the Chinese media. However, the Prime Minister and Premiers have also received criticism from some English media due to their targeted interaction focusing on Chinese media.

As we entered the 21st century, traditional Chinese media elites began to decline as new media started to prosper. In terms of print media, daily newspapers have started to shrink, periodical magazine publications have had to lengthen their periods between issues, while the weeklies have entered a state of fierce competition. The fierce competition for advertisements caused a decline in both the quality and the credibility of traditional Chinese media, particularly reports and commentaries. The new online media and social media face the challenge of effective integration and increasing their credibility. Through the next decade, Chinese media will all be experiencing a period of adjustment.

Chapter 8

Riding Out the Pandemic

Chinese Community Deserves Credits for Keeping COVID Cases Down[1]

The City of Richmond, British Columbia, with a large Chinese community, reported the lowest COVID-19 cases per capita in the province's major urban centres. Something must have done super in this city.

Many may believe in God's blessing. It is true God loves all his children unconditionally, from downtown to uptown and from midtown to market town. While new data released by the province shows Richmond has the lowest COVID cases per capita among major cities in B.C., other factors must have played a part.

As Richmond Mayor Malcolm Brodie puts, the city has a very large

---

1 Kenny Zhang, This article first appeared partially in the *Xinhua News* on September 7th, 2020.

Chinese community, and their early adoption of measures like wearing masks and staying physically distant helped keep the COVID caseload relatively low in his city. The city is the home of over 200,000 residents, making it the fourth populous city in the province. Among them, 54% are of Chinese descent, which is higher than 28% in the City of Vancouver, 12% in B.C., and 5% in Canada.

Being a Mayor for nearly 20 years, Mr. Brodie was right, that Chinese community not only was aware of what was happening in then infected areas of China, but also knew the dangers that were being faced. Furthermore, the Chinese community believed it is everyone's responsibility to do more together.

Amid the COVID pandemic, the responsibility means all individuals need to keep apart by taking accountable actions. The responsibility means all communities need to stand side-by-side by supporting each other. The responsibility means all nations need to combat the coronavirus by collaborating collectively.

In early days, the city's Chinese community started practicing social distancing in both conventional and innovational ways. They were one of the first groups to wear masks in public spaces despite being misunderstood, mistrusted, and mistreated as it was not deemed normal at that time. They still stuck to principles that the benefit of wearing a mask does not simply lie in protecting oneself, but also in protecting others.

They creatively drove two cars to pick up families or friends who returned from overseas to avoid their use of public transit, taxis or ride-sharing services, which would prevent this high-risk group's possible spreading of the virus to their family members and further to the local community.

Many Chinese residents put themselves in voluntary self-quarantine for

14 days after returning from overseas, long before it became a mandatory requirement for all international travelers.

There was a group of volunteers that used Chinese social media platform to provide pick-up services to passengers who returned from international trips, and helped deliver groceries to the doors of those who were in home confinement.

In addition to online shopping and delivery services, Chinese markets and stores were among the first in the industry to require customers to wear masks and to practice social distancing in the store.

When it comes to combat the coronavirus, sweeping the snow just in front of one's own doorsteps is far from enough. The virus itself does not respect human ages, skin colours, religious beliefs, social classes, or border walls.

At the time COVID cases exploded in the Iranian Canadian community, a joint initiative between a Chinese and an Iranian community organization was established to help members of both groups who returned to B.C. from then COVID infected regions.

Before the COVID-19 case emerged in B.C., many Chinese Canadians opened their hearts and wallets to support the Red Cross Canada's China COVID-19 Response Appeal, and Doctors Without Borders initiatives. Others spontaneously shipped protective gear to hospitals and to their families, friends, or other loved ones in the then epicenter of the pandemic.

What would you do if your peers of the same yacht or golf club, or companions in a corner bar or grill is suffering from an injury or threaten? If you believe love the God and love the neighbours as yourself, the answer should be simple as it is not just sympathy but empathy. So did the Chinese community. It was their strong faith that Canadians will be truly safe at home only if neighbouring countries manage to control the virus spreading.

When initial cases were reported in B.C., a group of community opinion leaders proposed five proactive measures to the B.C. public health authorities urging the government agencies to prevent the community spread of the coronavirus. Some of these recommendations later became mandatory practices in Canada.

Individuals and businesses were responding too beyond Richmond. Mrs. Chen, a 95-year-old Chinese grandmother and her group of volunteers, delivered home-made 3,500 scrub caps for health-care workers at Surrey Memorial Hospital, Richmond Hospital, Peace Arch Hospital and others. A 9-year-old North Vancouver boy surnamed Yang raised a total of $3,000 dollars, all of which was used to provide food and beverages for frontline staff. There were Chinese restaurants that provided free meals for health-care workers and many community organizations donate cashes and protective masks to hospitals and nursing homes.

Yet, some may still argue that the high COVID cases in other cities are the result of the outbreak in senior living facilities. There are over 36 senior homes in Richmond too, and why seniors are safer here?

It is the Chinese community that took early proactive measures, who deserves the credits for making the difference. Moreover, these practices allow analysts to compare measures used in different cities and see what's working and what's not to combat the COVID-19, and better prepare for the next crisis. A little responsibility goes a long way.

China's Coronavirus Outbreak Calls Out for Canada's help —and We Should Respond, in the Spirit of Dr. Bethune[2]

On Jan. 30, the World Health Organization declared the 2019 novel coronavirus (2019-nCoV) outbreak a public health emergency of international concern. But two days later, an even more surprising statement: Chinese Premier Li Keqiang asked the European Union to provide medical supplies to fight the epidemic unfolding in China.

This was highly unusual—top Chinese officials are not particularly known for their willingness to ask for international aid. But it points to the gravity and severity of the situation.

China is grappling with a severe public health challenge that is now outpacing the deadly SARS outbreak in 2003. As of today, more than 31,000 people in 28 countries and territories have been diagnosed with the new virus. The vast majority of those cases have emerged in China, where more than 600 people have died.

After 2019-nCoV was identified as originating in the city of Wuhan, the Chinese government took extraordinary measures to contain the outbreak. Wuhan and 13 surrounding cities have been locked down since Jan. 23 in a quarantine that affects more than 40 million people. It might be hard for Canadians to imagine this feat, but consider that Canada's entire population is about 37 million.

However, the biggest challenge China faces is on the front lines. Doctors and nurses are racing against the clock and struggling to treat thousands of patients with dwindling supplies. Somehow, they are standing

2 This article first appeared in *The Globe and Mail* on February 7th, 2020. Kenny Zhang is a Fudan University alumnus, Jenny Li is a graduate of Hubei University, ChiChi Wang is an alumnus of the University of British Columbia and Zhenyu Cheng is a Wuhan University alumnus. All are residents of Canada.

firm despite a shortage of hospital beds, staff, medicine and protective gear—even for themselves. Many doctors have worked throughout the day without drinking, eating or going to the bathroom simply to avoid replacing their protective suits. One doctor we know wore his son's goggles to work for protection.

That the Chinese medical community is in mourning only heightens the anxiety. Dr. Li Wenliang, the Wuhan Central Hospital ophthalmologist who was among the first to identify the disease, passed away Friday.

Canada has confirmed five cases of its own—three in Ontario, two in British Columbia—but it has been acting vigorously and vigilantly, monitoring the situation, providing travel advice and evacuating Canadians in China. It's remarkably brave of Ottawa to follow the WHO's recommendation not to ban Chinese and other international travellers from China from entering the country. Furthermore, as acts of racism against the Chinese-Canadian community increase, Prime Minister Justin Trudeau has made statements criticizing anti-Chinese sentiments and misinformation about the coronavirus. "This," he said, "is not something Canadians will ever stand for."

These are admirable steps. But it is our belief that Canadians will only be truly safe when China wins its battle. And history may offer a good example of what Canada can still do to achieve this goal.

In the late 1930s, Canadian physician Norman Bethune brought modern medicine to rural China. He was credited with saving thousands of Chinese civilians and soldiers during the Second Sino-Japanese War, and for this he is revered even today in China. His story confirms the most effective way to save lives: supplying Canadian medical treatment to China.

Doing so will require three courses of action. First, we would urge Ottawa to continue demonstrating respectful concern and vigorous support as China combats this virus during this critical period. Secondly, we would recommend the Canadian government play a vital role in facilitating the procurement of medical supplies for hospitals in affected regions. Trade-promotion agencies can help by adding a medical-supplies section to their information portals to connect qualified Canadian suppliers with Chinese buyers. Thirdly, we would encourage Canadian health-care professionals and specialists to work with Chinese and international experts in developing treatments and a vaccine.

Ottawa and Beijing have had their differences. A prominent Chinese executive is facing extradition to the U.S., while two Canadian citizens remain in jail in China and a crippling import ban hurts Canadian canola farmers. But Canadians remain highly respected and liked in China—in no small part because of the legacy of people like Dr. Bethune.

There is a Chinese saying: "Friends show their love in times of trouble, not in happiness." We hope we can focus on our shared humanity and give Chinese medical workers and citizens a hand during this extremely difficult time—for their sake, in the name of selflessness, in the spirit of Dr. Bethune.

B.C. Must Do More Testing and Urge More Use of Masks in Public to Defeat the Coronavirus[3]

Before mid-March, British Columbia might have been considered lucky to some extent, considering the total number of COVID-19 cases and daily increase in new infections in Italy and Spain. More recently, there have been sharper rises in Quebec and Ontario in comparison to our province.

The relatively low number of reported cases and a flattening of the curve of newly added cases in B.C. can be attributed to a number of factors.

Voluntary self-isolation has proven to be essential in preventing community transmission in the early days.

When federal and provincial health authorities repeatedly gave low-risk assessments of COVID-19's threaten to Canadians before mid-March, Asian Canadians wasted no time to stay on high alert to prevent the community spread of the disease.

Many B.C. residents placed themselves in a voluntary self-isolation for 14 days after returning from overseas. As of March 9, Canada had only nine cases among those who had reported recent travel history in China or were travelers' close contacts, accounting for 11.6% of the 77 then confirmed cases. Those numbers had shown no growth since February 23.

Practicing social distancing is more than just keeping two meters apart.

When Canada followed the World Health Organization's advice to keep our border unlocked to international travelers, the Chinese Canadian community started practicing social distancing in an innovative way. A group of volunteers was organized to provide pick-up services to passengers who were returning from international trips to avoid their use of public

3 Guo Ding and Kenny Zhang, This article first appeared in *The Georgia Straight* on April 12th, 2020.

transit, taxis or ride-sharing services like Uber.

These volunteers installed a separation barrier in their vehicle between the driver and passenger, and kept their vehicles constantly sterilized. These volunteers also helped deliver groceries to the doors of those who were in self-isolation.

Self-isolating and social distancing didn't stop cross-community care and support. When reported cases jumped in the Iranian Canadian community, a joint initiative between a Chinese community group and an Iranian Canadian organization was established to help members of both groups who returned to this country from the COVID-19 affected areas.

Such an initiative was quickly modeled by other neighborhoods in this province and Ontario; thus, many good practices of self-isolation and physical distancing were able to be shared by different groups across Canada.

Nevertheless, the early luck should not be regarded as B.C. having paved the way to defeat the virus. On the contrary, since mid-March, we have seen that B.C. missed many critical opportunities that could have prevented the community spread much earlier and faster.

The province is still lacking a forward-looking strategy to effectively prevent the community from spreading and control the pandemic.

Health authorities keep providing confusing messages of social distancing. For instance, on March 16 the provincial health officer limited the number of people allowed to gather at 50, whereas other provinces have set it at zero or two.

Dr. Bonnie Henry also insisted for quite a while that wearing a mask didn't help prevent transmission of the virus, while many other jurisdictions made it mandatory to wear a mask in a public space.

The most worrisome is that there is no test for those who have no or mild symptoms. Without proper testing, these individuals may not be aware that they are possible mobile infection sources putting their family and community at high risk.

Recent repeated community deaths of the aged rang an alarm of the failure of the current approach, which still offers no test to those individuals with no or minor symptoms.

To continue the early luck, B.C. can't afford to miss two more critical measures before a vaccine or a specific anti-COVID-19 medicine become available.

The province should encourage all British Columbians to wear a mask in public spaces and test, test and test as the WHO advises.

Wearing a mask in public might not seem normal for those who grew up in western society. Unfortunately, the reality is that we are all in an unprecedented moment and many jurisdictions in Asia and Europe have shown strong evidence that wearing a mask reduces the risk of transmission of the virus.

As we make our health-care workers the priority, the general public should also be prepared to wear masks when possible.

In addition, more testing will definitely help identify infected cases— i.e., screening those who are seriously ill, with mild symptoms. or with no symptoms at all.

While our existing hospital system is still able to handle and focus on those patients in critical condition, temporary field hospitals should be open to accept patients with mild symptoms.

In the meantime, those infected who have not seen symptoms should be placed in restrictive self-isolation to stop the spread to their family and community.

Better late than never. Let's wear masks and do more tests to defeat the virus in the most effective ways possible.

When It Comes to Wearing Masks in Public, Do We Want True Multiculturalism or White Cultural Hegemony? [4]

We are in the middle of the COVID-19 crisis. In the next two or three weeks, the outbreak in Canada will reach its peak.

During this critical period, the issue of wearing masks will rise to the forefront yet since the beginning of the outbreak in North America, wearing a mask in public areas has been a very controversial subject.

Chinese Canadians and other Canadians of Asian background who've worn masks while in public have been criticized, discriminated against, and, at worst, assaulted. Why is this happening in a country that holds multiculturalism as a core value?

The simple explanation is the divide between the cultural habits of Asian and Western countries. In Western countries, only sick people wear masks, so the appearance of people wearing masks brings panic.

Additionally, the World Health Organization and Canadian government officials at different levels have stated repeatedly that wearing masks will not protect against the spread of COVID-19. Sadly, the "professional viewpoint" seems to be distorted, with the resulting discrimination against people wearing masks in public.

---

4 Guo Ding, This article first appeared in *The Georgia Straight* April 19th, 2020.

This is wrong. According to Canadian values and the constitution, there are four reasons that discrimination should not be happening against mask-wearers.

First of all, it has already been proven that wearing masks is a successful way to prevent the spread of COVID-19. I understand that the government and medical professionals have stated that there is no need to wear masks because they may worry that if the entire community begins looking for them, it will affect the supply of medical masks, such as the N95 in hospitals and especially in the emergency departments.

However, from the experience in China and other countries that were hit earlier, wearing masks is a keyway to prevent the spread of COVID-19. Masks capture droplets carrying the virus before they can spread into the environment, which is the main method of transmission of COVID-19 in public areas.

Many countries, including Austria, have just made masks compulsory under certain circumstances in order to contain COVID-19, and other European countries may soon follow suit. Even the White House is now advocating wearing masks in public places.

Thus, the Canadian government and medical chief officers in different levels should not deliver a false message to the public, even if the ulterior motive is to prevent a shortage of masks for health-care professionals. I am glad to see the premier of Ontario wearing a mask in public. He is sending the right message to Canadians.

Secondly, attacking mask-wearers due to their cultural habits is an affront to the multicultural values of Canada. It is ethnocentric to ridicule the act of wearing masks, which is seen as a sign of cleanliness and protecting others' health in Asian cultures. The uproar over mask-wearing has only made it clear that the talk of cultural acceptance in Canada is hypocritical, and many Canadians still believe that Western culture is intrinsically superior and 100 percent correct.

According to the principle of multiculturalism, even if you don't like to wear a mask when you are not sick, you must respect other people's choice to wear the mask.

Thirdly, in discussions about mask-wearing, the one point that has not been brought up is that it is a basic human right to wear a mask. It is the same thing as choosing what clothes to wear, or which tattoo to ink. Above the cultural and medical discussion, basically this is a human rights issue. The government must clearly state that discriminating against or verbally attacking a person who chooses to wear a mask is an attack on basic human rights. In the most egregious cases, it should go before the judicial system.

I strongly believe that in a crisis such as this pandemic, cultural barriers must be overcome. When we see the United States and Canada make decisions to close down cities and restrict travel, we must realize that we are facing unprecedented times. Why are masks such a big issue?

It is ridiculous to make a fuss over cultural differences when wearing masks can save lives. If the mask supply is adequate, I hope that everyone will wear a mask when they leave their homes.

When I see people wearing masks and practicing social distancing in public areas, I start believing that Canada will prevail over COVID-19 soon.

Malignant McCarthyism Is More Dangerous than Coronavirus[5]

When a wildfire sparked the evacuation of more than 80,000 residents from Fort McMurray and its surrounding region four years ago, Canadians at home or abroad lent helping hands through all possible means to their fellow citizens. They were in urgent need to cope with the unprecedented natural disaster in northern Alberta.

Four years later, when a novel coronavirus broke out in Wuhan, China on an unprecedented scale, thousands of the city's care workers were in life-threatening danger due to a shortage of personal protective equipment (PPE). Concerned Canadians, regardless of ethnic backgrounds, opened their hearts to support the Red Cross Canada's China COVID-19 Response Appeal, as well as initiatives by Doctors Without Borders.

Some Canadians spontaneously shipped protective gear to hospitals and individuals in the then epicentre of the pandemic.

These are just a few of many examples demonstrating Canadians' care and compassion for others, reflecting their fundamental principles and humanitarian values. But on April 30, 2020, these Canadian principles and values were attacked and smashed by Sam Cooper and Abigail Bimman on Global News.

Their stories painted an incomplete, unbalanced, and distorted picture of Canadians of Chinese heritage. These reports conveyed an erroneous message to readers that China's Communist government deliberately

---

5 Guo Ding is a Vancouver journalist, columnist, and historian on the immigration history of Chinese Canadians. Kenny Zhang is a Vancouver-based writer. Guangwei Ouyang has a PhD and is a professor of philosophy based in New Westminster. Lu Chan is a Burnaby-based immigration lawyer. All are Canadian citizens. This article first appeared in *The Georgia Straight* on May 10th, 2020.

stockpiled PPE supplies and that certain so-called secret groups controlled by China were behind all this.

They distorted the humanitarian responses to the pandemic by hundreds of thousands of Canadians, including those of Chinese origin, while attempting to confuse readers with their conspiracy theory of the Chinese government hoarding PPE from Canada and all over the globe

They used the term "Chinese nationals" in Canada to downplay the loyalty of Canadians of Chinese heritage, when the fact is that the majority of them are Canadian citizens and some of their ancestors came to Canada as early as in the 1800s, long before the Chinese Communist Party (CCP) was created. Chinese Canadians are not foreigners but nation builders of this great country.

The Global news report racially stereotyped Chinese and Asian Canadians by calling "every overseas Chinese a warrior", whereas the original meaning of the source should have been read as "every overseas Chinese is a warrior against the pandemic."

In fact, every Canadian should be a warrior against the pandemic.

The profiling and attack on Chinese Canadians reeked of McCarthyism, which was popular in the United States from the late 1940s to the 1950s, finally abandoned, and gradually forgotten at the end of the Cold War.

If a new McCarthyism malignancy breaks out in our society, unfortunately, it will become a most dangerous political virus amid the COVID-19 spread and in the post-pandemic era.

With fuel from narrow-minded populism and biased media, it will sooner or later evolve into a real witch hunt with great damage to Canadian society.

Like the coronavirus attacking people regardless their age, gender, ethnicity, cultural background, or level of wealth, this political virus will eventually threaten all ethnic groups, starting with the Chinese Canadian community. From the country's chief public health officer to elected officials of all levels of government, a groundless assertion and accusation of "working for China" will put them in a situation where a political intensive care unit (ICU) wouldn't be able to save their careers.

Even businesspeople conducting legitimate businesses with China, academics involved in normal cultural and academic exchanges with China's partners, and politicians undertaking regular contact with their counterparts in China are likely to become new victims of such charges from the new McCarthyism.

It would be deadly wrong to take this news report only as an armchair exercise without any social consequences.

A dramatic increase in random attacks recently on innocent Chinese and Asian Canadians, from pushing a 92-year-old senior onto the ground to knocking a young girl down to the street, demonstrates the impact that irresponsible journalism can play in this new wave of racism and hatred in Canada.

This new McCarthyism may evolve into "ethnic cleansing", which would create an unprecedented human rights disaster and humanitarian tragedy in the modern history of Canada.

It would be shameful to repeat the Chinese Exclusion Act or the Japanese Canadian internment in the 21st century. Many Chinese immigrants came to Canada after the horrifying Cultural Revolution, hoping to embrace a multicultural democratic society without having to live in fear of attacks.

History also tells us that if McCarthyism were to be reborn in Canada, Chinese Canadians would likely become the first victimized group, but they would definitely not be the last.

In the past, the targets of McCarthyism were not just those under the influence of the Soviet Communist Party, but also politicians from opposition parties and innocent people in the United States.

The new malignant McCarthyism is more complicated and dangerous than ever before. In addition to the widespread attacks on targeted groups, it also shows symptoms of various political stains such as racism, white supremacy, contempt for Asians, extreme ideology, anti-globalization, and division of community groups. It not only has a strong infectious ability but also easily triggers violence and racial attacks.

Fortunately, we have seen a sign that the curve of the coronavirus pandemic has flattened, and it will ultimately be cured with a vaccine and specific medicines being developed.

But unfortunately, the fight against a political virus remains a challenge for everyone in Canada for the foreseeable future.

I'm Wong, not Wrong[6]

Wong, a Cantonese and Hakka romanization of the popular Chinese surname Huang, originated in the Huang Kingdom of China in 704-648 BC. In recent times, it has spread across Southeast Asia, North America,

6 By Kenny Zhang, Guangwei Ouyang, and Lu Chan. Kenny Zhang is a Vancouver-based writer. Guangwei Ouyang has a Ph.D. and is a professor of philosophy based in New Westminster. Lu Chan is a Burnaby-based immigration lawyer. All are proud Canadian citizens. First published in *The Georgia Straight*, June 20,2021.

and other continents through centuries of chain migration.

Many overseas Chinese have kept a tradition of self-identifying as descendants of the Yan and Huang emperors.

When the phrase "every overseas Chinese is a warrior against the pandemic" was manipulated by a 2020 news report—intentionally or unintentionally—into "every overseas Chinese is a warrior", Wong was seen as "wrong".

Such a news thread has been evolving step by step into an alleged "warrior theory" by producing "detective stories". These tales regularly rely on shadowy unnamed sources rather than standing as investigative reports that can be replicated by other reporters.

This "warrior theory" is being advanced by stereotypical narratives rather than logical reasoning and by following the path of political extremism rather than objective journalism. This is wrong.

From the simple fact that many overseas Chinese, including some from Canada, donated or helped purchase an unimaginable amount of personal protective equipment (PPE) for their loved ones in China for humanitarian care and support during an unprecedented COVID-19 outbreak, fans of the "warrior theory" derived that all overseas Chinese are warriors of the United Front Work Department (UFWD) of the Chinese Communist Party (CCP).

And by using their creative imagination to insert many false assumptions, exciting and horrifying "detective stories" are then produced.

Even if stockpiling PPE was the Chinese Communist Party's strategy and even if it were organized by UFWD, there is still a distinguishing line that could be possibly drawn between humanitarian aid and political operations, or between individual spontaneous efforts and organized activities. The "warrior theory" conflates all of this.

The theory's flawed syllogism goes on: the UFWD represents the evil CCP government; some Chinese Canadian community organizations and their members are seemingly involved in the UFWD efforts in Canada; and therefore, those Chinese Canadians are deemed to be foreign agents—national security threats to Canada—and part of an organized criminal network operating in Canada, as a 2021 book subtitle suggests.

The theory's slippery slope is a classic case of the fallacies of reasoning.

Fans of the "warrior theory" stand firmly against Beijing. If one disagrees with them, this person must be pro-Beijing.

In the same vein, if someone holds a similar view as Beijing's on any random topic, this person must be an agent of Beijing. This reasoning makes people wonder if these fans took a course in logic taught by an art teacher, willfully brushing white, black, red, or yellow together to create colour blindness.

The theory's impaired logical argument further goes off into the far extreme. In its view, attacking overseas Chinese in Canada or elsewhere becomes a means of attacking China and its CCP. Thus, attacking overseas Chinese is not racism.

When immigrants from China or around the world prepared for the Canadian citizenship test, they learned and embraced Canada's democratic principles and fundamental characteristics of Canadian heritage and identity, such as the rule of law; freedom of thought, belief, opinion, and expression; and multiculturalism, along with many other Canadianisms.

It is not clear if the author of the "warrior theory" has ever passed the citizenship test, but the half-cooked theory obviously missed many blind spots, as he failed to do a shoulder-check.

In a country with the rule of law, it is not a journalist, nor a politician, but only a judge or jury who can convict suspected individuals or groups of being criminals.

Calling out names of Chinese Canadians as being part of a criminal network without a proper judicial proceeding is far beyond the discipline and ethical standard of basic journalism. Let alone if it is in line with the spirit of the Canadian Constitution.

Equally important, in a country upholding human rights and freedom, it is a sacred right for individuals to have freedom of speech, regardless of whether it is pro-Beijing, against Beijing, or somewhere in between.

A quote often attributed to the French philosopher Voltaire (but actually written by one of his biographers to reflect his thinking) declares: "I disapprove of what you say, but I will defend to the death your right to say it."

The "warrior theory" and its fans have every reason and every right to dislike the CCP or attack Beijing, but they definitely have no single reason nor any right to stop others from expressing different and independent views unless prohibited by Canadian laws.

When the "warrior theory" was cooked up, many Canadians of Chinese heritage—including those who were born in Canada, moved to Canada at a time before the founding of PRC or came from sources other than People's Republic of Cihna—were frightened and outraged.

This time, instead of always remaining silent, many members of the Chinese community spoke out to defend their rights and freedom. They protested such nonsense in Canadian ways, including signing online petitions, writing letters to the editor, publishing commentaries in newspapers, and seeking legal aid to hold the author accountable to Journalism 101.

More importantly, in a country where diversity is celebrated and differences are respected, personal characteristics such as one's skin colour, ethnic surname, and emotional tie to the place of origin is not a sign of doing anything wrong, but an indication of being a member of a big multicultural family.

Seeing the Chinese Canadian community's protests, fans of the "warrior theory" turned this upside down, suggesting those demonstrations were mobilized by the CCP trying to shut up the Canadian journalists. They went on to investigate individuals participating in the protests, including other Canadian journalists who had criticized the theory, attempting to make up another story of them being secret agents of CCP in Canada.

The "warrior theory" seems so comfortable and enjoyable riding to victory on the Four Horsemen of Calumny: Fear, Ignorance, Bigotry, and Smear.

It's unfair to say that the "warrior theory" specializes in attacking all overseas Chinese. In fact, it is also good at praising selected ones who are like-minded fans, including some with anglicized Chinese names.

In a controversial 2015 study of housing transactions, a researcher with an anglicized Chinese name specifically isolated "non-anglicized Chinese" names (romanized in the way of the PRC) listed on land titles. Among his findings were that 66 percent of the buyers of the 172 homes in the study had names spelled in the way used in the PRC.

This suggested to the public that they were likely recent arrivals from mainland China. That led to media reports arguing that people from China had pushed housing prices to an unaffordable level.

With such overgeneralizations about "foreigner buyers" weaponized against a community with Chinese surnames, they had found a scapegoat.

The foreign ownership study was released when housing prices were soaring, and politicians and media were rushing for a quick answer to respond to the public outcry.

The foreign buyer was an easy target. Using the "non-anglicized Chinese name" as a proxy, it was creative thinking, for good or bad, because at the time no real data was available reporting foreign buyers in the B.C. housing market.

No wonder this study was praised by fans of the "warrior theory" as "fearless".

Fearless of what? While some community groups criticized the foreign ownership study as racist, the author was fearless in defending his questionable methodology.

Despite the small sample of 172 homes in a few blocks on Vancouver's West Side, the proxy of "Chinese buyers"—advanced by the media based on anglicized or non-anglicized Chinese names—had serious flaws and limitations.

Here is why. The coauthors of this article, Lu Chan and Guangwei Ouyang, would be classified as "non-anglicized Chinese" names but Kenny Zhang would be considered an "anglicized Chinese" name, if things were that sample.

Opposite to the way this ownership study was widely interpreted, both Chan and Ouyang came to Canada in 1986 whereas Zhang came to Vancouver in 2000.

By the time of this infamous ownership study, the two with non-anglicized Chinese names had been in Canada for 29 years and the latter had called Vancouver home for 15 years. None of them was a newer immigrant, nor a foreigner.

Arguably, the three names of this article's coauthors are a tiny example that may not accurately represent an entire population. That is exactly why we would expect the author to update his pioneering but outdated ownership study by adding more samples, perhaps by including surnames such as

Einstein, Mohammed, Singh, or Suzuki, if he is serious about this subject.

This is the kind of evidence that the "warrior theory" uses in its narratives scapegoating a Canadian community with the surnames of "Zhao, Qian, Sun, or Li"—the most popular family names representing public people in Chinese literature. As such, the theory tries to prove being Wong means wrong.

MP embraces warrior theory

The "warrior theory" also has many high-profile fans. People remember that just over a year ago, a rookie member of Parliament (MP), then running for the leadership of the Conservative party, released a video attacking Canada's chief public health officer Dr. Theresa Tam, declaring that she was "parroting" misinformation about COVID-19.

This MP asked if Dr. Tam, who was born in Hong Kong, was "working for Canada or working for China".

Ironically, this MP, then in the caucus of the Official Opposition, listed the United Nations, the World Health Organization, and the CCP together as his objects of opposition on his Twitter feed. This came when international collaboration was widely accepted as critically important for every nation in responding to the pandemic.

That was apart from his groundless accusation about Dr. Tam based on her Chinese surname.

It is no wonder this MP's attack on Tam drew backfire. Prime Minister Justin Trudeau declared that "intolerance and racism have no place in our country." Even his Conservative caucus mates described this kind of attack as "outrageous", "embarrassing", and "garbage".

Clearly, any disagreement over "warrior theory" is not an argument if it is right or wrong to be against the CCP. Nor is it an argument about whether there are or aren't secret agents of CCP in Canada.

Rather, it's to argue if it is right or wrong to accuse every overseas Chinese of being a warrior of the CCP.

If anyone had told us that such "detective stories", stereotyped narratives, and political extremism would have nothing to do with recent rising anti-Asian racism and resurgence of McCarthyism, we would have called that man an idiot who is losing his sight, losing his mind, and losing his wisdom.

Historically, the settlement of Chinese immigrants in Canada can be traced back to the late 18th century, long before Canadian Confederation in 1867. Over the centuries, waves of Chinese immigrants sought their livelihoods in this country to avoid wars, famines, horrors of personal attacks, or lack of freedom in their regions of birth under different regimes.

Many immigrants from China could have enjoyed a peaceful life here as they knew that this is a land of prosperity and hope, which is safeguarded by the rule of law.

They could also have kept their peace of mind because they've learned that this is a society where no one deserves to live in fear or danger because of their skin colour, their rooted family names or their emotional ties to where their heritage originates.

They could even have achieved peace of heart as they embraced the belief that this is a community in which every member lives equally and respects each other.

But on that day when they saw the shaking weak body of a 92-year-old senior pushed onto the ground, and when they saw such a tiny young girl knocked down to the street, they were seized with fear.

On those days when they heard the endless slurs of "f--- you Chinese," or "go back China," and when they had seen this repeated hate graffiti in Chinatown, they were seized with anger.

On that day when they read the news that Vancouver was named the anti-Asian hate crime capital of North America, and when they had watched footage of leftover coffee being thrown in a shop manager's face, they were seized with despair.

Canada is a land of hope.

Love All Your Neighbours, a message taken from the Bible, is an art piece created by local artist Jocelyn Wong during the 2020 Vancouver Mural Festival.

Wong's mural comes as a heartfelt reminder—being Wong is not wrong.

Let's embrace love not hatred, harmony not calumny, and hope not horror.

Chinese Canadian Museum Will Counter Flawed Narratives about B.C. and Canadian History[7]

Last month, the B.C. government announced $10 million in funding for the Chinese Canadian Museum project.

This marks the first time that a North American government has supported such a project. And $10 million is only the beginning.

This shows that Premier John Hogan is a leader who fulfills his campaign promises.

I still remember when I wrote an article in Sing Tao Daily on May

---

7 Guo Ding, This article first appeared in *The Georgia Straight* on August 2nd, 2020.

1, 2017, suggesting that B.C. should build a Chinese Canadian history museum to identify the contributions of the Chinese community since 1860. The next day, I received a phone call from NDP headquarters, telling me that the party leader, Horgan, endorsed my idea.

I then suggested that Horgan should make this a campaign promise. When he visited Sing Tao Daily, he pledged to build the Chinese Canadian Museum.

After the lieutenant-governor asked Horgan to form a government, I was invited to Victoria to attend his swearing-In ceremony as premier. Horgan reconfirmed with me that he would build the museum.

I also spoke to the newly appointed attorney general, David Eby, and the minister of state for trade, George Chow, on that day as well. They delivered the same message.

The $10-million announcement has come at a very critical time. During the COVID-19 pandemic, anti-Chinese and anti-Asian hate crimes have more than doubled. "Go back to China" has become a slogan of this wave of discrimination.

This shows that people in B.C. lack historical knowledge of their province and Canada.

Even though it seems to be a little late, as Chinese people have lived in B.C. for over a century and a half, the Chinese Canadian Museum is a step in the right direction.

Museum will advance understanding

I believe that the Chinese Canadian Museum can have three big impacts on B.C. and Canada as a whole.

Firstly, it will make B.C. history more complete. The early Chinese migrants made huge contributions to B.C. and Canada.

Their role in the B.C. Gold Rush, construction of the Pacific Railway, the Second World War, and in overturning the Chinese Exclusion Act and bringing back voting rights to all citizens are some of the ways in which they have shaped B.C. The museum will finally fill those gaps in B.C.'s history.

Secondly, the museum can fix the Eurocentric viewpoint of Canadians when it comes to our history. Since B.C.'s early beginnings, multiculturalism has been a focal point of the province.

Europeans, Chinese, First Nations, Japanese, and people of various backgrounds worked together to create the province as it is now, and it is time for Canadians to recognize this fact.

Thirdly, the museum will cement the identity of Chinese Canadians as true Canadians. By learning the stories of the early Chinese migrants, all Canadians will know that they were not just a source of cheap labour, but played key roles in building B.C. and the nation.

We have to admit that B.C. has very deep roots in discriminating against Chinese Canadians, but that racism is based on an incorrect view of historical facts, as well as ideology.

The Chinese Canadian Museum will help uproot those sources of discrimination. This is very important in our current times, because we have seen how quickly and strongly the political virus of discrimination has infected our community.

The museum will show that multiculturalism is not a recent fad or policy: it is part of the Canadian gene. I, for one, have a dream that young Canadians who visit the museum will never utter the words: "Go back to China."

Finally, I believe that the museum will teach new Chinese immigrants that they are not outsiders to this country. They will be reminded of the hard work and sacrifices of their ancestors to create a home for them here, and be encouraged to adopt the culture and values their ancestors did, giving back to Canada as they have done for the past 150 years.

Chinese Canadians in the aftermath of COVID-19[8]

Even as the country prepares for a second wave of COViD-19 infections, a debate is emerging about whether the disruptions to Canadian society and economy since March 2020 are temporary or permanent, and if governments should plan on a return to "normal" or something very different.

One of the key lessons of COVID-19 is that the virus has affected different segments of society differently, with minority groups bearing the brunt of infection, due to economic and social circumstances which put them at greater risk of exposure.

What about Chinese Canadians? There is evidence to suggest that Canadians of Chinese descent had lower rates of infection compared to the general population—contrary to expectations, given the higher likelihood of community members travelling to hot spots in China. For example, infection rates in Richmond, B.C.—with its majority ethnic Chinese population—were significantly lower than in surrounding municipalities. Epidemiologists put the lower infection rates down to measures taken voluntarily by the Chinese community to don face masks well before public health officials advocated the use of such, and an early willingness to accept social distancing as a necessary precaution to control infection. This

---

8   Yuen Pau Woo, Ottawa September 2020

reflex in the community likely stems from direct experience with SARS, which raged across Asia in 1997, resulting in a higher comfort level with face masks and intrusive social isolation policies.

While face masks may have been an important reason why communities with heavy concentrations of ethnic Chinese were less likely to be infected with COVID-19, this humble accessory also turned into a lightning rod of animosity towards some Chinese Canadians. In the early days of the pandemic, wearers of face masks—mostly of Asian descent—were treated with a mixture of derision and ostracism by those who misinterpreted the wearing of masks as ignorant, anti-social, or a sign of illness.

With mask mandates now commonplace across the country and around the world, this prejudice has largely faded away, but the fact that it emerged in the first place raises uncomfortable questions about intolerance in Canadian society. Some of the vitriol towards Asian mask wearers was very likely a form of subliminal racist expression made respectable by focusing on the scourge of a virus rather than on a racial group as such (even though racist symbolism has long borrowed from the language of contagious diseases).

The mask controversy in Canada was complicated by actions on the part of Chinese community groups that organized campaigns for face masks and other personal protective equipment (PPE) to be sent to the People's Republic of China when the latter was at the height of its COVID-19 crisis. By the time Canada some weeks later entered its own period of rapidly growing infections, PPE were in short supply, and a narrative emerged that Chinese Canadians were being disloyal by putting their native country ahead of Canada. Worse, there were accusations of complicity with the Chinese government in mobilizing and sending PPE to the People's Republic, at the expense of Canadians.

Curiously, when some of these same groups some months later made efforts to source PPE from China for use in Canadian hospitals and seniors' homes, they were met with skepticism about ulterior motives, claims of inferior quality products, and—again—collusion with the Chinese government.

In many ways, the most profound impact of COVID-19 on Chinese Canadians has less to do with the virus as such, and much more to do with parallel events in 2020 that did not have much direct link to the coronavirus. Some of these factors predate COVID-19, and were magnified by the fact that the virus was initially associated with a particular racial group and country, and hence was able to flourish in a social petri dish of prejudice and fear.

Prior to COVID-19, resentment against recent immigrants from China was directed mainly at the high cost of real estate in cities such as Vancouver and Toronto. This led to taxes and surcharges on foreign owners of Canadian property and on vacant homes in designated areas. The result of those policies so far, it would seem, has been to make some of the most expensive homes in greater Vancouver more affordable for the very rich, but the foreign buyers' and vacancy tax has done very little to improve housing affordability for average Canadians.

COVID-19 provided a fresh outlet for resentment against Chinese (and other Asians/indigenous peoples who look "Chinese"), with many incidents of physical and verbal abuse reported across the country, and a host of efforts by community groups to combat these acts of racism. Just as mainstream attention was starting to recognize the problem of COVID-related discrimination against Asians, the spotlight on systemic racism shifted dramatically and profoundly after the George Floyd murder in the United States, which provoked a massive national reckoning about the plight of African Canadians. Anti-Asian racism efforts quickly aligned with the Black Lives Matter movement but many of these groups felt the need to downplay their previous focus on discrimination against Asians, for fear of being misinterpreted as a "competing" anti-racism initiative.

There is of course no reason why minority groups cannot work together on the systemic racism that all of them face, and there are many productive alliances that attempt to do so. The reality, however, is that many of the challenges faced by Chinese Canadians are quite different from those faced by Black Canadians, and the key to combating racism across society is to not only work on common issues but to also identify challenges that are specific to affected communities.

The most important factor in anti-Chinese racism today is anti-China sentiment. This is true both for Chinese Canadians who are sympathetic to Beijing and those who are opposed to the Communist regime. While the Chinese community in Canada has always had a diversity of views on the PRC, Taiwan, HK, and the broader Chinese world, anti-Chinese racism has tended to not make a distinction among the different sub-communities. Hostility towards wealthy mainlanders buying up expensive homes in tony Vancouver suburbs in recent years is not much different from the hostility towards Hong Kong and Taiwanese immigrants who did the same 30 years earlier.

There is, however, an increasingly public split between the most vocal of Chinese Canadian supporters of the PRC and those who identify with Hong Kong and Taiwan. This split has been laid bare by Beijing's imposition of a National Security Law in Hong Kong, which is deeply unpopular among Hong Kong residents and their many relatives in Canada. The issue has spilled into the political arena, with calls for the Canadian government to impose sanctions against Chinese officials who have suppressed protests in Hong Kong and for alleged abuses of human rights in other parts of China, notably Xinjiang.

Canadian public opinion towards the PRC is at its most unfavorable in decades, and there is immense pressure on all political parties to take a tougher stand towards Beijing. The detention of Michael Kovrig and Michael Spavor, apparently in retaliation for extradition actions against Huawei's Meng Wanzhou, has only added to the sour mood towards China. While Canada has not come close to the kind of escalating diplomatic and commercial actions by the Trump administration against China, Ottawa will be hard pressed to resist pressure from Washington, DC to treat China as, at best, a strategic rival, or increasingly, an "enemy"— regardless of who prevails in the November US Presidential election. With virtually all public commentary in the Canadian media now lined up on the side of getting tough on China, it will take enormous political courage on the part of any government to resist such a reflex and instead focus on longer-term considerations.

The first victims of a heightened strategic rivalry between China and the US will be ethnic Chinese who are seen as suspect because of ties to the mainland. Canada has some built-in protections against this kind of discrimination, but the weight of opinion is already shifting towards a much more skeptical attitude towards recent and former Chinese nationals in the country, such as was seen in recent discussions around "mask diplomacy". Indeed, a kind of "litmus test" has been set up by the media and some China commentators whereby participation in "United Front" organizations, meeting with Chinese officials, and expressing views that may align with Beijing are automatic markers of suspicion and symbols of disloyalty to Canada.

It is not that the community should have one voice on issues related to the PRC and Ottawa's relations with Beijing. On the contrary, the diversity of opinion is healthy and essential in the formulation of Canadian foreign policy towards China. But it is a problem if the Chinese Canadian community is defined by its differing views on the PRC/HK/Taiwan because Chinese Canadians will come to be seen as "foreigners" advocating for issues in their motherland, rather than citizens who contribute to the totality of Canadian society—through political life, business, the professions, social service, and much more. The tendency of Canadian politicians of all stripes to view ethnic communities as vote banks and important only insofar as they connect to "diaspora" issues is a disservice to the true meaning of multiculturalism and to the immigrants who make up multicultural Canada.

The challenge then for Chinese Canadians Post-COVID is both the same as before the crisis, and also different. It is the same in that Chinese Canadians must not allow themselves to be defined by their ties with and views on the Chinese world. Chinese Canadians have already demonstrated their capabilities and success in a variety of professions and pursuits, but the community as a whole is grossly underrepresented in leadership positions across politics, the justice system, corporate and not-for-profit boards, and higher education.

That is not to say that Chinese Canadians should in any way downplay their ethnicity. However, the cultural identity of Chinese Canadians and the organizations that purport to represent them should not be defined by a government (whether Beijing, Taipei, or Ottawa). The Chinese Canadian community can and should express its rich cultural heritage without the need for approval from or association with governmental authorities, least of all the People's Republic of China.

At the same time, Chinese Canadians must not allow distrust of the PRC and strategic rivalry with Beijing led by the United States to force their own "decoupling" with the Chinese world—whether in business, scholarship, philanthropy, cultural relations, or other fields of endeavor. Whatever reservations the Canadian government may have with China on specific problems related to Hong Kong, Xinjiang, extradition, and hostages, it is important for civil society to maintain and strengthen ties with counterparts in Greater China.

What is different, however, is that the pressure to disengage with China will grow in the immediate future, due to a mixture of perceived self-protection, a desire to retaliate, repugnance over Chinese actions within its own borders, and fears about national security. More than ever, a longer-term view of Canada's interests vis-a-vis China, and indeed a longer-term view of China's place in the world, is needed. Chinese Canadians can be an important contributor to that conversation.

Epilogue

The Dual Challenges of Canada's Chinese Gene

The idea of "Canada's Chinese gene" is becoming more widespread. After reading the prologue to our English version of the book, my good friend, Professor Stan Remple was so happy that he wrote me a long letter to express his reaction. This scholar who once held deputy positions in crucial ministerial offices in Alberta and British Columbia told me that our research and perspective would reforge the 150-year-old book of Canadian national history. It would help other Canadians, especially those of European heritage, to understand more about Chinese Canadians. The history we cover not only includes contributions made by Chinese Canadians to the founding of this nation, but also the historical connections between our Chinese, Aboriginals and other ethnic groups. Professor Remple also pointed out that the historical and modern contributions made by Chinese immigrants to Canada have never been sufficiently appreciated by other Canadians. What is really sad, he said, is the lack of awareness of history by many Canadians, wherein their understanding of recent Canadian history falls too far behind compared to our research; this is also what prompts Chinese Canadians to pay more attention to the history of Canada's founding than most Canadians of Western background. Professor Remple also made the profound observation that if Canadians do not learn from the mistakes in history, they may be doomed to repeat the same mistakes today.

After his criticism of the general disregard towards history by the Canadian population, however, the professor also pointed out some shortcomings of his beloved Chinese people based on his profound understanding of their communities and of China. One of the most decisive barriers that prevented the general Canadian society from learning about the Chinese gene and the Chinese people's contributions to Canada was that Chinese Canadians tend to stick together rather than spreading out and intermingling with other Canadians. This caused their own lack of knowledge about, and limited visibility to, other Canadians. Eventually, an invisible wall formed between the Chinese and Canadian communities in general.

His idea of "breaking down the wall" resonated strongly with me. It gave me an epiphany that the idea of "Canada's Chinese gene" not only needs to make a breakthrough in the blank or blurry pages of history to ensure that Chinese Canadians receive rightful recognition for their contributions and status in the founding of Canada, but also create a new narrative for the last hundred and some years of Chinese Canadian history, as the cultural positioning, emotions, mentalities and literature would all need to be reviewed as this historical fact becomes confirmed. This means that "Canada's Chinese gene" is a double-edged sword that brings two challenges: one reveals the "fragmented and incomplete" Anglocentric and Francocentric historical narratives so as to open up a new path to resolve the problem of discrimination against Chinese from its historical roots. The other reveals the historical "victim" mentality of Chinese Canadians that has hindered them from seriously exploring their true status in Canadian history, which in turn has deterred them from proactively integrating into history as its masters, able to learn about the historical progress of others. In other words, Chinese

Canadians have always treated Canada as "a sanctuary" and "gold mountain of riches", ignoring the "gold mountain of history" that was built by their ancestors. They constantly pace back and forth begrudgingly between "going back to their roots" and "taking root where they stand", but they have always remained on the outskirts of mainstream Canadian history. If Chinese Canadians a hundred years ago were sure of their "genetic position" as founders of Canada and worked hard addressing such a position, just think what would have been the outcome for Chinese communities here today!

Thus, "Canada's Chinese gene" is not only an idea for the non-Chinese mainstream to consider, but is also one for Chinese communities themselves to use as a mirror that helps them to reflect on their hundred years of history as well as their current situation; the mirror will reflect both the wrongdoings of others as well as their own blemishes.

Guo Ding

Manufactured by Amazon.ca
Bolton, ON